Lacie's Lessons In Dating Confidence Is Alluring

Lacie Mae Gabor

Cover and eBook design by

Susie Acheson ~ featherstonestudio.com

Interior book design and publication by

Jen Harty ~ clearcoursecreation.com

For my daughter Aubrey:
"With men this is impossible, but with God all things are possible."

- Matthew 19:26

Preface

Have you ever found yourself at home alone during the prime social hours on a Saturday night wondering how the hell you got there? Maybe you're like me and thought you had life all planned out. A modest house, babies, a white picket fence, and family swim parties. A Golden Retriever running in the yard, perhaps.

Then it happens.

Your husband asks for a divorce. You're left in a total state of shock. Before you is an unforeseen detour from the beautiful life that you saw in your perfectly planned out future. After the initial shock wears off, you teeter between being lost without your husband and wanting to get back on track with someone new. Quickly, you realize, you know nothing about dating.

Fast forward a few years and you're still stuck at home, eating bonbons, feeling lonely as fuck, while watching HBO. You ask yourself, "How the hell did I end up here?" It's far from the single life portrayed in movies and TV shows.

I don't know if you can relate, but I can shamelessly admit that this is where I found myself in my mid-forties, a few years into singledom.

My self-esteem was starting to diminish. I was totally confused about how to attract the type of relationship I wanted. At this time, I really didn't love myself enough to expect the treatment I deserved from men. I didn't know *how* to live my new life, since being a wife and mother were the only roles I'd known for so long. I definitely didn't know how to date in my forties.

Single… a status that I thought I'd left behind forever.

Marriage, to me, was a contract that would last forever. Period. Unfortunately, two people make up one relationship and if the other half taps out—you're fucked.

Prior to getting married, my life was fairly sheltered and uneventful. I had dated my high school sweetheart for five years, and was heartbroken when we broke up halfway through college. I turned my focus to finishing my bachelor's and master's degrees, dating very little for the next five years, mostly due to the unresolved pain I carried from my breakup. I had a few casual dates during that relationship hiatus and eventually, I met and married the man who would become my ex-husband.

Consequently, having very little dating experience in my twenties, I was left utterly confused, not knowing where to begin, when I found myself single and ready to move on— post divorce—in my forties.

Prior to my divorce, I'd never been drunk, never gotten high, and had only slept with a handful of men. This, most people will find surprising to learn about me—especially as I am now. The majority of my prior sexual experiences could be summed up with two serious relationships. I had almost zero life experience outside of going to school, working, and traveling. Needless to say, my sex life was severely lacking.

I fully admit that I was naïve and I believed what men told me, even if their actions didn't align with it. I might as well have been colorblind when it came to spotting red flags. I had zero experience in setting boundaries, nor standing up for myself when I was wronged.

I learned from a very young age that standing up for myself was a no-no as it disrupted the illusionary peace required in relationships. Biting my tongue was ALWAYS the safest route—no matter what. Unfortunately, that rationale led to the acceptance of getting less than what I deserved from men and left me with an inability to speak up for myself.

For as long as I can remember, I have been a textbook type A personality: overly responsible, always punctual, over achiever, and perhaps a bit repressed. I was a rule follower for most of my entire life and even came home five minutes before my curfew as a teenager.

Unfortunately, as a single adult, all of these character traits translated into a boring, predictable, and lonely life. I allowed people to treat me any way they pleased, regardless of the pain and suffering it caused, so as not to rock the boat.

That's not to say that I didn't have great friends and family. By all means, I have the most loving, supportive, caring, and thoughtful friends and family. With that being said, we all know that friends and family won't fill the void when one is missing companionship—of shall we say—the physical type.

Don't get me wrong; it wasn't my personality that was the problem. My life may have been considered boring, but I definitely wasn't shy. I've always been very outgoing, friendly, and energetic—my friends say I'm hilarious and fun to hang out with. However, I had spent the majority of my life making sure that every I was dotted and every T crossed—I guess you could say that my fun was always a little restrained and my confidence was in reflection a bit lacking.

So, as you can see, it was completely out of character for me, Ms. Responsible, to begin having casual sex with men that I barely knew and who were also nearly half my age.

Sometimes life throws you a curve ball. And that was where I was—on one such lonely fateful night—sitting on my couch feeling broken, tired of my predictable safe life. I made the choice then to throw caution to the wind and began sleeping with significantly younger men. By answering the call of one of the assertive and handsome young guys who had repeatedly tried to match with me on Bumble, I changed for the better.

Despite having set age parameters, younger men seemed to slip through the cracks and message me from time to time. I ignored it.

Little did I know that by taking this first step, it would lead to the validation and personal discovery that I had no idea how badly I needed.

In my mid-forties, the only identity I'd known was gone. I really didn't know who I was, what I wanted from life, nor how I deserved to be treated. I knew nothing about setting boundaries, which resulted in one unhealthy relationship after another.

Who could've guessed that the twelve months of sexcapades that would follow, helped to lead me to emotional healing, a renewed sense of self-confidence, self-acceptance, and a level of self-empowerment that I hadn't previously possessed.

Some of the men I spent time with helped me learn to love my body and made me feel sexier than I ever had. Other experiences forced me to stand up for myself and allowed me to finally find my voice after a lifetime of repressing it.

I was also able to get a glimpse into the world of online dating and "hooking up" as those involved call it. I learned quickly there is a niche for middle aged women going through midlife crises and that nook is in the arms of men in their twenties. These men also happen to be in their sexual prime and looking to improve their skills in the bedroom. What better way to improve one's skills than to sleep with older, more sexually experienced women, who also happen to be in their sexual prime?

I can tell you first-hand that the myth of twenty-something-year-old men looking to hook up with forty-something-year-old women is not a myth at all. It's real and flourishing. And while this may not sound like something you can imagine yourself doing—for a myriad of reasons—sometimes pushing your comfort zone beyond its limits is the only way to learn what you want and how to get it.

As you can imagine, with this new perspective comes some amazing experiences and stories to tell. Stories that are occasionally hilarious, a little bit scary at least once, and a few that are unbelievably sexy.

My friends hung onto every word as I began to tell them about my year of sexcapades.

"You should write a book," they said at first.

Then their persistence ramped up to, "Oh my God, you *have* to write a book," as I reached the end of each new story.

So, after a year of casual sexual encounters with younger men and an abundance of persuasion (oftentimes bordering on threats) from my friends, I did just that.

I wrote this book hoping that you or someone you know might be able to relate to my experiences, be motivated to discover yourself through your own journey, and ultimately find the strength to go after what you deserve in life.

There's no question that dating can be uncomfortable and messy, but I learned the key to it is a combination of uninhibited communication and setting clear expectations, which can minimize the agony for both people involved.

I think everyone can understand what it's like to be tired of being alone and confused as to why Mr. Right seems to be a fictional character than a man in the flesh. I may have yet to find Mr. Right, but I can say with certainty the learning and growing I've experienced as a result of my sexcapades have set me up to be more ready than ever for when that special man does enter my life.

The most important transformation for me by the time I ended my journey was the great amount of confidence and trust in myself. I can say with certainty, I will NEVER make the same mistakes when dating again, as you will see in the chapters before you. That is something I'd never been able to say until now.

I may not have extensive degrees deeming me an expert on dating, but I've found learning through living and experiencing. This has been the most powerful education I could receive.

So, moving forward, know that I'm a hardworking, single mom, who knew close to nothing about dating until I graduated from the school of hard knocks (i.e. I made a shit ton of mistakes with men and slowly; but surely, learned from them all).

I hope you will read and enjoy my tantalizing adventures (Oh my God, that sex was fucking incredible!), learn from my heedless mistakes (Why on earth did I sleep with him again?), and possibly embark on your own path to healing—albeit unique and tailored to your needs (i.e., figure out what the fuck you need to emotionally heal and make it happen, so you can move on with your life!)

As you begin to read, please have an open mind and rest assured, I'm much, MUCH, more than the needy and insecure woman you meet at the beginning of this book!

Table of Contents

Chapter 1: Let's Get It On

TONIGHT? I texted, my heart beating a mile a minute. I CAN'T MEET WITH YOU TONIGHT. IT'S MIDNIGHT AND WE'VE NEVER MET.

Thomas texted back. LET'S FACETIME AND YOU CAN SEE THAT I'M NOT A SERIAL KILLER.

LOL! OK. I wrote back.

Oh shit. I thought. Was I really doing this? It was only a few hours since I lowered the age range of the men I was looking to date to twenty-five years old.

Thomas was twenty-six. I swiped back over to his profile. He was a single dad of two young ones both under three. He was Hispanic with dark hair and was clean-shaven.

He didn't *look* like a serial killer.

All of his profile pictures were of him and his two kids. During our initial texting, he told me that he shared a two-bedroom duplex with his brother and fifty percent of the time his little ones were with him.

He had dark flame tattoos coming out the sleeve of his shirt, which were sexy as hell. In fact, every damn thing about this man was sexy. He was insanely handsome and his body was chiseled to a T.

A FaceTime request from Thomas started ringing and my heartbeat sped up.

Oh shit. Oh shit, oh shit, oh shit!

It was just FaceTime. It didn't mean that I was inviting the guy over. It was harmless; just a little excitement. It didn't mean that I had to actually go through with anything.

I took a deep breath, bit my lower lip, and clicked the green accept button.

"Hi. It's you. You look just like your pictures." I replied cheerfully, despite feeling nervous. I felt myself overcompensating, trying to hide my nerves with an overly excited tone.

He smiled. "Hi. You look even better than your pictures. You're beautiful."

I smiled back. "Thanks. You're fucking handsome yourself."

He was charming. And those pictures on his profile… they did not lie. He was shirtless (I was sure that was calculated). I could see his chiseled chest, shoulders, and arms. I must have had a goofy grin on my face, but I wasn't too self-conscious about it, because his smile was just as big.

He liked what *he* saw too.

And damn if that didn't send my temperature through the roof. This man, this gorgeous god of a man, wanted me. It was becoming very clear to me that if I gave the go ahead—said god would book it over to my condo in a matter of minutes, take me in his arms, and… and…

I cleared my throat and tried to focus on what he was saying. Nope. That just had me staring at his mouth, imagining all the things he could do to me with it. There was no question, I was attracted to him and wanted to get my hands all over his body. I was just so scared of what could happen.

I looked behind him at his bedroom. His open closet was packed with clothes. I could see tiny children's clothes

2

hanging on one of the rails. He noticed me looking around him and proceeded to give me the tour of his small room. Moving his phone about to show me as much as he could on FaceTime. A bed shoved up against the wall and a portable crib for his one-year-old daughter. Thomas wanted to reassure me that he was who he advertised.

He wasn't a serial killer. He was in the same boat that I was. Single, busy, and wanting company—when time permitted.

Or was that just what a serial killer *wanted* me to think?

Being the forthright woman that I am, I told him straight up what I was afraid of happening. I'd find out later that I wasn't alone in this fear. Turns out, the number one fear for women when dating online is that they'll be murdered by— *ding, ding, ding*—you guessed it, a serial killer.

What's men's number one fear, you may be asking yourself? That when they show up in person, the woman meeting them doesn't look like her profile pictures.

I'll give you a moment while you go punch something. *Ahem.*

Back to Thomas.

"I really want you to come over. Trust me, I do," I said while looking him up and down. I really, really did. "But I'm scared. I really don't want to die tonight."

Thomas laughed. "I swear, I'm not going to kill you. Let me come over."

We talked for two more hours.

I disconnected FaceTime, but we kept texting. He made me laugh. He'd send me these texts about the other Bumble women he had killed and where he hid their bodies.

THERE WAS THIS ONE GIRL, I KILLED HER WHOLE FAMILY, INCLUDING HER PETS.

3

I rolled my eyes but laughed at the same time.

It took him a lot of time to convince me. I'd never done anything like this before.

Hours and hours of texting and a couple more FaceTime calls later, the arousal, adrenaline, and curiosity won out against my initial reluctance. I decided to take the leap.

It was 1:30 am.

We'd been texting on and off since 8:00 pm.

I typed out my address and hit send before I could overthink it to the point of nausea.

I stared at my phone while feeling all the blood drain from my face. Oh God, what was I doing? I could have at least said that we should meet up in a public place. The Starbucks nearby had closed at nine, but I could have thought of someplace else to meet him. I have two police officers in my family. If my brother—in particular—found out what I was doing, he would literally kill me.

Okay, Lacie. You can sit here thinking of all the ways you're about to be carved up and worn as a skin suit or you can go freshen up, in case the hot as fuck man is exactly who he says he is.

I ran for the master bath. I brushed, flossed, and started to tend to my hair. I fixed my bangs and smoothed my crazy curly hair, spraying them back into place. Then, I stopped and looked at myself in the mirror. For a second, I just stood— frozen.

Now, let's just pause here to say this—men tell me that I'm a beautiful, down to earth, funny, sexy, a forty-three-year-old MILF (yes, ladies, sometimes it takes all forty-three of those years for us to gain the confidence to say this, loud and proud! Well maybe not the MILF part—that comes a bit later). I've grown to love my curvy body. Although I eat healthy most of the time; ultimately, I eat whatever I want. I may highlight my dark brown hair a honey blonde to keep the gray hair from showing, but I wear my hair naturally most days: long and wavy with some tight curls against my neck. My neighbor is always telling me that I have skin she would die for. But… my gym membership expired, eh, six or seven years ago. And let's just say that I've never been in a hurry to renew it. I'm curvy in all the right places. I know how to dress to accentuate my assets and hide my problem areas (thank you *What Not to Wear*). But if tonight goes where I think it will go, there won't be any clothes to hide under.

As I said, forty-three-year-old woman.

And Thomas was twenty-six and cover-model hot.

For a second, I couldn't breathe. My eyes traced the small crinkles around my eyes and the lines on my forehead that appeared whenever I lifted my brows.

I glanced back down at the phone.

He'd be here in ten minutes.

I whispered to myself, "I can't believe I'm fucking doing this." Then turned away from the mirror. He was on his way over and I was doing this. Well, okay, I was *mostly* sure that I was doing this, like three-quarters sure—anyway.

I finished getting ready. I ran my hand down my legs. No stubble—check. Underarm sniff—all good. Should I put on fresh perfume or would it seem like I was trying to hard?

Gah! Why was I wasting time thinking about perfume? What was I going to *wear*? I opted to keep my sweats and tank top on. I was comfortable in them and my loose sweats were flattering—definitely diminishing my muffin top to almost nothing. In the middle of the night, he wasn't coming over just to see me dressed up anyway.

Thomas got to my house at about two. I'm not a night owl, so pure adrenaline was the only thing keeping me awake.

Typically, I'd meet any new guest at the parking lot to help lead the way to my front door. However, since it was so late, I chose to let him find the door while I waited safe and warm inside.

I'M HERE, I THINK.

I'LL OPEN MY FRONT DOOR AND COME OUT.

I opened my door and took a few steps outside. I could see down the pathway to the parking lot. I immediately saw him ten yards down with his cell phone in his hand, the screen lit up. His face was somewhat illuminated by the glow of it.

I smiled and waved.

"Hi," I whispered as not to wake the neighbors.

Thomas smiled and sped up his pace. He walked right up to me and hugged me. He was so much taller than me, which was pretty typical for anyone I meet over the age of ten. I'd stopped growing when I hit the five-foot mark.

After he stepped back, I finally got my first full impression of him—in person that is.

I was shocked at how much hotter he was.

We walked into the house and I closed the door behind us. I had a hard time keeping my eyes off him. He was wearing sweats, sneakers, and a basic sweatshirt. I could tell that he wasn't using his clothes to cover or hide anything: he had a perfect physique.

Thomas broke the ice. "Wow, you're gorgeous in person."

I smiled looking him in his eyes as I replied, "Thanks. I guess I look like my pictures then?"

"I already knew you looked like your pictures after facetiming, but your pictures don't do you justice. You're much better looking in person."

6

I smiled again. "Thanks. You're super handsome yourself."

The truth was this: Thomas was an Adonis and I could not believe that a guy who looked like him was standing in my house. He literally looked like he could be a calendar model. Not just because of his perfectly chiseled physique, but also because he was—I don't know—hot. His hair was perfectly coiffed at two in the morning no less.

I invited him to sit on my L-shaped couch. Thomas sat on one side and I sat on the other. Although we had already talked for hours, we continued doing just that, really getting to know each other.

Honestly, I was nervous. What I needed most was to get even more comfortable with him.

Luckily, he obliged.

About thirty minutes in, Thomas gave me a smile—he had a gorgeous smile. Full lips and white teeth.

"Come sit closer to me." I'm sure that he was tired of beating around the bush, although he had been gracious in entertaining my need for comfort.

I moved closer. Still feeling very nervous, yet knowing now that I definitely wanted to get my hands all over him.

Shortly after I moved closer, Thomas placed a hand on my thigh. The other came up and started rubbing my back. Could he tell how nervous I was? I was so thankful that he was taking the lead.

I was not some well-versed seductress. In fact, before all of this began, I would have called myself a borderline prude.

I rarely kissed a man on the first date—unless I felt wildly attracted to him. Before that night, I had only slept with a man on the first date once and that was because it was one of the best dates I'd ever had. So, for me to contemplate kissing a stranger at 2:30 in the morning, it took a lot of effort to drop my walls and open up to the moment.

Clearly, Thomas was well versed in the casual online dating world. He leaned in and kissed me. I wasn't sure what to expect, but I was pleasantly surprised.

Thomas kissed me tenderly and gently. His breath tasted like peppermint, I assume from a mint or gum that he chewed on his way over.

He slipped a hand behind my head, underneath my hair. It was the first time that I had kissed another man since my last serious boyfriend—I couldn't think about him now. My stomach did flip-flops. I felt weak even though I sat comfortably on the couch.

I lost my breath and felt completely swept up in the sensation. Almost unaware of whom I was with. His kiss was something that I had needed for months—and here I was finally getting it.

After he broke that barrier, I was ready for whatever came next. We kissed for a few minutes. Thomas had his hands all over me. They were strong and warm gripping me firmly. His hands hungrily moved around my body

Though, we'd spent the evening talking, the truth was that these were a stranger's hands. I had a stranger in my home. He was groping my breasts and pinching my nipples, reaching down between my legs.

I felt like a deer in headlights. I wasn't scared—exactly. More like there was just so much sensory input coming at me, all at once.

Oh damn, Lacie, you're just sitting here like a limp noodle while he does all the work!

I woke up and started reciprocating the physical contact. I began touching his face and body while we kissed. His face was smooth and freshly shaven. It felt great to finally touch a man after such a long hiatus.

Thomas adjusted his position on the couch, turning to face me better. My back was pressed firmly against the back of the couch as we continued kissing.

It was quickly becoming clear that we were never going to make it to the bedroom. It was all happening so fast. Or was it? Maybe this was the normal speed these things happened at, what the hell did I know?

What I did know was how *good* Thomas felt. That couch I'd been sitting on alone and bored, was now seeing more excitement than it ever had.

We continued fooling around. Luckily, he brought a condom; that was something I hadn't planned for when this night started. Protection never occurred to me, not until we started making out. I didn't even know what would happen when he came over, but I knew what I wanted now, and there was nowhere to get condoms at this time.

We started undressing each other. Thomas had showered. I could smell the faint scent of soap. It was overpowered by sweet, yet masculine smelling cologne, he must've put on before coming to my house.

Thomas was the full package—I had no idea just how full until we completely undressed each other. Thomas had a huge dick.

Wow. Where had this guy come from? I'd hit the jackpot. Not only was he insanely attractive and fit, but he was also hung like a damn horse.

After putting the condom on, Thomas moved me to the corner of my couch, placed himself on top of me, and slid his dick inside me.

He was huge. Very rarely does a man's dick hurt me, but I knew Thomas might need to hold back a little. It had been six months since I last had sex. As much as I wanted him at that moment, I'll admit I was apprehensive.

After a few minutes, Thomas flipped me over onto my hands and knees. I was balancing on the edge of the couch. He kneeled behind me then slid himself back inside.

I loved the way Thomas took charge and moved me how he wanted. It's such a turn on when a man has that kind of masculine energy and takes charge during sex.

I felt wanted and desirable.

Suddenly, I felt a wave of insecurity surge inside me. I had been in a rut the past few months and my body felt soft and flabby. The lights were still on, being so caught up in the moment, I never turned them off. There I was, naked as a Jaybird, on my hands and knees. I didn't want to do anything that would stop the forward momentum we were in, so I pushed my insecure thoughts out of my mind.

At the same time, Thomas started pounding me. I could tell that I couldn't handle the full force of his thrusts.

I tried to bite my lip.

"Ow," left my lips a few times.

He slowed down and took it more gently. I could tell by his immediate response to me that he was used to having to hold back while having sex with women.

And when he did—oh my God, finally, finally, I was able to feel it. That huge dick sliding in and out of me. His hands on me. Powerful. Strong. Taking me exactly where I wanted to go.

"How do you like to cum?" he asked.

"Missionary." Maybe it was vanilla, but it was the truth.

I loved the feeling of his strong arms and hands as he moved my body from one position to the next.

He flipped me onto my back, slid himself back inside me and made me cum quickly. I asked Thomas to straddle my legs, so I could close them. He did as I asked and continued fucking me. My hands were all over his smooth pecs while he pounded me on top.

I could not believe how great his rock-hard chest felt in my hands. His body alone was such a huge turn on, not to mention his huge dick. Thomas didn't have to fuck me very long in that position.

I started screaming.

"Oh my God, I'm going to cum. Fuck your dick feels so fucking amazing." I exploded with a huge orgasm, my fingernails scratching his back from shoulders to waist—a purely instinctual reaction I have to a big orgasm.

God, did I need that orgasm. Thank you, Thomas!

My body relaxed immediately after.

When I had finally drifted into awareness again, I apologized for shredding his back. It was quite frankly out of my control.

I asked how he wanted to cum. Thomas wanted to have sex doggy style again, but this time he stood on the floor with me kneeling on the edge of the couch. He put one leg up on the couch while he pounded me from behind. I tolerated his thrusts much better after my orgasm. I felt calm, relaxed, and ready to lie down.

When Thomas came that night, he was louder in expressing his pleasure than most men I had experienced. My knee jerk reaction was to laugh, but instead I took it as a compliment that Thomas was more than satisfied.

He arched his back forward and threw his head back screaming.

"Oh my God!" he yelled. I could feel his dick pulsing inside me. One of the many benefits of having sex with a man who's hung.

After he came, he grabbed the condom, holding onto it as he pulled out.

"Where should I take this off?"

"The bathroom is down the hall on the right."

He walked down the hallway and into the bathroom. I moved onto the couch and laid there on my back, pulsing from the extremely erotic experience I just had. *So, this is what it's like to have sex with a man nearly half my age?* I smiled knowing I already wanted more. I put my clothes back on and waited for him to return.

I was hoping Thomas would cuddle me. I hadn't realized it until that moment, but I'd been looking forward to this as much as the sex.

When he returned to the living room, I asked him, "Please tell me you cuddle?"

Thomas laughed. "Yes, I cuddle." I could tell he was amused by my direct approach.

Thomas laid down on his side. I moved myself next to him, lying with my backside facing his front. It was a perfect. Big spoon, little spoon.

I closed my eyes and relaxed into his body—or at least I tried to relax.

I could feel the tension strung throughout him. This was officially the most reluctant cuddle I'd ever received.

Sure enough, not five minutes passed before Thomas was climbing off the couch. "I gotta go. I have to work early in the morning—I'll be tired as it is."

I got up and followed him to the door. He slipped on his sneakers without tying them. I opened the door for him. Thomas leaned down and hugged me. I hugged him back.

"Thank you for coming. I had a great time. I really needed that."

"Thank you for letting me come over. After all that—you're still alive."

We both laughed at that. Thomas walked out the door. We both said goodbye, then I watched him disappear into the dark.

It was so late after he left that I crashed shortly after.

The next morning, I wondered if it had actually happened. Then, I stood up and was reminded exactly how real last night had been. A body doesn't deal with a dick like that and not feel it the next day.

God, the sex was *fantastic*.

See, now *this* was exactly what I'd been looking for, some excitement and companionship for the night, maybe with a little more cuddling next time, but overall great sex and *fun*!

I could live a more colorful life than just being a divorcee and a mom—I could do more than just be at home eating fresh baked cookies and binge-watching episodes of Game of Thrones, while my daughter, Aubrey, was at her father's house.

I could be more than the woman pining after a man, I like to call 24, whom I thought at this time was the love of my life—lost. The same man who literally pulled me from the depths of despair after my painful divorce. And finally, the man whose last words to me were in a text, declaring angrily that he'd never speak to me again.

I wanted to feel like I was living after my divorce. The only problem was this: I didn't feel that way at all and my relationship with 24 had left me in a terrible state. In my mid-forties, the vision of my life did not consist of being divorced, living paycheck to paycheck, and raising my daughter by myself. My vision had been set in concrete since I was a child.

Education. Marriage. Children. All in that order.

I only knew how to live one life. The one I planned. I really didn't know how to live as a single, divorcee. What did my life look like when all of my plans were gone?

Most of my friends were married, so going out on weekends was limited to dinner with them—a rarity in itself. Most of the time, I spent my weekends feeling like a total loser.

Above all, I missed the companionship of a man. Lacking that physical connection, left me feeling unhappy and unsatisfied. Thanks to Thomas and his amazing dick, I felt young, energetic, and full of life again.

Maybe Thomas could be the cure to all my ails. *He* was a single parent. *I* was a single parent. Neither of us had an interest in a serious relationship.

But sex—now that was a whole other story. I could offer him what guys always say they want—no strings attached sex. I could be his booty call. When I needed my itches scratched, I could message him.

Easy peasy.

That's all I was looking for right now. A regular number to put in my little black book. Consistent access to great sex. Something to shake up my weekends and give me the one thing I was missing most from a relationship. I was sure I could get him to warm up to cuddling afterwards, too.

But nothing in life is ever simple, is it?

You—my friend, are no doubt far savvier to how dating in the modern world works than I was when all of this began. You can probably imagine how my encounter with Thomas is going to end… right?

But before we go into all this, you need to really understand who I was and how I came to this point, we need to go back to the very beginning. Before that night.

Chapter 2: Toxic

It was a few years post-divorce. The wreck that was left in the wake of my broken marriage had been cleaned up as best as it could be. We, Aubrey; myself; and our little dog, Chewie; now lived in a small condo outside of Denver. It took a lot of work to get there, I was bound by the divorce agreement to remain close by, but couldn't afford much in Aubrey's school district. Somehow, we made it!

But with all the essentials now cared for, my emotional needs finally started coming back up, demanding to be addressed.

I had fifty percent custody of my daughter and we always made the most of our time together. We had a large circle of friends and family that we were always getting together with during my half of the week. However, when Aubrey was at her dad's, I was quite often alone.

In part, it was my choice. That particular night with Thomas, my friend Alex had invited me over to dinner— usually I said yes, but this time I declined. The last thing I wanted to do was sit through *one more dinner* with my married friend and her family. The kids would ask awkward questions, wondering aloud where Aubrey was. I'd get the delightful task of explaining that she was at her dad's house, while their mom tried to shush them, then quickly change the subject. It took its toll on me.

Please, don't get me wrong. At the beginning of my divorce, I needed nothing more than my friends around me, especially to keep me busy. But, after years of healing—first from my divorce and then from 24—the man whom I had an intensely karmic post-divorce relationship with (more on him later)—I was ready to start living on my own.

Sometimes friends would ask me to come to their children's sporting events, often in the hope that a hot single dad would be there. No such luck. My close circle of friends continued to include me in their family dinners and couples' parties regardless of the single status.

Yet, even when nothing awkward happened, it just felt... *off*. Something was missing. It was like I was in a Sesame Street skit of "Which One of These Things Doesn't Belong?"

So, I started staying home.

All alone.

Thinking of... 24.

My almost soulmate. Or hell, maybe he was my *actual* soulmate. But 24 and me, our timing had been off and I'd given up hope of us ever syncing.

I clicked off the TV and tossed the remote onto the coffee table. I closed my eyes and ran my hand along the soft suede of my couch.

The thing that no one tells you about being single is that after a while you begin to crave touch. Sex, you're expected to start missing—eventually. But something as simple as human contact. No one ever told me how much I'd miss that.

My thoughts went back to the last man who touched me. *Really* touched me in all the ways that mattered.

I nicknamed him 24, because that was how old he was when I met and started dating him. Back then I was 36. Yeah, yeah I know, I was a cougar even then, although he called me a puma, since I wasn't quite in my forties.

We were two broken people who fell in love quickly, despite the fact that neither of us were in the right place in our lives. Somehow we saw a future together. Our sexual and emotional connection was unlike anything I have ever had—with anyone. It was the first time I felt connected to a man. It was an incredible feeling. Intoxicating.

No matter how perfect we were for each other, we couldn't manage to stay together. All throughout 2012, we were on again, off again. On again. Off. Then—

Well, you get the picture.

It was at this point when I had the first realization that something needed to be healed inside me.

Let's face it, no self-respecting, confident woman with healthy boundaries would allow herself to remain in an unhealthy cycle with a man who didn't show evidence of change or commitment, upon his numerous reappearances in my life.

Relationships all came down to timing, a concept that I had never truly understood before. 24 wasn't a bad person, I would learn that he was actually going through the same sort of growing up that many of the men I dated were also working towards.

The fact was this: some people meet at the wrong time and there is no forcing it; because simply, it won't work. I'd wanted it to work so badly. I saw the man that 24 could become. Would become (I hoped). I wanted to be with that man. Till death do us part.

The problem was… 24 was still, well—24! He was young. The immaturity hadn't had time to burn off yet. He wanted to be with me and made that crystal clear, but he didn't know who he was, nor what he truly wanted out of life. Until someone knows definitively who they are and what they want, I don't see how any romantic relationship can be successful.

Lucky for him, he had many alluring and desirable traits. He could be thoughtful, affectionate, take charge, masculine, generous, and many other things that I could hope for in a partner.

Every time we broke up, 24 would eventually come back... and I'd always open the door. Sometimes it would be a few weeks later. Sometimes a few months. The last time it was a year or two.

24 came back to my life in the summer of 2017. He had just broken up with his girlfriend of two years and, as usual, he wanted to throw himself into the arms of a woman.

It started with a text.

24: HEY, HOW ARE YOU DOING?

Me: I'M GREAT. HOW ARE YOU DOING?

24: NOT GOOD. I BROKE UP WITH MY GIRLFRIEND 2 DAYS AGO.

Me: I'M SORRY TO HEAR THAT. AT LEAST I KNOW WHY YOU'RE TEXTING ME NOW.

I wasn't happy to hear from him and I had no intention of hiding my feelings.

24: IT'S NOT LIKE THAT.

Me: OH REALLY. WHAT'S IT LIKE THEN?

24: I'VE NEVER STOPPED THINKING ABOUT YOU. I WANT TO SEE YOU.

Me: I HATE TO BREAK IT TO YOU, BUT YOUR WORDS MEAN NOTHING TO ME ANYMORE.

Our conversation went on and on like this—all night long. Sometimes, I'd have the final word and he'd scamper away with his tail between his legs. Sometimes, he'd have the final word, because I wouldn't take the bait and buy into his bullshit. Finally, at around 7:00 am the next day, I caved and agreed to let him come over—5 years had passed, yet I still

19

had no boundaries and no more self-respect than back in 2012. The shame I felt was a heavy. He'd asked at least a handful of times during our texting marathon and I'd finally surrendered.

24: SERIOUSLY?

Me: YES. I MOVED. HERE'S MY NEW ADDRESS. TEXT ME WHEN YOU'RE IN THE PARKING LOT SO I DON'T HAVE TO GET OUT OF BED UNTIL YOU GET HERE.

24: OK. I'M GETTING AN UBER NOW. I'M EXCITED TO SEE YOU.

I didn't reply.

I wasn't excited to see him. I had tried for years to close the door on my relationship with him. Yet, his coming back into my life meant that I'd regressed and had completely failed to move forward.

Twenty minutes later, I got a text. He was out by my car. It was now 7:30, thank goodness it was Saturday.

Me: COMING.

I hopped out of bed and threw on a skirt, keeping on the tank top that I had worn to bed. I grabbed my flip-flops and sunglasses. Even though it was early, it was already a beautiful sunny day.

I squinted at the bright light as I opened the door and walked out onto my front step. I had barely slept a wink. I was tired and not really happy with myself.

I still loved 24 and probably always would, but I had no desire to be used and discarded as I had been in the past with him. I knew he wanted temporary comfort and I told him before that I wasn't the person to give that to him.

Regardless, I found myself on my doorstep waiting for him. Just like I always did. Pathetic.

When he showed up at my house, he was still drunk from the night before. He'd obviously been up all-night partying, taking God-only-knew what kind of drugs that had allowed him to stay up late and still look wired.

I knew immediately that he was doing drugs other than pot and alcohol. Both would make someone pass out—eventually. Whatever he was on, it allowed him to party for 12 hours straight.

24 was nervous as he walked into my house. He had never been to my new place. The décor and Chewie were unfamiliar to him. Everything about my life had changed and he was like a foreigner in a strange land.

He was on edge (or maybe he was just now coming down from whatever he took). He made a beeline for my fridge and took out the half empty bottle of Chardonnay my mom had left. 24 pulled out the cork and put his lips to the top of the bottle, threw his head back and guzzled the wine.

"Holy shit, it's 7 am!" I followed him into the kitchen. "What the hell are you doing, 24?"

"Fuck. I needed that." He took a couple more swigs from the bottle. "I can't believe I'm here—in your living room." He looked around slowly, taking it all in. "Do you still smoke weed?"

I nodded. I could not wrap my mind around the fact that he was standing in my kitchen. How many sad lonely nights did I have over the past few years, yearning for him? Yearning for comfort. Now, here he was. In the flesh, yet—I really didn't want him anymore.

What I had desired for so long was now not as appealing. Physically speaking 24 was a ten in my book. Tall, dark, and handsome pretty much summed him up. He was six-foot-three and biracial, with curly hair and a thick black beard. 24

was masculine and hot with a confidence that bordered on cocky.

His greatest grace was his amazing personality and his ability to make me laugh with just a facial expression.

Personality has always been that top character trait I look for in a man. 24 was a ten in that category, too. We could spend a long rainy day getting high, watching movies, and playing games—doing whatever and it was always a great time.

I snapped myself out of reminiscing then replied to his question, "Yes. You'd be surprised. I have my own pipe and my own weed. I smoke pot on occasion, not just when someone else has it."

"Wanna smoke some now?" he asked.

"Sure, why the hell not? My day is already going to be wasted from being up all night and having zero sleep—due to *someone* texting me."

24 laughed that deep heartfelt laugh of his. He always did think I was funny, even though in this case, I was actually speaking with mild sarcasm.

I headed towards the patio and opened the slider.

"Come on, let's smoke on the patio. Do you have bud?"

24 gave me his signature half laugh which said: *Are you fucking kidding me?*

I stepped out onto the patio. The tile cold on my bare feet. I opened the storage door and grabbed my hidden weed pouch, then sat down in one of the two small wicker chairs. The blue cushion beneath me and the brightly-striped pillow at my back did not reflect my current mood. 24 sat in the other chair.

"Your place is great, Lacie. You must be so happy that you have all this. I want something like this too, someday."

"Yeah, I love our condo. It's perfect for us. I miss not having a house and a pool, but it's great that we have our own place. It gives me a great sense of stability."

24 pulled a medicine container of weed from his pocket. He pulled out a bud. I pulled out my grinder.

"Damn, you even have a grinder?"

He took it from my hands and inspected it. "This is top notch."

"I know. I love it. It's magnetic and super heavy duty. It was expensive so it better be good."

24 broke off little pieces of marijuana and stuffed them into the grinder. Once it was full, he put the lid in place and turned the top and bottom in opposite directions, grinding up the buds. He opened it, pinched some weed between his thumb and forefinger, and then packed the bowl of my pipe.

He handed me the lighter and pipe. He was the most well-mannered man I ever smoked with and always insisted I take the first hit. I covered the carb with my thumb, lit the weed, and inhaled deeply.

24 was used to me being a novice weed smoker. He was genuinely surprised that I took such a long drag without coughing or choking. The Lacie he used to know would've been coughing and needing water.

"Damn. You sure do smoke weed."

I laughed and nodded in his direction. "I learned from the best."

24 laughed again—louder this time. Apparently, I was killing it without even trying.

I handed him the pipe and lighter. He lit the bowl and took a long deep drag. He exhaled, his lips forming thick white smoke rings that dissipated in the air as they floated higher. He handed the pipe and lighter back to me. I took a big hit again, tilting my head back, closing my eyes, and exhaling slowly. When I released all the smoke, I turned to look at 24.

He was staring at me with sad eyes. Eyes that seemed to say: *God, I fucking miss you.*

I smiled slowly even coyly, continuing to keep our unwavering eye contact. My movements felt slow and drawn out.

"Damn, this is some fireball weed. I just took two hits and I'm high as fuck."

24 smiled. "I only smoke the best."

"Clearly. But then again, it doesn't have very far to go. It goes down and it comes right back up." I looked at my feet.

24 laughed. "God, I forgot how fucking funny you are."

"I don't know if other people think I'm quite as funny as you think I am. Let's go inside. It's early and people may still be sleeping."

I grabbed the pipe, lighter, and case before heading in. 24 followed behind me, locking the slider as he entered the house. He was always a guy who noticed the small details like that. You'd never have to check that he'd locked the door or turned off the lights when he'd leave.

We sat at opposite sides of my L-shaped couch.

"So, how've you been, Lacie? It's been a minute."

"Yes, it has. As you can see, I've bought a condo. We've been here for almost a year. We love living here—the school is within walking distance. Everything is great. But what's up with you—aside from your recent breakup?"

He spread his arms across the back of the couch, then crossed his ankles as he prepared himself to speak. "I'm still installing cable. I like what I do. Not much else new."

We continued chatting, catching up on his family and mine—he asked about Aubrey. We talked about everything we wanted to know about each other's lives.

After some time had passed, our conversation had reached a lull. 24 said, "Let's smoke again"

"Ok."

Still sitting on the couch, I opened my pipe case and pulled out the pipe and lighter. I lit the bowl and took a hit.

24 looked surprised. "You smoke in here?"

"Fuck yeah I do. It's my house."

The truth was that I mostly smoked outside. I didn't want my house smelling like a dispensary. On occasion though, I'd smoke inside knowing full well the smell would dissipate by the time Aubrey returned.

I handed him the pipe and lighter. He grabbed both and took a hit then handed them back. I took another hit, knowing it would be my last. His weed was so strong. I handed the pipe and lighter back. He took another hit.

Before he blew out the smoke, he got up off the couch, walked over to me, and leaned over my body. His hands braced the back of the couch on either side of me as he closed the last bit of distance between us.

He pressed his big, full lips against mine. Holy shit! Largely due to the weed and the wow factor of that moment, I lay my head back onto the couch cushion and took in the sensations of his lips touching mine.

What. The. Fuck. Was. I. Doing?

Here, I was with a man whom I had broken up with countless times before. The outcome never changed. Always the same result. He wasn't ready for a commitment or adult life for that matter. And this time I was set on moving on.

I knew this time would be no different from our previous ones. I knew any interaction would be a temporary fix, a momentary break from my loneliness. I knew what I needed, and I knew that 24 still could not give that to me.

Even though I knew all this. I knew that having him over could only lead to the same repercussions and rebounding into the same old routine, something I certainly didn't want any of, he was still here with his lips on mine.

I hadn't been longing for him or looking at him lustfully before. Sure, I noticed he was still the fine man I once dated; but otherwise, I didn't feel the sexual energy we once shared. Before this moment it almost felt like we were old friends, catching up.

That was why the boldness of his kiss took me so off guard. I was completely turned on by the moment and swept off my feet.

24 exhaled as I inhaled. I took a full shotgun hit from him. As he had exhaled all of the smoke, he pulled me into a long gentle kiss. He kept our lips connected long enough to make me want more.

24 knew just how to tease me, how to entice me. Like a perfectly placed puzzle piece, my right hand reached up to cup the side of his face. My thumb gently rubbed his smooth cheek. I turned my face away long enough to exhale, then slowly turned back and kissed him.

It was so easy. So familiar. So, fucking *good*.

At first, I barely opened my mouth, letting him feel and taste my lips. When he started using his tongue, I started using mine as well, just a little. I wanted to make him want more, to increase his appetite for me.

Finally, I opened my mouth wide and caressed his mouth with my tongue. I kissed him tenderly, my right hand held his

26

face while my fingers were running through his beard. He tilted his head towards my hand, as if he were longing for my touch. His cupped my face, tilting my head back. Then ran his fingers through my hair.

I could feel myself melting into the couch. All of my muscles relaxed at once. I felt my heart race. The desire returned—God how I missed this. I was completely immersed in the moment. My body pulsed. The apex between my legs was lit with sensation. I could not believe that I was under 24 again. Every time, I thought it would be the last, yet here he was. Psychoanalyze that.

"Fuck, I forgot how fucking great you kiss," he whispered, his voice husky.

I smiled and looked at him with the kind of bedroom eyes that only weed can give.

"You mean how great *we* kiss."

I don't know how long we made out in that same position—it felt like an eternity—I was ready for more. I wanted 24 in every way possible. Just like I always had.

"Let's go to my bedroom."

"Ok."

He pulled back and held out his hand to help me up. 24 needed me to lead the way. He walked into my room and sat on the edge of the bed. I closed the door, sauntered straight up to stand between his legs.

I grabbed the bottom of his shirt and pulled it up over his head. 24 lifted his arms to help. I was surprised by how toned his body was. He was working a physical job, but for a man who had no desire to spend his time working out when he could be smoking weed, he looked surprisingly fit.

"Holy shit. Look at your body."

24 laughed. "Yeah I use my arms every day at work. I'm tall enough that I don't need a ladder, so I am constantly lifting my hands over my head."

I didn't think I could be anymore turned on than I already was—but damn. "You look fucking great."

24 smiled. "Thanks."

I dropped his shirt onto the ground. My hands went straight for his pecs. I wanted to get my hands all over his upper body.

How was it possible that he could be hotter to me now, than he was before? If I had to answer that question, I'd probably blame it on the weed. I ran my fingers all over his body from his pecs, to his shoulders, and down to his biceps. His smooth skin was firm to the touch. I trailed my hand back up and down his pecs again. Never once pausing my contact with his body.

24 started kissing me while my hands rediscovered him. His hands grabbed my tank top and pulled it off. He exhaled loudly when he saw my breasts. He immediately grabbed them with both hands, lifting them up and kissing one at a time. 24 buried his face in my breasts and took turns sucking on each nipple.

"Fuck, I forgot how amazing your tits are."

I ran my fingers through his dark curly hair while he enjoyed my body. I was reminded of how much I loved his hair, his soft tight ringlet curls slipping through my fingers.

I could feel wetness between my legs. I was ready to feel him deep inside of me. He was always able to turn me on, more than other men, this time was no different.

I stopped him from playing with my breasts by running my fingers through his hair and gently pulling his head back. He looked up at me and we kissed hard and passionately. I knelt down between his legs, grabbed his pants, and started to slide them off. He stood up and let me do the rest. I set his pants and underwear to the side on the floor.

I got on my knees and grabbed his familiar amazing dick in my hand. 24 was already fully hard. I started stroking it up and down. 24 took a deep breath and moaned with pleasure from my touch. He continued staring intently at me, even putting a hand on my head, running his long slender fingers through my hair. It turned me on to know he enjoyed watching me give him head.

I was a giver, there was no doubt about that. I grabbed his balls in my free hand and felt the surge of electricity run through his body.

For a moment I felt the connection we had once shared. I knew how to give this man pleasure. It made me feel powerful and desired. The time we had spent apart felt like a mistake between two passionate needy people spooked by the perfection of our chemistry. Of course, this was my heart talking—mixed with some fireball weed.

In my head I knew nothing had changed. This wouldn't be different than any of the times before. 24 was not a man who liked to feel pain or discomfort of any kind. I was a comforting body to him. He was using me for his immediate gratification and to soothe himself after a breakup, I knew this, yet—

It was 24. We had history with a capital H. As much as I knew that this morning would be just another dead end with him, I'd missed him. His body was warm and strong beneath me.

He was kryptonite.

But I was whole now, strong and confident, I'd never let myself slide back into old, unhealthy patterns of behavior which I knew would only result in pain—or so I thought.

I was horny as fuck. I let that feeling guide me.

I started focusing on giving him great head. I wanted him to remember this when he left my house, how good I was. I wanted him to remember me. I grabbed his balls firmly and fondled them while I sucked his dick, stroking it with my other hand.

24 groaned. "I will never find anyone who gives head as good as you."

I smiled. 24's verbal expressiveness was one of his most redeeming qualities. Genuine expressions of pleasure fueled my efforts.

As I continued working him, he lay back onto the bed and moaned, breathing heavily from his own arousal. I gave him head for a few more minutes.

No way was I going to keep this up until he came and run the risk of him leaving. Up until that moment, he was the best fuck of my life. I wanted to get a piece of him while he was under my roof.

I crawled onto him and propped myself up with my hands on each side of his head, then leaned down to kiss him. He reached his long arms down and pulled off my skirt and panties in one fluid motion.

Luckily, he had a condom in his wallet.

As soon as I slid him in, I was reminded of how exceptional his big thick dick was. A damn near perfect dick.

Any time we were together, whether high or sober, fireworks would fly. I'd think every time that there was no better sex than the caliber of what we had with each other.

What's even more amazing is that we had perfect kissing styles, which sent our passion and chemistry off the charts.

I rode him while we lay across the bed. His hands on my hips, moving my body up and down. My feet dangled off the bed.

After a little bit we switched positions, he climbed to the middle of the bed and I laid next to him.

He immediately rolled to his side and put his hand on my legs, turning his head to kiss me. He slid his hand up my thigh. My heart raced with anticipation. I was dying for him to put his hand between my legs. I wanted him to move faster. He chose to torture me, moving his hand slowly up my thigh until it reached my wetness. He put his finger inside me.

"God, you are so fucking wet. I forgot how wet you get."

"You make me wet. I'm horny as fuck for you. I want you to fuck me."

"Yes ma'am."

He rolled on top of me in one swift move. He propped himself up on his elbows and slid his dick deep inside me.

"Oh my God," I groaned. "You feel fucking amazing."

"Fuck, I've missed you," he responded, kissing down my neck.

I jerked back, shaking my head.

I didn't want to hear the player playing in this moment. I didn't need lip service. For him to tell me what he thought I wanted to hear. "Don't—don't tell me that. Please just fuck me."

And fuck me, he did.

24 knew exactly how to please me. I didn't have to give him any direction. He knew when I was aroused enough that all I needed was to close my legs and cum. He straddled my

legs and fucked me slow and deep. He remembered exactly how I liked to cum.

After a very short time, I was screaming, "Oh my God!"

24 gave me a huge orgasm that morning.

Now it was his turn.

I knew he liked to cum doggy style. After I came, I moved onto my hands and knees getting into position for him. He knelt behind me with his knees between my legs. He slid his dick inside of me and started fucking me. I could feel him hitting my cervix as we had sex. He felt amazing. He was so incredibly hard.

24 held my hips with both hands, as he drove his dick deep inside me. He arched his back as he moaned loudly. I didn't even have time to grab his balls or do any of the things that I know men like. After he came, he sat there for a few minutes with his dick still deep inside me. Finally, I had to lay down on my stomach. He pulled himself out.

I headed for the restroom, quickly cleaned up then returning back to bed, all the while remaining naked. 24 cleaned up as well and came back. He cuddled up to me immediately and passed out within minutes. I could hear his breathing get heavier and heavier until it was the calm steady rhythm of sleep. I lay there listening to him.

What the hell did I just do?

I buried my face into my pillow. How did I let him back into my life, let alone my house and bed? After many times of us breaking up and getting back together, I had vowed to never let him return to my life in that same way. Yet, here he was coming into my house, getting me high then fucking me—just like every other time before. I felt so shitty in that moment.

Nothing was different about him. Or me. Or us. It made me feel sick.

But did I pull away from him or get out of bed?

No, of course I didn't.

Because this was 24.

We slept until 11 am, cuddling the whole time. 24 never took his hands off me. He loved to cuddle and it made me realize how starved I was for a man's comfort.

Human touch. You only realize how hungry you are for it after going without for so long. Yet, I was never the kind of woman to date someone just for comfort. I wanted a mature, responsible, emotionally-healthy, committed, fun, and communicative man. A real man. Sadly, they're so very hard to come by.

I woke 24 up. "Hey, you gotta go. I have plans. I need to shower, get ready, and leave." I was cold and matter of fact.

"Are you serious?" His eyebrows scrunched all the way up to his hairline. "I'm still drunk and I have no car."

"Well, lucky for you, I have a car and you live two minutes away. I'll drop you off on my way out."

It was the first time I had ever kicked him out of my house. I could tell he was hurt and shocked. He stayed in bed sleeping until I was ready to leave. I woke him up for a final time.

He was miffed and had a total attitude with me. I didn't care.

I drove him back to his house. He made me stop a block away. He said he wanted to smoke a cigarette on his walk back, but really he didn't want his parents to see my car. He didn't want to explain why he was with me.

He opened the door to get out. There was a definite awkwardness to all of it. In spite of everything, this wasn't

33

how I wanted to leave things between us. I held out my fist in his direction. "Sooooo… fist bump?"

24 laughed as he stepped out of the car. He turned around and fist bumped me.

"Have a great rest of your weekend."

"You too."

He closed the door and stepped onto the sidewalk.

As I drove away, I could see him walking down the street smoking a cigarette, carrying his collared shirt over his shoulder. He was wearing his pants and an untucked under shirt. He looked exactly like what he was, a man who had been up all-night doing drugs and getting drunk.

Pathetic.

As soon as he was out of sight, I realized I felt numb towards him. The guilt and shame I had felt after letting him in the door—yet again—had subsided. I simply felt nothing.

I called Chloe before I even got home.

Chloe lived a couple hours away, but we remained close through regular communication. Chloe was a lifesaver after my divorce. For years we talked almost nightly as she supported me on my path to healing.

She was by my side when I first dated 24 and had seen all of the ups and downs of our relationship. She was always the first one that I'd call when I had something to discuss involving him. She knew what made him tick and was able to help me see things that I couldn't or didn't want to.

"Well, you may or may not be shocked at what I'm about to tell you… 24 came over last night and we had sex."

Chloe responded, "Oh wow! I'm not exactly surprised, but how long has it been? Years, right?"

"Yes, it's been years. Not surprisingly, he just broke up with his girlfriend of two years. So, he pretty much wanted comfort and I let him weasel his way back in. I hope one day I will actually be able to say no to that man."

"You loved him deeply. You may never be able to do that."

"I really hope that's not the case. How are you doing? What's new with you?"

"I'm good. I've still been seeing Steve on occasion."

"Why only on occasion?" I asked as I pulled into my parking spot. "I thought you were really into him."

"I felt like I was at first, but maybe it was just the excitement of something new. The intoxication of a man showing interest and wanting me."

"Yeah, I get that. A new relationship is like a drug. What are you going to do?" I parked but stayed seated in my car.

"We have plans to have dinner this week, so I plan on talking to him about it. Telling him that I'm not in a place to be in a relationship. The fact of the matter is, we aren't compatible—I knew that from the beginning."

"Talking to him at dinner sounds like a good plan." I unbuckled my seat belt. "In the meantime, what are you going to do to tackle and resolve whatever issues are keeping you from being ready? That way—when the next man comes around—you don't have the same problem."

"Yeah, I've thought about that. I am going to reach out to my counselor and schedule an appointment to talk about it".

"That's great! I'm proud of you. It doesn't always feel so good to tackle our problems." I caught a glimpse of myself in the mirror. "It's painful."

"Yeah, I figured that I've been putting it off long enough. Time to move forward in my life."

I shook my head at my reflection knowing I needed to follow Chloe's lead. "Good for you!"

***

24 and I communicated very little that week, but the following weekend the same thing happened. He texted me at 4 am seemly lost and upset.

24: I DON'T KNOW WHAT I'M DOING WITH MY LIFE. I'M A FUCKING MESS.

Me: WHAT THE HELL ARE YOU DOING? WHY ARE YOU UP AT 4:00 AM? YOU ARE AN AMAZING MAN, THE MOST INTELLIGENT MAN I KNOW. GET YOUR SHIT TOGETHER.

I was pissed. Not because he woke me up, but because the 24 that I knew was better than all this. Much better.

He felt like he needed me during this time. I knew based on our past that I wasn't the person to be there for him—not now or maybe ever.

I told him this—again.

Me: I'M NOT THE PERSON TO COMFORT YOU. I'VE TOLD YOU THAT BEFORE. YOU NEED TO FIND SOMEONE ELSE TO MEET YOUR NEEDS. IT CAN'T BE ME. IT'S TOO PAINFUL FOR ME AND IT ALWAYS WILL BE.

My phone started ringing. I was surprised that he was calling, especially since I was being harsher with him than I had ever been before. I thought for sure that what I was saying would be too much and it would push him away.

Still, I answered the call. "Hello."

24 started crying. "I fucking love you, Lacie. I'm so grateful God brought you into my life. You truly care and I know that."

I sat up in bed, leaning against the headboard. I hated that he was hurting so badly. I softened my tone. "I love you too, 24, but you gotta get your shit together. Being up all night, doing drugs and drinking, it's a waste of your life."

36

"I know." A short silence came from the other line. And then he said, "Can I come over?"

"Sure… OK."

The words were out of my mouth, before I could think better of it. I knew I was fighting an uphill battle. However, I had never seen him this emotionally distraught before. Something about his tone... it made me want to comfort him.

Two confusing Uber rides later, he arrived at my house for the second weekend in a row—in the wee hours of the morning. I opened the door in my panties and a tank top— because who were we kidding, we both knew where this would lead.

24 crawled into bed with me and immediately cuddled up. He was still emotional and started crying again. I'd never seen him like this. Ever. I held him and reassured him that he would be fine that he'd get through this.

24 stayed until 7 that night. A total of 14 hours. We smoked weed, watched movies, and had sex six times that day.

Somewhere in the middle of the afternoon, I had two realizations. One, I couldn't see 24 again. It wasn't healthy for my own somewhat fragile state. Two, he had a problem with drugs and alcohol, but I wasn't sure what I should do about it—if anything.

His hyper-emotionality. His staying up all hours. The erratic behavior—this wasn't the 24 that I'd known.

The following weekend was his thirtieth birthday. He was going to celebrate at a beach house in Southern California with his cousins and friends.

I texted him 'Happy Birthday' at midnight. By 6 pm the next day, I still had not gotten a response. 24 *always* texted back. I am not typically an anxious person, but I grew more and more worried as each hour passed.

I'd never had someone in my life before that I had considered to be an addict. And as each hour ticked by endlessly, I kept envisioning the worst. What exactly was he on? What if he took too much? Would he even know how much *was* too much if he was that out of it? What if he got into a car with someone who took too much and drove? What if he died?

Finally, around 6:30, I texted him again.

Me: ARE YOU OK? I HAVEN'T HEARD FROM YOU AND I'M WORRIED.

When the answering ping came, I felt a wave of relief crash over me. Followed by anger.

24: YEAH, I'M FINE. JUST SUPER FADED.

I knew in that moment that 24 had a major problem. This wasn't a case of someone who occasionally smoked weed to relax on the weekends. If I (the least anxious person) thought he was either dead or in harm's way due to his drug use, then there had to be a problem with it.

Over the next week, I thought about 24 and what I should do to help him. I debated whether it was right of me to do anything at all. I reached out to friends who were recovering alcoholics. I talked with other friends who knew about our past and asked for advice.

I called Claudia. She was also a single mom and was as no nonsense as me. I knew she would give it to me straight.

"What should I do?"

"Nothing," Claudia said. "He's not your problem. He comes back after three years to fuck you and you think you are responsible for him? Fuck no. That guy has other people who can help him. Not you, Lacie."

I could see Claudia's point, but I still cared about 24. I was not the type of woman to do nothing. I take charge, get shit done. And right now, I felt helpless. I had to do something. I decided to call another friend, Samantha.

Samantha had been in recovery for many years and was still connected with the AA program. She was one resilient and inspiring woman. Not only had she conquered addiction, but she had also survived breast cancer. All while being a single mom. Sam was one of the few people that I could call and who would be willing to be vulnerable enough to openly share her inner struggles.

"Wow, that's tough," Sam said. "You definitely should say something to his family—if you're comfortable with it. Decide the best way to do it—for yourself. However you're most comfortable communicating with them, that's how you should do it."

"Yeah, I think I'd like to say something in person—the next time I see them," I said. "I don't really feel comfortable showing up at their doorstep, but if I see them, I'll definitely say something. I run into them maybe a couple times a year, just running errands."

Sam and I talked for an hour. She explained all of the help that is available online and the support groups offered to people struggling with addiction. Samantha was a driving force in helping me follow through with talking to 24's parents.

A week after his birthday, I prayed before going to bed.

God, if you put 24's family in front of me, I will tell them my concerns. I will tell them that he has a problem and how fearful I am for his life. If you want me to tell them, then please put them in front of me. I promise, if you do your part, I'll do mine.

The following day, I had breakfast plans with a friend. She texted saying she was sick and couldn't make it. Because it was Sunday, I laid in bed until close to 11 am. I watched a movie before throwing on clothes to head to Starbucks then to the bagel store near my house.

While walking through the parking lot, I looked up and saw 24's dad and sister in the window seat of the bagel store, they were waving at me like crazy.

Fuck! Are you kidding me? The very next day?

I smiled and waved back pointing to Starbucks. Letting them know that I'd be right there. FUCK! All I wanted to do was turn around. There was no way that I could tell them. What was I thinking? Why would I make a deal with God like that? But now that they saw me, there was no turning around and going home. Fuck, fuck, fuck!

In that moment, I truly didn't think that I could do my part. When I walked into the bagel store, they both stood and greeted me with hugs. His dad had pulled a chair up to their table for me. I ordered my bagel (his dad insisted on paying for it) and sat down to eat with them.

I loved 24's family so much. I felt genuine warmth and love from them every time I bumped into them. They immediately wanted to know how Aubrey and I were doing.

After a few minutes of catching up, I asked about 24. I had to keep up pretenses, since they had no idea that I had just spent the last two weekends with him.

"He's good," his dad said. "Still working in cable installation. We barely ever see him. He works during the week and is gone all weekend. His birthday was last weekend. He went to Southern California to celebrate with his cousins."

I forced a smile. "Oh, that sounds like fun!" (Or like a death wish.)

We continued to catch up as we ate our bagels. Every minute that passed, I could hear the two angels sitting on my shoulder:

Good angel: *You promised if He put them in your path, you'd—*

Bad angel: *You're the fucking ex-girlfriend! This is none of your business! Just say goodbye and be on your merry way.*

Good angel: *And if he ends up dead and you never said anything?*

After a while, his dad got up to close out his tab. When he walked away, I looked at his sister. Taking a deep breath, I opened that can of worms I so badly wanted to keep closed.

"I'm worried about your brother. He came by about two weeks ago. I'm really worried about him. He doesn't seem well at all." My eyes began to tear up. "I'm afraid of him dying."

His sister, who was only twenty-five years old, placed her hand on my arm. Her eyes wide. "Lacie, I've been worried about my brother for *years*. I've told my parents repeatedly that I'm concerned about his drug and alcohol use. My mom sees it and fears for his life. She even started going to counseling. Every night she goes to bed afraid that he is going to die that night."

I started crying as quietly as possible. I asked if we could go outside. I wasn't ready to talk to his dad and I didn't want him to see me crying. When we got out to my car, I went into more details regarding what I had witnessed. I was truly afraid that he was going to die if he didn't make a change in his life.

His sister looked me in the eye. "Would you be willing to talk to my parents and tell them what you're telling me? My mom sees it, but Dad's in denial. I think hearing it from you would make the world of a difference."

"But I'm just an ex-girlfriend. Won't your parents take it the wrong way, coming from me?"

She reached out and put a hand on my arm. "Not at all. My parents love you and have so much respect for you. We all know how much you loved 24. When you communicate your concern for him, they know it comes from a place of genuine love and caring."

I took a deep breath and nodded. "Okay. I leave for Maui in two days, but I can meet with them today or tomorrow. Here's my phone number. You can text me and let me know."

She texted me within the hour and let me know that she, her mom, and dad would come to my house to meet with me the next afternoon.

I called Sam to let her know what happened.

"So, guess whose parents and sister are coming over tomorrow to talk?"

"You're kidding me! You already ran into them?"

"The morning after, I prayed and told God that I'd talk to them if he put them in front of me. Go figure."

"Wow. Talk about divine intervention."

"Seriously," I shook my head. "I'm so nervous. I feel compelled to talk to them; yet at the same time, I feel scared he's going to hate me forever."

"He may. You have no idea how he's going to react. But trust me, you'll feel better speaking up—especially if you can end up helping him. If something happened and you didn't speak up, you'd never be able to forgive yourself."

"Yeah, I know it's the right thing to do—I'm just scared."

"God will give you the strength. He put you in 24's life to save him, Lacie. I'm confident of that."

"I agree—I am too."

The next day, 24's mom, dad, and sister came to my house. I baked oatmeal, milk chocolate chip, and walnut cookies for them. They are 24's favorite and I wanted them to be able to take some home. We all sat at the kitchen table with a plateful of cookies sitting in the middle. Just as I started speaking, I broke down crying. His sister placed a hand on my back in an effort to soothe me.

"I feel like I'm betraying him. I feel horrible. I know that I have to do this, but I also know that the tradeoff will be him hating me forever. With that being said, I couldn't live with myself if he died and I did nothing."

All three of them reassured me that I was doing the right thing and they knew how much love 24 and I had for each other.

After their encouragement, I told them everything that had happened over the past two weekends. I told them about him being awake all-night long partying, that weed and alcohol are not the kind of drugs that will keep you up all night. I told them about the things he did while we were dating, his reckless and irresponsible behavior. I told them that I have never been *so* scared for him before now.

In the end, his parents were very grateful. They knew he had a problem and they were going to meet with his mom's therapist to develop a plan for how to handle it.

Lucky for them, 24 still lived at home, so they had major leverage over his actions—if he wanted to continue staying where he was, he was going to have to take a look at his behavior.

Before they left my house, they all hugged me, thanked me, and expressed that God had sent me to help with 24. I believed the same and told them so. I sent all the cookies home with them and told them that they could figure out how to explain how they got them to 24.

I stayed in touch with 24's sister—to find out what was going on once the shit hit the fan. I also bumped into his parents at Costco a couple weeks later and was updated on his progress.

In a nutshell—he denied having a problem when they first confronted him, which resulted in them needing to tell him that they had talked to me. After their second conversation with him, when my name was brought up, 24 admitted to everything. He agreed to attend weekly counseling with a drug and alcohol specialist and to join an AA group.

The last time I saw a member of his family, I learned that he had been sober for a few months and that he was continuing weekly drug and alcohol counseling. At the time he had attended ninety consecutive days of AA meetings. He had transformed back into the son that they hadn't seen in twelve years. His family was beyond grateful to me, especially for my vulnerability and honesty. It was one of the most difficult things I'd ever done, but the love and affection his family showed me made it all worth it.

On a less happy note, I received a text from him about a month after all of this went down. He blamed me for the rift in his family and for all of his other problems. He was angry that I didn't come to him first before talking with his family.

As if that would've accomplished anything.

He told me that I would never hear from him again. He wished Aubrey and me a nice life.

I'd expected something like that, but it still hurt to know that this man, who I loved so much, hated me because of my actions that could have ultimately ended up saving his life.

And that was it. Seven years post-divorce and I was back where I started.

Alone. At home. Full circle.

The first few nights were tough. Not only was I hormonal and horny, which is an insatiable kind of horniness, but I was also in emotional pain from the fallout with 24.

I turned on the TV and when that wasn't enough of a distraction, I picked up my phone. I had been on dating apps for years—on and off. I'd always close down my account then log back in weeks later with high hopes of finding Mr. Right, only to get frustrated and disgusted by the sampling of men who frequented them.

Out of loneliness and boredom, I checked for any new matches. I read old messages and sent a few replies—albeit to old and outdated messages I had received months before. Afterwards, I started swiping right and left—in search of a new man.

But this night, as I said before, was different. Unlike my typical dating trends—this time, I was only swiping right on men who were hot and had fairly chiseled bodies. My hormones and subconscious longing for comfort after the pain and rejection I felt after reading 24's text drove me elsewhere—to a fantasy man.

Sure, maybe I was trying to replace 24; but at the time, all I knew was that I needed a distraction.

It's usually quick and easy to get matches and begin a conversation with a man. However, this night, after an hour of swiping, I still had no luck in starting a conversation. I lowered my age range from 35 to 30. What the hell? I had nothing to lose. The men only got hotter and why should I give a shit? I was home alone—on the weekend, no less. It wasn't like I had something better to do.

I got a few more matches after lowering the range to 30, but still had not engaged in a single conversation with a man. All I wanted was a connection and I hadn't made a single one.

After spending more unfulfilling time swiping, I lowered my age range—yet again.

This time to twenty-five, a year older than 24 when I first met him.

OK, I was clearly trying to find another connection like the one I had with 24; but like I said, I wasn't letting my mind think about that. This was about filling the void I was feeling at that moment. And all of a sudden, I was seeing the light at the end of the tunnel!

Again, the men got hotter, but this time I… was getting matches left and right. Matches with men who looked like models.

How was this even possible?

A very handsome Hispanic man popped up. He took pride in how he looked and was sculpted to a T. His hair was perfectly styled, and his photos showed him holding a young child.

I swiped right.

It's a match!

I clicked on the message icon and began messaging Thomas, the twenty-six-year-old single dad.

Chapter 3: You Shook Me All Night Long

I sat on my patio enjoying the crisp morning air, still in a daze from the much-needed gratification of the night before. Everything about that first night with Thomas couldn't have gone better. Well, at least as far as the sex was concerned. The cuddling on the other hand? Disappointing.

It *was* late and maybe he really *had* just needed to get home in time to rest before work. Next time, I'd try to entice him to stay a little longer afterwards. I could even make it clear up front that for me, cuddling was almost as important as the sex. I'm not shy about making my needs known. I'm a firm believer in: if you don't ask for what you want, you probably won't get it. The few men I had been physical with before had always appreciated my straightforwardness anyway.

I checked my phone just in case he'd texted while I was asleep.

No messages.

I chastised myself for being silly (and needy). He was at work. It wasn't like he was going to text me right away or send me flowers—or something. Honestly, I didn't expect or want any big show. I wasn't looking for a relationship with a twenty-six-year-old.

We had amazing sex. I knew it had been as good for him as it was for me. What guy wouldn't want more of that? I certainly did!

The day passed.

No text.

By sunset, after having spent the day with my phone glued to my side not unlike my pre-teen daughter usually did, I had to roll my eyes at myself. I had gone against my plan. I didn't want to kid myself—Thomas wasn't waiting around for my call or text. I shouldn't be either. We were mature adults. I continued doing my usual weekend routine of laundry, grocery shopping, and food prep, all while trying to convince myself that I wasn't focused on the phone or holding my breath waiting for Thomas to text.

Finally, out of neediness and desperation, I texted him asking when he'd be free to come back.

No reply.

Feeling deflated, I settled onto the couch for the night. Back to my usual routine of HBO and dessert.

When I hadn't received a reply twenty-four hours later, I texted him again. Maybe my first message had just gotten buried in a bunch of other messages and he hadn't seen it. Thomas was young and probably had a bunch of friends. It was entirely plausible.

Still, no reply.

I knew the messages were getting delivered. The confirmation message popped up almost immediately after I sent them. So why would he not have the decency to reply?

Now you, my friend, are no doubt catching on way quicker than I did.

What, I just experienced was a one-night stand… more like a one and done.

Thomas eventually answered, a blow-off reply along the lines of *I'm very busy and I don't know when I'll have time.*

I was stumped. Genuinely baffled.

I didn't want a relationship, but I also didn't like being dismissed like that. I'd made it clear to Thomas during our many hours of conversation on FaceTime and in text that I wasn't looking for anything more than the physical, yet he was treating me like I was disposable.

The whole encounter had not changed my mind about being in a relationship with Thomas. I genuinely just wanted someone I could—I don't know—set up some sort of informal arrangement with. I wanted to sleep around but also be safe. I was horny, bored, and wanted some great sex on the regular. Thomas and I had great sex, so why was he against the regular part? What guy wouldn't want to come back for more of that?

I shook it off. Thomas just wouldn't be the person that I'd be putting on my speed-dial under *Bootycall*. Surely someone else would be interested in setting up a regular no-strings situation. Wasn't I offering something that all guys supposedly wanted? A woman who just wanted sex.

It was time to get back on Bumble.

***

Little did I know that my next online experience would arguably lead to being one of the best sexual experiences of my life…

I met Colton—surprise, surprise—on Bumble. What initially drew me to his profile was his pictures. He was twenty-six, handsome, fit, and holding a very large gun while dressed in military issued camo. There is nothing more appealing to me than a man who has served his country. Colton, by every definition, was truly a masculine man. The very type of man that I was most attracted to—at least during this ravenous stage in my life.

We agreed to meet at the Starbucks near my house, but his time was limited. He worked at a security company. It was

Halloween and he had to be at work early that night. Unfortunately, this was the only day that we could meet, so an hour and a half would have to suffice.

ME: SO, I JUST REALIZED, I'M WEARING A SNOW WHITE COSTUME. I CAN STILL MEET YOU AT STARBUCKS AFTER WORK, BUT WOULD YOU PREFER IF I RAN HOME AND CHANGED FIRST?

Was it cheesy that we dressed up at my office? Yes, okay, maybe it was. Was I happy that I still fit into the costume I'd bought back in college and wanted to show that off? You bet your ass I was! Especially since Colton texted back quickly with—

Colton: FUCK NO! THE SNOW WHITE COSTUME IS PERFECT!

Me: LOL! REALLY?!! OK, SEE YOU AROUND 3:30 THEN!

So, the whole women-in-sexy-costumes thing actually *was* a turn on for guys? Huh. I always thought that was just an out-of-date, silly sex game that no one really did anymore. Either way, I was game. There was something about that costume that had always made me feel petite and innocent. The idea of getting fucked while wearing it was sort of a turn on.

I pulled into the Starbucks parking lot. He was already parked (right next to a police car) and sitting in his gray Chevy Silverado. I parked, got out, and walked over to his car. With my yellow Snow White costume blowing in the wind and a bright red bow in my curly blond hair, I was pretty hard to miss.

Colton got out of his truck and hugged me. We made small talk for a few minutes, but we both knew the clock was ticking due to him having to work in two hours. This added a new dimension to the sexual tension. We had very little time before he'd have to leave for work and I knew once I set my eyes on Colton, that I wanted to make the most of our time together.

Colton made me feel bashful with the way he was looking at me, which was something I have felt with very few men. I was instantly attracted to him and had trouble taking my eyes off him. I could tell by his permanent smile that he was mutually interested. I felt like he was already imagining what he wanted to do to me in my innocent costume.

"Since a cop saw us and you totally don't seem like a serial killer, let's go back to my house," I suggested more quickly than I might with other men, knowing we were somewhat rushed. Although, I knew in my head that I was just trying to justify what I was doing by making light of it.

Colton smiled revealing dimples and gave me an endearing, "Yes Ma'am!" as if he was a soldier who had just been told he was shipping out for a tour of duty at a four-star resort.

He followed me back to my house.

When we arrived, he immediately asked if he could go onto my patio to make a phone call.

"Sure," I said, feeling a little perplexed.

"I'm calling in sick," he said. "Something I haven't done in four years."

My eyes opened wide and he could see the look of surprise on my face. "Is that ok? I don't want you getting into trouble."

"If they can't find someone to cover for me, it might be a problem. But I've never called in sick. So, the way I see it, it's their problem to deal with."

Holy shit! Did I just hear what I thought I heard? Colton was calling in sick to work so he could spend his night with *me.* I was very taken aback, feeling flattered and turned on all at the same time.

Colton went out onto the porch and made his call. A few minutes later, he came back in and sat on the couch.

"You okay with me smoking some weed?" I was still a bit nervous about this casual sex thing and the courage Mary Jane gave me was just what I needed to feel more comfortable. I gathered Colton knew it would make for a better time for the both of us, because he had no problem with it. He encouraged me to do what I needed to relax and enjoy myself.

While I stood and smoked, Colton and I chatted, getting to know each other a little. Colton came from a big family and was really into dirt bike racing. He didn't offer up too many details, but he seemed pretty close to his family.

Something in the combination of the marijuana and Colton deciding to spend the evening with me—had me so turned on. Coincidentally, I just read somewhere that people who smoke weed have 20% more sex. I'm surprised that number isn't significantly higher.

I put my pipe down and walked over to Colton. Lifting up the hem of my Snow White dress, I straddled him. The Snow White costume and how well he responded to it gave me the confidence I needed to make this bold move.

Colton was not shy at all. In fact, I think the spontaneity of my action turned him on. He immediately slipped a hand under my hair to grip the base of my neck and wrapped the other hand around my waist.

I discovered in an instant that Colton was an amazing kisser, very passionate. He immediately held me firmly while gently caressing my mouth with his. We had pretty much perfect chemistry and kissed the same, slow and gentle.

Kissing tells you everything you need to know about what a man will be like in bed.

It's true, I swear!

Every man that I have ever kissed, who demonstrated both passion and skill while doing so, was an equally skilled lover.

The way Colton was kissing me—sensuous and slow, but still very in command, definitely taking the lead in this dance—told me that tonight was going to be off the charts.

Colton made no rush of taking me to my bed. It was different from my night with Thomas. Instead, he took his time making out and learning the curves of my body with his hands.

Undressing me was a little challenging. As mentioned earlier, I originally purchased my costume twenty years ago. Now that I was in my forties it didn't *exactly* fit the same.

Colton was patient and laughed as I struggled to get the tight dress over my chest. My breasts were definitely different from my early twenties. Having a child helped with that. With Colton's help, the dress finally fell to the living room floor.

We moved to my bedroom.

I sat Colton on the edge of my bed and stood between his legs. I was in my bra and panties, he was still fully dressed. A situation, I was happy to remedy.

I lifted his shirt and pulled it up over his head—holy shit! Colton was ripped! I could see every outline of muscle in his chest, stomach, shoulders, and arms.

I don't know what I did in this life to deserve a man like this in my bed; but fuck, here he was and I was ready to take advantage.

Colton's strong hands wandered all over my body and I couldn't get enough of them. He strategically supported my neck and back with one hand as he used the other hand to explore my breasts and hips. I've never been so turned on by a man's hands before. They were strong and moved with such purpose. He was confident and touched my body with equal confidence. Nothing gets me more excited than a man whose hands are hungry for my body and Colton's firm caresses showed me he was starving.

Colton wasn't the most verbally expressive man, but he was sure to tell me that I was sexy.

His breathing, the firm pressure of his hands, and the noises he made told me I was turning him—the fuck—on. His nonverbal reactions as he suckled and teased my nipples, running his tongue down my body aroused me even more. I realized that I had never been tasted and experienced like this before and I fucking loved it!

After undressing each other, we moved to laying on the bed. I was pleasantly surprised that Colton was hung.

Could things get any better? Fuck yeah, they could!

Colton and I were perfectly aligned. He knew just how to touch my body to get a response, as if we had been lovers for years. His body engulfed mine. Colton intertwined our bodies so our legs were woven together while we had sex. We moved as one—in complete unison. Our passion and chemistry were through the roof.

In hindsight, I still don't know if it was the sex or if it was him calling in sick, because of his desire to have more time with me that contributed to this mind-blowing experience. I think it was all of it. Colton and I were a perfect storm of desire and passion.

He came just after me and continued to hold our bodies pressed together.

We stayed like that for a few minutes while we both caught our breath. Having sex with Colton was so intense. I wanted more.

After we were done and cleaned up, I returned to bed to cuddle. Colton laid next to me, but he wasn't touching me. I moved my body over to his. He allowed me to lay touching him but made no move to cuddle.

"Don't tell me you're not a cuddler?" I asked.

"I fucking hate cuddling. Can't stand it!" he replied vehemently.

"Well, you can lie there then, I want to feel a man's body after I've had sex with him. Is that ok?" I asked.

"Yeah, that's fine," he murmured.

So, we ended our first round of sex lying next to each other, my back pressed up against his side and my head lying at the top of his arm. I cuddled his ripped arm that was stretched down against my body.

I can't tell you how many men I've had to explain to that cuddling is literally forty percent of the sexual equation. You may have just given me the best sex of my life, but if I have to choose between that with no cuddling or plain simple good sex *with* cuddling, I'd choose the latter every time.

Regardless of his distaste for cuddling, I still made sure to get the physical contact I needed to feel fulfilled.

As we lay in bed, Colton began to bend his legs, moving them around and stretching them out. I heard cracks and pops coming from various body parts.

"Why are your legs cracking like that?" I asked.

"That's from jumping out of airplanes with a hundred pounds of gear on my back," he replied.

Oh my God. Here was a man in his mid-twenties with aches and pains that would be with him for the rest of his life.

This elicited emotions in me, I wanted to care for him, but I was also insanely aroused by his ruggedly sexy veteran experience.

After a few minutes, Colton announced that he was hungry and wanted to get dinner. Apparently, he hadn't eaten at all that day, because he was sleeping. The pains of working graveyard. His day began with meeting me then driving to my house.

"There's a good Mexican restaurant close by. We can walk there."

He nodded. "Sounds perfect."

We had dinner and talked some more about our lives. I gave Colton the short version of my story with a lot edited out. He told me about his hopes, dreams, and the plans he had for his future.

I sat across from Colton listening intently. He looked up a few times to connect our gazes. It seemed like he was checking to see if I was truly listening. I find that a lot of men do this with me. They want assurance that someone is listening and he could tell I definitely was. I find that most men I talk to seem to really like this about me. I absorb their words, encourage their dreams, and give them solid advice.

He was desperate to get back to Afghanistan. He loved being there. Loved the excitement. He told me that private security was very lucrative, especially in the Middle East— where danger was everywhere.

He had hoped to work in Afghanistan for two years with the goal of saving money and moving to Nevada, where his family currently lived. The money he saved while working in Afghanistan would be enough to return to Nevada, purchase a home and start a business. That was his end goal: to be by his family's side and be in a position to support them.

I was so impressed by both his courage and his clear plan. I told him so.

For the record, I also told Colton that he was crazy for wanting to return to Afghanistan and put himself in harm's way. No amount of money is worth possibly dying for—in my opinion.

He smiled at me and tried to grab the check. He was an absolute gentleman through and through. I wouldn't let him pay for my meal though. He had too much that he was saving for and shouldn't be spending his money on me. We split the bill and walked back to my house, talking the whole way home.

When we returned home, we had sex a second time. Later we watched a movie then had sex again (Don't worry, I made sure to get my half ass side arm cuddle).

The sex was just as mind-blowing as the first time. Absolutely incredible. I felt like I had won the lottery with Colton.

Around 9 pm, Colton said he had to get going. I was still lying naked in bed, savoring our final sexual encounter. He was standing at the foot of my bed getting dressed.

I will never forget the vision of Colton standing at the foot of my bed, dressed in only his jeans with a big belt buckle. It's hands down the hottest mental snapshot I have to date.

"Holy fuck Colton! You are so fucking hot!" I said in disbelief while shaking my head.

He smiled the biggest smile, crawled back onto the bed and in between my legs. I grabbed the waistband of his pants, hooking his belt in both hands then pulled him towards me until he was hovering over me. He proceeded to give me a long gentle sensual kiss.

My stomach flip-flopped even as my vagina screamed. *Hell no, not again!*

Colton had done quite the hat trick that night and my body was done!

For those of you who don't follow sports, a hat trick refers to scoring three times in one hockey game, just as Colton had scored three times that night with me.

After kissing me, Colton finished getting dressed. I threw on my tank and stretch pants then walked him to the door. He sat on the cushioned entryway bench and put his shoes on.

He pulled me between his legs and started kissing me again. I grabbed his hand, pulling him to the couch. Where I sat him down and straddled him again. I could tell that Colton didn't want to leave. I didn't want him to leave either. Comfort and connection of any kind is addicting, even if it has no real meaning or feeling behind it. We kissed for a few more minutes as I sat on his lap.

Then he stood up while holding me, set me down gently on my feet, and reluctantly said goodbye and left.

The next day I eagerly texted Colton. He didn't reply.

Just like Thomas, I never heard from nor saw Colton again. I'd love to say I didn't care and simply brushed it off; but the fact was, it hurt.

It pained me to have such an intense physical connection with a man, only to have him discard me as I'd been so many times before. I don't think it matters how strong a person is, the sting that comes from being used never dulls.

I occasionally think of that night. It may or may not have been the best sex of my life, given the lack of cuddling, but it definitely makes the top three!

When I reflect on my time with Colton, I am convinced that it is possible to have immediate chemistry with people.

My experience with Colton may not have been the first time I had felt that immediate chemistry, but it was so strong that it made the biggest impact. I would soon find out that I could also feel this way with other men.

Chapter 4: Hungry Like A Wolf

Despite the disappointment and rejection that sprung from Colton's lack of reply—and that this was becoming habit for my Bumble encounters, I remained on cloud 9 after our night together. Not only was the memory of him standing there shirtless—in all his glory, enough to bring a smile to my face, I was also beginning to see myself in a new way. I had always been a sexually confident woman, regardless of my lack of experience, but this new pastime was giving me a whole new understanding of men. I certainly didn't know it at the time, but this new wisdom would eventually end up benefitting me in ways I couldn't have imagined.

Even if they were only turning out to be one-night stands, I was definitely enjoying it, not to mention the caliber of sex I'd been having lately. With this new pep in my step, I was also looking forward to my upcoming girl's weekend. Who wouldn't? To go from great sex during the week to a weekend getaway with friends, clearly my life had taken a turn for the better.

As a single mom, I carried the weight of the world on my shoulders and getting some girl time and relaxation in was always something I looked forward, especially when I needed to boost my spirits and rejuvenate myself.

Neither my friends nor I made a ton of money, so we always tried to choose destinations within driving distance or at least a cheap flight away.

This weekend we were headed for a mountain getaway. The drive wasn't too bad and our main goal was to relax and enjoy each other's company.

My car was in the shop, so I was driving a loaner. Lucky for us, the only loaner the dealership had available was a brand new fully loaded Yukon XL. Needless to say, I offered to drive that weekend. I picked up Sarah, Ingrid, and Maria. They were just as excited as I was about the loaner car.

Leather interior, two television screens, Wi-Fi, and every other luxury you can put in a vehicle. It was a comfortable drive to say the least. Our ride was plush compared to the old jalopies we were accustomed to driving.

"Wow," Sarah said as she jumped in the car. The last to be picked up. "Can I use this to drop my kids off at school next week?"

We all laughed. The four of us were always commiserating about how humiliated our kids were by the cars we drove.

Maria said, "Tyler insisted I drop him off a block away from school last week. He would be beside himself if I drove him to school in this thing!"

As we drove on, I turned up some old school 80's music and we sang like we were teenagers. Yes, this was the perfect distraction from my thoughts of Colton and the rejection I felt from not hearing back from him. It was hard to stop myself from wondering about him and that night. If he didn't have a good time, then why did he appear to be so conflicted about leaving that night? Was I mistaken in my assessment of that night?

I had so much to learn.

After a laughter-filled two-hour drive, we arrived at our condo in Breckenridge. Much like our good fortune with the rental car, our pad for the weekend turned out to be exceptional. It was located right downtown with a spectacular view of the mountains all around us. Everything seemed to be working in our favor and the smiles on our faces couldn't have gotten any wider.

We moved the car so it was parked just in front of our building. Our condo was number 69. We all cracked up when we saw the room number. Sarah even took a picture of it, making sure to document every part of the weekend as she always did.

We walked in and couldn't believe how big our place was. It had two bedrooms, a full-sized kitchen, dining area, family room, and back patio. It was huge compared to the places we were accustomed to staying at and it was centrally located to everything we wanted to do that weekend.

Sarah and Maria claimed a room, while Ingrid and I took the other one. We settled in and unpacked a little before getting ready for dinner. After we were all freshened up, we headed out to walk into town and find food before going to see a local blues band that had made a name for themselves in the annual Art & Music Festival.

The band was playing at the Historic Brown & Fox's Den, which was a rustic old hotel converted into a music venue. We discovered it was a favorite local's hangout that also had decent food. It had great energy so we decided to make it a one-stop shop for us that evening.

The best part of hanging out with these women was how easy it was for us to get along. I'd always had eclectic circles of friends that I kept in touch with, but this group was definitely my fun travel group. No one was picky and we could all find what we liked in just about any environment.

After ordering our meals, we sat around the table chatting and waiting for the music to start. The food wasn't fancy, but the vibe in the bar was just what we were looking for. There were a lot of your typical sophisticated hippie types that you find in most Colorado ski towns. The patrons all seemed open to welcoming 4 weekenders into the mix.

The music was awesome, once it finally started, and kept us all on our feet dancing until we agreed it was time to go out for some fresh air and head back to the condo.

Ingrid and I smoked weed on our walk back. Sarah and Maria had a bottle of wine waiting for them. We had stopped at the grocery store on our way up the mountain for snacks, wine, and dessert to have in our room. A girl's weekend wouldn't be complete without them, sweets were a universal "relaxation drug" of choice that we could all agree on.

On the walk back, Sarah turned the conversation over to something she had been flirting with most of the night—my dating life.

"So, Lacie, are you still hanging out with hot twenty-five-year-olds?"

I laughed, knowing they all wanted to know what I'd been up to recently.

"Yes, I am—when I have the time," I said coyly. "I've actually been texting with a guy who lives a few minutes away from here. We've never gotten together before because we live so far apart."

Sarah was giddy. "Invite him over. We want to meet him!"

"No way. Are you kidding me?" I was completely taken aback by her suggestion.

I had been talking to Mario, a fire fighter recruit for a couple weeks. He was from the Denver area—near me, but he was commuting back and forth to Vail, a small town not far from Breckenridge, until he became a permanent member of the station. We had talked and facetimed many times but had yet to meet because of our schedules.

Before going any further, I want to point out that I have very few single friends. Almost all of my friends are married with families; exactly where I was at in my life until I got divorced.

Sarah, Maria, and Ingrid all had husbands and kids. My singledom was a source of their entertainment. Whenever we got together, they loved navigating my dating app. Since they were married on upwards of ten and twenty plus years, they loved hearing about my most recent adventure. They especially loved swiping on men's profiles for me.

I had no real investment in online dating, so I didn't care who they swiped left or right on.

I finally tried to change the subject and distracted them from further vicariously matching. "Let's talk about what you all want to do for the rest of the weekend." I said.

They all rolled their eyes and Ingrid exclaimed, "We want to live life through you this weekend!"

"Exactly!" said Maria. "Is virtual flirting behind the mask of someone else's profile considered cheating on your spouse?"

"Yes!" I said laughing. "Give me my phone back before you get yourself in trouble."

When we got back to the hotel, we sat on the couch eating our dessert.

Sarah brought Mario back up. "How far away is he?"

I handed them my phone. All three of them huddled around it. They started looking at my matches and current conversations. They saw that Mario was only three miles away.

"Seriously Lacie, invite him over." Sarah was not going to take 'no' for an answer.

"And do what?" I asked.

Ingrid chimed in with an enthusiastic, "Fuck him!"

I started laughing. "Where? We have two bedrooms with two women in each room. It's not like I have my own room."

Gesturing around the living room where we were sitting. They rang out in unison, "Right here!"

I shook my head. "I could never have sex with him in our hotel room. I have never had sex with someone when other people were around. I'd be too uncomfortable."

Sarah didn't want to hear it. "Get over it. I have."

"So have I," Ingrid chimed in again.

"I wouldn't be able to do it either, so I don't blame you." I thought for a moment that Maria might be on my side. "But I still want to meet this guy. We want to see the guys you're sleeping with, Lacie. Come on and give your married friends a thrill."

This was all too much for me. "Are you all serious?" I said incredulously.

I was completely shocked that my friends were goading me into inviting a stranger—for all intents and purposes— over to our hotel room. Two of which seemed to support me having sex with him while they retreated to their rooms.

In unison—again, they shouted in an exasperated tone. "Yes!"

"You'll go into your rooms, turn on your TVs, and close the doors? You agree not come out at all while he's here?"

I knew there was no way that I could sleep with a man without complete privacy. I wasn't a hundred percent trusting that they'd give me what I needed.

"Yes!" they shouted.

I finally caved. "Okay, I'll text him and ask him to come over."

"Tell him to bring his swimsuit, so he can go in the hot tub with us."

I laughed but hesitantly said, "Okay."

Getting Mario to come over was more of a task than I thought it would be. He made a million excuses like having to iron his shirt and polish his shoes for training on Monday.

What the fuck? It was Friday night, he was passing up on hanging out with a woman—to do fucking laundry? Unbelievable.

I eventually talked Mario into coming. By the time he agreed (hours later), we were already out of the hot tub and back relaxing in our condo.

While we waited for Mario, we shared the variety of decadent desserts we brought. Maria and Sarah drank wine while Ingrid and I smoked some more weed. We were feeling great and it was a beautiful evening. We opened the slider to the patio to let in some fresh mountain air. We also discovered a stereo in the living room. Between the wine, weed, and good music; we all felt carefree.

Apparently, our patio was right next to the master bedroom of the neighboring condo.

Around 10:30 pm, there was a knock at the door. I knew it wasn't Mario as he said he'd text, when he was on his way.

Like a good girl, I asked, "Who is it?"

"Security."

I opened the door to find a handsome young man.

"I'm really sorry to bother you ladies. I can tell you're having a good time, but we've received a noise complaint coming from your suite."

By now, the girls were crowded around the door to see what was going on.

"Our music isn't that loud."

"Closing your patio door might help, since their windows are right next to your patio."

"Sure, no problem. You should come join our party. What time are you off?"

My friends all chimed in. "Yeah, come join us. Hang out."

What better way to fix a noise complaint than to hang out with security? If only it had worked.

"I'd love to, but I'm working until the morning. I'm on the night shift."

"That's too bad. We'll close the slider and turn the music down. Sorry to be a nuisance."

"Ah, it was no problem at all. You ladies enjoy your night and keep having fun."

"Oh, we plan to."

The security guard left. We turned the music down and closed the slider. Ingrid wanted to take a joint next door as an apology to our neighbors, but we all agreed it probably wouldn't help.

Finally, around 11 pm, Mario texted me to let me know that he had arrived. All three of my friends went wild with excitement. You would have thought we had a stripper coming to our room.

"Don't keep him waiting. Go get him and bring him up here!"

I quickly ran down the steps and met Mario in the parking lot. He was very muscular and tall. I was pleasantly surprised. Let's face it, no amount of FaceTime calling will really show you what someone will actually look like in person. He had dark hair that was shaved close to his scalp. He was SUPER handsome in person.

I could tell immediately that he was a little socially awkward, which totally explained his hesitancy in coming over. We did not have our normal back and forth conversation now that we were in person, and there were a few awkward silences as I walked Mario to our condo.

My friends immediately greeted us when Mario and I walked in. They started firing off questions at him right and left wanting to know more about his life and career aspirations. He answered them and conversed like a champ. He was much better at answering rapid-fire questions than trying to make small talk with a woman one on one.

I'm not sure what my friends were expecting. They seemed genuinely surprised at how good-looking, well-spoken and personable Mario turned out to be. After they expressed all of these things out loud to Mario, I stuck my foot in my mouth.

"You think he's great, huh? Take your shirt off for them Mario. Show them your abs."

Following that statement was the longest most awkward silence of my life. I played it off like I had been joking—but I wasn't. Mario didn't have an ounce of body fat and I knew my friends would love to see him. I didn't really know how to recover, so I asked him if he wanted to go sit on a bench outside. He agreed, so we said goodbye and left.

We found a bench close by and took a seat next to each other. It was a cool crisp evening and the fresh scent of the trees was comforting.

"Isn't it gorgeous out? It's so quiet and refreshing." I asked while trying to break the ice.

"Yes, the fresh mountain air never gets old," he replied.

We chatted for a while on the bench getting more comfortable with each other. I could tell he was still somewhat new to the online world of hooking up and needed to get to know me as much as I needed to get more comfortable with him.

After chatting for about an hour, we went back to my room.

It was quiet when we walked in. My friends had already retreated to their rooms. I could faintly hear their televisions. I guess they were serious about wanting me to sleep with Mario, because they left the living room and kitchen completely vacant. I still felt somewhat apprehensive.

How could I possibly focus on having sex with Mario while my friends were literally in the next room? I was definitely out of my comfort zone.

I dimmed the lighting to set the mood and turned on the gas fireplace. We sat on the couch close to each other. Mario started kissing me almost immediately. I was surprised that this socially awkward man took charge the way he did.

I could feel his strength and determination. He knew what he wanted—and clearly it was me. It was a huge turn on to feel that energy flow from him—feel the strength of his hands as he grabbed me. Mario was hungry for me that night.

Our kissing got hot and heavy very quickly. I climbed on top of him and started grinding my body against his. I could feel that he was hard. We were both grinding, moaning, and kissing—things were heating up quickly!

Suddenly, the thought occurred to me... I didn't have a condom. I sure as hell hoped he did. Especially since things were really getting hot and heavy.

I stopped kissing him and moved off his lap onto the couch.

"Do you have a condom?" I asked anxiously.

"Yes."

I was relieved. Clearly, I had not anticipated having sex with a man on my girl's weekend and was not prepared with protection. In that moment, I decided I'd carry a condom in my purse at all times. That decision might've been overkill, but I'd rather be safe than sorry.

Mario leaned forward and started kissing me again. I melted and was immediately reengaged. I got back onto his lap and resumed grinding on his dick.

After a few minutes of making out, I slid off his lap and stood between his legs. I pulled his pants off. I stood in front of him while he undressed me.

Mario was wild with excitement. If I was a betting woman (which I am), I'd say he hadn't had sex in a while.

I crawled back onto his lap and he gently slid himself into me.

We had sex like that, his hands on my ass, him bouncing me up and down while we kissed. I held my breasts up for him to suck on. My legs eventually started feeling fatigued and it was time to change positions.

I slowly lifted myself off Mario, making sure to keep his hands on me until I broke the connection and walked over to the fireplace. I wanted him on me while I was on my back, so I laid down on the carpet and invited him over. Mario came right over, climbing on top of me and sliding himself back into me. He fucked me until I came, which was very quickly due to the impulsivity of the night and the downright naughtiness of having friends just on the other side of those walls.

Mario had great self-control and was able to cum just a short time after me.

We cleaned up and laid back down on the carpet in front of the fireplace. Like most men I had met online, he proclaimed to hate cuddling. I told him that I didn't care and cuddled up against his warm muscular body.

We cuddled in front of the fireplace for a few minutes, until I saw him start to get hard again. (This is exactly why I love sleeping with twenty-something-year-old men. Most can literally get hard and have sex to completion two to three times in an hour!) To a hormonal, forty-three-year-old single mom, it doesn't get any better than that.

I grabbed his erect dick and began stroking it. I could feel him getting harder in my hand. He started moaning with pleasure. We were ready for round two.

I climbed on top of Mario's now rock-hard dick, put my hands on his chiseled chest for balance, and rode him in front of the fireplace. He grabbed my hips to help me move. I was getting very aroused, arching my back and moaning as quietly as possible (so my friends wouldn't hear). I leaned forward onto his chest, closing my legs straight down his body.

Mario fucked me like this until I came. And it was a huge orgasm. The whole experience: the fireplace, the ambiance, the mood, all of it was sexy as fuck and helped me climax just as quickly as Mario.

After I came, Mario moved me onto my hands and knees. He kneeled behind me and fucked me from behind. Mario felt great. He had a big dick and was an excellent fuck for sure. He grabbed my hip with one hand while his other grabbed one of my breasts. Mario came fast the second time. I could tell he liked our sex. We cuddled for a few more minutes and chatted.

Mario smiled. "That was great."

"Yes, it definitely was," I agreed.

"I had a lot of fun, but I have to go."

Mario didn't waste any time. He'd gotten laid twice that night. It was very late and he was ready to leave. I'm sure he had ironing and shoe polishing to attend to.

"No problem. Thanks for coming over."

"I'm glad that I did," he smiled.

We both got up and put our clothes back on. I walked Mario to the door expecting to never hear from him again.

Mario left and I went to bed.

The next morning, my friends were dying to hear all the nitty gritty details. I couldn't believe I got coaxed into having Mario over; but alas, I had a great time.

I described in detail how our night went and thanked them for pushing me into inviting Mario over. I think my friends got just as much enjoyment out of the glimpse they had into my new-found lifestyle as I did.

I texted Mario a few days later to see when we could get together again.

He never replied.

I texted one more time—because I was pissed and wanted to tell him that the least he could do was reply. That wasn't very helpful, still no reply. Don't worry. At this point, I was starting to see a pattern. Yes, when it comes to this, I was a bit of a slow learner but I was coming to the conclusion that if I truly wanted to see a man again, I needed to leave him alone. I needed to stop texting these men and let them come to me. If they didn't, well… it was their loss.

I deleted Mario from my contacts and moved on to communicating with my next catch.

***

Six months later I received a text from an unknown number. HEY. HOW ARE YOU? ARE YOU STILL ON THE ONLINE DATING APP?

Me: WHO IS THIS?

IT'S MARIO FROM VAIL.

Me: MARIO FROM 6 MONTHS AGO? ARE YOU KIDDING ME? I TEXTED YOU AND YOU NEVER REPLIED. I DELETE PEOPLE WHO DON'T REPLY TO MY TEXTS.

Mario: YES, IT'S ME. AND YEAH, I'M SORRY. I WAS SUPER BUSY WITH TRAINING AND HAD NO TIME FOR ANYTHING ELSE.

Me: WELL, JUST SO YOU KNOW, I WON'T TOLERATE A MAN NOT REPLYING TO MY TEXTS. IT'S RUDE.

Mario: I'M SORRY AND I TOTALLY UNDERSTAND.

Me: SO, WHAT'S UP?

Mario: I'VE BEEN THINKING ABOUT YOU AND WANTED TO SEE IF YOU MIGHT WANT TO HANG OUT AGAIN SOME TIME.

Aka… Mario was horny and willing to drive two hours to fuck me, because he had nobody else to fuck close by.

Me: SURE, IF YOU CAN AGREE TO COMMUNICATE BETTER.

Mario: I CAN DO THAT.

Mario literally wanted to hang out that night. Clearly my theory was spot on. I was just finishing up at work and had Aubrey. We agreed to meet that following week, I would be off work for a chunk of the summer and Aubrey would be at her dad's. He could come over then during the day.

Just when I thought I'd never see a man again—there was Mario, texting me to hang out after six months of silence. I started to realize that maybe men will come back… just in their own time. Most likely when they're desperate and going down their list of potential women. Whatever the reason, Mario was back. He was the first one thus far. I wondered if there would be more.

Only time would tell.

That next week, Mario came over in the early afternoon. He was hotter, taller, and more masculine than I remembered. I was reminded of my attraction to him immediately and began fantasizing about the sex we would be having together in this unrestricted environment.

My mind raced thinking of how great our sex was before, even with my friends close by in the next room. It was going to be way better alone at my house and on a bed. It was strange how in six months he went from a guy who lacked confidence and was socially awkward to looking like a strong, confident, take charge kind of man. Maybe the training at the academy had given him a boost. Whatever it was, I was wildly attracted to Mario and wanted him immediately.

Mario sat on the couch. I wanted to smoke weed since sex was infinitely better when high. I got my supplies out, packed a bowl, and lit up. There I was, smoking weed and about to sleep with a twenty-seven-year-old fire fighter recruit. Boy had my life done a 360 since this all began.

Even though Mario was less socially awkward this time, I could tell he was still mildly uncomfortable when I sat down. I intimidated him a little. He sat at the edge of his seat and had his hands on his bouncing knees. We engaged in small talk about his job, the commute, anything I could think of to distract him. Shortly thereafter he began to look more at ease.

After updating me on his training progress and some general chatting about our lives, Mario grabbed me and kissed me. Mario was very aggressive in how he took me. It was intoxicating. He didn't play games. He was here to fuck me. I liked the obviousness of it all.

Mario was a Cross Fit coach before joining the fire academy. He was in insane shape. Muscular everywhere in ways that were more advanced than most, due to his training, no doubt. I felt tiny next to Mario.

I climbed onto his lap (just because it feels so sexy with big guys). We continued making out. Despite his strength and dominance, he took his time and enjoyed every minute of our connection. He may have been there to fuck but he wasn't going to rush it. He thoroughly enjoyed my body.

It made for great sex.

As things got a little more heated, I led Mario to my bedroom in an effort to get more comfortable. I reclined on the bed. Waiting as Mario crawled on the bed until he was between my legs. His face hovered over me and he began kissing me. I grabbed his dick firmly and began stroking it. With my free hand, I began playing with his balls. Mario went wild with arousal.

With my enthusiastic permission, he drove himself into me. Mario couldn't wait another second and that was a total turn on. He was there to have fun and he was horny as fuck. He started pounding me hard, over and over in just the right way.

Due to the lapse in time, I forgot how big Mario was. He had a big dick! Like before, he had great control and lasted as long as I needed him to. With my guidance, he made me cum easily. He wanted me to make him cum in return by giving him head.

Not my favorite way to make a man cum, but I know it's at the top of their list so I obliged.

Mario lounged on his back. I started giving him head while he fondled my breasts. He grabbed a handful of my hair and helped my head move up and down over his dick. I didn't have to work for very long until Mario yelled, "I'm going to cum!"

I took his dick out of my mouth and began giving him a hand job to finish him off. Although he would've loved it, I had no desire to let Mario cum in my mouth even with a condom on. I loved the fact that I got him there with my head. I felt so powerful next to this huge man because of how I could affect him.

Mario removed the condom and came all over his chest and belly. I could feel his dick pulsing and throbbing in my hand.

Mario reluctantly cuddled me for a few minutes after cleaning up. I was definitely familiar with this pattern. Younger men seemed to lack any desire for physical connection after sex. It continued to be a letdown.

It was late afternoon and he wanted to get going before the commuter traffic started. We got up and dressed. I walked him to the door.

Mario and I reached out to each other a few more times, but were never able to get our schedules to match. We never hung out again after that day.

Such is the world of online dating.

Chapter 5: Don't Fear The Reaper

Warning: The following chapter includes forceful sexual acts bordering on sexual violence, which may trigger survivors of sexual assault.

I waited in anticipation at Starbucks. Zack's pictures were insanely attractive. I was dying to see him in person. I sat at a table outside, facing the parking lot. A nicer than average BMW pulled in—and a Greek god stepped out.

Tall, slender, blond, very well dressed with swag to infinity. Zack made a beeline for my table. He saw me from the parking lot and knew who I was. Once our eyes locked, we never took them off each other as he walked up and sat down.

Zack looked like a Calvin Klein model. Tan, sculpted, looked great in sunglasses. It might sound like I'm exaggerating. I'm not. There's apparently a whole segment of the hot young male population who are into older women. I'll eventually get clues as to why, but in the meantime... God! What did I do to deserve this?

I may sound like a broken record; but at this point in my life, I didn't feel deserving of the time and attention these men were giving me, even if it was only sexual in nature. I'm not sure why I felt so undeserving given my natural sense of self-confidence. I can only assume it was the age difference and the emotional scars that I still had from my bad divorce and my breakup with 24. At any rate, all I could think of was that this sexy man walking toward me was going to be naked in my presence in a very short amount of time.

When Zack got to the table, I stood up and hugged him. He was well over six feet tall. That in itself made this a win for me.

"Hi, how are you doing?" he asked. "Have you been waiting long?"

"No, not at all. I just got here a few minutes ago. How was your day?"

"Great. Glad to be off and hanging out with you. You look great. I'm pleasantly surprised." This would become a theme. I've been told I'm one of the few women who actually look better in person. I always take it as a compliment. Either that or I'm just not very photogenic.

I smiled. "Thanks. I take it you've been catfished before?"

I had one man tell me a story about showing up for a date to meet a woman he met online and she looked nothing like her photos. Apparently, it's more common than one would think.

He laughed then said, "Yeah, you could say that."

We chatted for about fifteen more minutes. That was all the time I needed to know I was game to sleep with him. He was hot, well spoken, and educated. I couldn't take my eyes off him.

"So," I began much more confidently now having done this before, "do you want to head over to my house and get comfortable?"

Zack's eyes heated. "Absolutely." He flashed a broad flirtatious smile.

We got up at the same time and headed towards our cars. I nodded toward mine. "I'm in the SUV. Follow me. You can park in the guest parking lot—on your immediate left when you pull into my complex."

"Sounds good."

I pulled out of the parking lot and Zack followed behind me. We drove a half-mile to my condo. He turned into guest parking and found a spot. I drove ahead and parked in my usual spot, then grabbed my purse and headed to guest parking to make sure I didn't lose him.

He was already walking towards me when I got to the pathway. We both smiled as we walked to each other. I could tell by the way Zack looked at me that our attraction was mutual.

We walked to my door and went inside. Zack stepped into the house and immediately removed his shoes. His mother clearly had him well trained. He squatted down and held his hand out to Chewie. Chewie inched closer wagging his tail as he cautiously strained to reach Zack's hand with his nose. After getting a sniff of Zack's scent, Chewie started barking uncontrollably.

In hindsight, Chewie's reaction was slightly foreboding. At the time, I chose to ignore it. I swooped him up and locked him in Aubrey's room.

After getting Zack some water, I put on music. We walked over to the living room and sat down on the couch.

Zack had confidence for days, it was something I'd found so attractive about him at the coffee shop. I figured that we'd continue chatting like all the other times and warm up to the main event.

But as soon as I sat down, Zack immediately grabbed me and started kissing me. *Hard.* I could barely even kiss him back. He smashed his mouth against mine.

I squirmed and blinked.

It's okay, Lacie, I told myself as I struggled with whether or not to pull away from him. I'd been all-in only moments before. But this kiss was far from enjoyable.

Just because he was a bad kisser, didn't mean the whole night would be bad. Maybe he'd prove my kissing philosophy wrong.

He was just… dominant in an intense and forceful sort of way. I'd never experienced that before. I liked confident men who took charge, right? *Just see where it goes*, I told myself.

His kisses didn't ease up and it turned out that Zack did everything hard and rough. After kissing me for what seemed like an eternity, he grabbed me by the shoulders and force me flat on the couch.

Whoa, whoa, whoa.

Zack lied on top of me and started grabbing my body roughly. He was turning me off. He kept kissing me, shoving his tongue in my mouth and grabbing my breasts. Hard. None of it felt good. He pulled off my dress and unsnapped my bra.

I felt like a blow up doll manipulated by him. But I didn't say anything, partially because his tongue was halfway down my throat, but also because I was just so… stunned. Was this really happening?

He continued groping my body, painfully squeezing my breasts, sucking my nipples so hard that it hurt, and slapping my ass harshly. I liked when other men showed their appreciation for my body, but this was different. This was not desire, it was more like punishment.

After several minutes of painstaking "foreplay", Zack asked to go to the bedroom. I felt like a deer staring at headlights. I reluctantly agreed and we headed down the hallway into my room.

At this point, I wasn't sexually aroused. Everything Zack had done thus far turned me off. I had honestly never been in this position before, I felt it would just be easier to sleep with him then try to get him out of my house.

That rationalization may sound crazy, but I admit… I was scared. One thing I can say about myself is that I typically never have a problem with responding at times of crisis or knowing how to take action. But for the first time in my life, I felt so completely vulnerable that I froze.

In reflection, I realize that I had quickly weighed my safety and whether or not asking him to leave was an option or if I risked really pissing him off. If he was this forceful during his "pleasure", how would he be with rejection?

You've already gone this far, Lacie. It'll be fine. You wanted to have different experiences, right? I wasn't a wimpy little wildflower. If he took it too far, I'd make him stop.

Would he stop, though? The question came from an insidious little voice in my head. It's just you and him, all alone in this condo. If you scream, will the upstairs neighbors hear and call the cops?

We were already in the bedroom. He grabbed me and shoved me onto the bed. I stayed where I was, totally stunned, my back flat on the mattress with my legs dangling over the side.

He got onto the bed and hovered over me. He picked my hips up and swung me around, so that I was lying where he wanted.

Fuck, this guy moved me around like a piece of meat.

Zack had put a condom on while he undressed. He climbed on top of me and rammed himself into me. Zack was a tall guy and had a big dick.

He pounded me fiercely. I started moaning and screaming loudly hoping my responsiveness would make for a quick end. I could tell Zack was getting closer to cumming. Good. The sooner I could get this crazy bastard out of my house, the better. This had been a total mistake.

But then—

He grabbed my neck hard as he continued to fuck me. I looked up and his eyes never stopped staring at me. He was watching himself choke me and it looked like it turned him on. Zack squeezed so hard that both of my hands shot up and I grabbed his wrists.

"Fuck!" I gasped. "You can't squeeze that hard."

Zack was already cumming, though. He left his hand on my neck while he came. He did loosen his grip after I reacted so harshly.

Then, just as fast as he had started all of this madness, he got up, took off the condom, got dressed, and left. He clearly had this routine down and I wanted him the fuck out of my house.

After he left, I locked the door and took a shower. I didn't want any trace of him left on me. I crawled into bed and let Chewie sleep with me that night, which is a rarity. I felt violated and stunned all at the same time.

Did that literally just happen?

I thought about how things could have been even worse that night. I needed comfort and little twelve-pound Chewie was right there for me. I couldn't call my friends and talk about this yet. Part of me fell right into that place of self-blame. I had put myself in this situation from online dating. I justified the whole event by telling myself, even though my encounter with Zack was horribly unpleasant, I knew it could have been worse. Much worse.

Zack scared the shit out of me. For the first time, I saw how extremely vulnerable my position was, I had been almost completely defenseless.

I couldn't believe I was casually sleeping with men that I didn't know. What was wrong with me?

No, nothing was wrong with me.

I had several great experiences. This was just one bad one. I pulled my covers up to my chin.

How is Facetiming these men or meeting up for a quick coffee any different than talking to them at a bar? I know countless women who have met men at bars and hooked up with them, something I had never done before and yet they were okay.

But that rich boy could've killed me and there would have been nothing I could have done about it.

I was officially *done* with this shit.

I deleted the Bumble app off my phone.

Lonely and bored was better than dead.

I didn't need Bumble. I'd either meet a man the old-fashioned way… or I wouldn't. All my friends thought I was a little crazy for doing this anyway. Even if half of them (most of them actually) couldn't wait to hear my stories, they were still concerned.

Claudia and Chloe would be chomping at the bit to hear what happened when I talked to them next.

They would be pissed if I told them this story though. They would both be protective and want to hunt Zack down. No, I would not share this one right now.

I washed off the whole experience in the shower that night. I was not going to let it affect my life. I would simply use this experience to be safer in the future… and without Bumble!

I had no idea how much I sounded like a sexual assault victim at that moment. All I kept telling myself was that it was over and I was lucky nothing worse happened.

Lesson learned: the fact that you survive abusive unwanted sex does not make you lucky. If any of you find yourself in any situation like this please reach out for support. **Sexual violence is not justifiable in any situation.**

If you or anyone you know has been the victim of rape, here are some resources:

https://www.rainn.org/about-national-sexual-assault-telephone-hotline

Hotline: 800-656-4673

Chapter 6: Mom

I had tried for the first time in my life to be a single, carefree woman looking to take care of her own needs. I admit that I needed to open my mind and stir the pot a little. After all, I was famous in my circle of friends for being a serial monogamist, and that sure had not brought me the satisfaction that I was looking for.

However, I had let the pendulum swing way too much in the other direction.

This whole thing had just been, I don't know, a horny mid-life crisis? Either way, I was done with it.

Done.

One hundred percent.

Did not need it, no thank you *ma'am*. My life was fine the way it was before this started. I had a great daughter, a good job, fabulous friends, and a loving family.

Okay, so the job wasn't like, a *dream* job or anything. Working in human resources might be a good fit as it utilized my people skills; but really, who wanted to listen to people complain all day?

But a job was a job, it afforded me the life of luxury and leisure that I'd become accustomed to. Clearly kidding.

The reality was that my life was fairly boring and uneventful, so the sexual encounters I was having added excitement and fun to an otherwise monotonous and sheltered life. At least it had been up until the latest horrifying connection.

I checked my text messages as I turned off my monitor then pushed my chair back from my desk. Aubrey had sent a text to let me know she got home from school.

I typed out a quick return message.

Me: OK. THANKS FOR TEXTING ME. PLEASE TAKE CHEWIE OUT TO POTTY, GET A SNACK, AND START YOUR HOMEWORK. I'LL CALL WHEN I'M DRIVING HOME FROM WORK.

Aubrey: OK.

On weekdays, Aubrey got home from school a little before I did. At twelve years old, I could tell she enjoyed the time to herself. That it made her feel grown up and responsible. Often times, she'd rotate the laundry for me or empty the dishwasher before I got home. And yeah, I do know just how rare that is.

I dialed her number just before pulling away from the curb.

"Hey, Mom."

"Hi love. How was your day?"

"Good except for when we had to run the mile in PE and I hated it. I have a math test that I need help studying for. It's tomorrow."

"Sounds good. When I get home, we can take Chewie for a walk then make dinner. I thought you could help tonight, we can take pictures for your Instagram account."

"Ok. What are we having for dinner?"

"Chicken and shrimp fajitas. I bought an avocado and sour cream so they should be extra yummy. We both can take leftovers in our lunches tomorrow."

"Yes!"

"I should be home in fifteen minutes. I'll let you go so you can keep working on homework."

"Ok. I love you."

"I love you most."

I was still smiling long after she hung up. See, this was what it was all about. I didn't need a man. Being a mom was more than enough.

As I pulled onto the highway to head home, I thought about Aubrey and how much people say she looks and even acts like me. It's funny, when you have a child you never know what he or she will be like.

Aubrey was her own person that's for sure, but she definitely had a lot of my attributes. She was a smart kid who had a knack for witty replies that made most adults laugh. She loved to have fun! Sometimes we had dance parties in our small living room—all by ourselves.

Aubrey and I spent a lot of time together when she was home. We ate dinner every night at the kitchen table and spent that time talking about friends, boys, or anything else of interest to her.

I kept waiting for the age when she wouldn't want anything to do with me, but it hadn't hit yet. Maybe it never would—I could only hope.

I knew my house was more peaceful than her dad's— where there seemed to be constant drama. I thought she might see me as something of a safe haven. Her unhappiness at her dad's was a situation that might eventually need to be addressed and was something I worried about a lot, but there was nothing I could do about it at the moment aside from encouraging her to use her words and speak up.

When I walked through the door, Aubrey and Chewie both greeted me with hugs and smiles. Chewie would do his dog smile while shaking his booty back and forth, letting out an occasional snort.

"Hi Mom." Aubrey hugged me tight. "I missed you. I'm so happy to be home."

"I missed you too, love. I'm soooo happy you're home."

Aubrey usually gave me an extra-long hug on the days when she returned from her dad's. I could tell she was starving for love and affection as she clung to me. I was happy to be the one to give it to her.

"What did I do to deserve such a long hug from my favorite pre-teen?"

"I missed you a lot." Her voice was muffled from being pressed against my shoulder.

I had to wait a beat before answering, swallowing back my emotions. "I missed you a lot, too."

I never broke the hug, letting Aubrey hug me as long as she needed to. Once she let go, I headed into the kitchen and took out the frozen shrimp.

"I'm going to throw on some sweats and tennis shoes, then we can head out to walk Chewie." I turned to look at her. "But not until after you've finished your homework. Let's study for the test after dinner so you can have a little break."

Aubrey nodded. "Okay."

I went to my bedroom to change while Aubrey went back to her homework. We headed out to walk the dog about twenty minutes later. Chewie might as well have been a twelve-pound sled dog with the way he pulled on his leash. Aubrey held his leash and ran with him occasionally so he'd stop pulling. It didn't really make a difference since Chewie never seemed to tire.

"How was school today?"

"It was ok." After a long pause she quietly said, "I didn't eat with Ashley though."

My eyebrows lifted simultaneously. Ashley and Aubrey had been best friends since elementary school. They had always been connected at the hip, I couldn't imagine what had come between them?

I asked, "Why's that? You and Ashley eat together every day."

Aubrey kicked the dirt and looked at the ground as we walked. "Yeah, well, I told her I liked Jon and she told me they were messaging last night."

My heart sank a little. Here it was, the first crush versus friend debacle. "I can see how that would be upsetting. What are you going to do? You can't just avoid her and not eat lunch with her. That's not the right way to handle it."

Aubrey nodded her head. "I know. I don't want to talk to her though, not now."

"I know it's tough and uncomfortable, but it's an important thing to do for yourself and your friend. A phone call is a good idea, if you think you might get upset. You don't have to do it at school."

"That's true... I guess I can call her."

"Let me know how it goes. Just tell her how you feel."

Aubrey nodded reluctantly. "I will."

We walked a couple miles around the school track near our house and headed home. Hopefully a walk would allow for Chewie to relax the rest of the evening rather than being a pest as was usual.

"Let's start dinner," I said as soon as we got back inside and unleashed Chewie.

"Ok. What do I need to do?"

"Look at the recipe book and start getting out the ingredients. I'll cover the pan in foil and get out the bowl and spatula."

Aubrey started filling the counter with spices, olive oil, chicken, peppers, and an onion. I did my tasks.

"First we prep. Get the peppers and onion chopped up then put them into bowls. Then we'll chop up the chicken and get everything tossed with oil and spices."

Aubrey grabbed the knife that I'd set on the counter and began cutting the peppers into strips. I was proud that she had already learned enough that I didn't have to give her much direction anymore. Once she chopped up all the vegetables, she put them into bowls and set them aside.

"Grab the chicken tenders and cut them into one-inch pieces."

Aubrey made a face. "I hate cutting the chicken."

I laughed. "I know you do, but it's part of the meal and it doesn't seem so yucky the more you do it."

Aubrey opened the chicken and tried to touch it as little as possible while cutting it.

We tossed everything together then poured it out onto the pan.

When it was done baking, we filled fresh tortillas with avocado, sour cream, chicken, and shrimp. Then, sat down to eat together.

"Great job!" I snapped a photo of our plates. I had taken some pictures of her chopping and mixing, and of the fajitas once they came out of the oven.

"You can use the pictures I took if you want to make an Instagram post tonight?" Admittedly, the cooking Instagram account was my idea. I wanted to teach Aubrey how to cook and I thought it might motivate her to mix in something modern like Instagram. Plus it kept a record of our time together and the recipes we made.

"Ok. I will after we eat."

We finished our meals and Aubrey posted her cooking pics to Instagram while I did the dishes. After dinner, I helped Aubrey study for her math test. We got it done with only a minimal amount of frustration and eye rolling, so I counted it as a win.

We watched some TV. For the most part, I really couldn't stand Aubrey's favorite shows, but in order to spend time with her, I'd suck it up and watch. Around 8:30, Aubrey had to get ready for bed. I let her stay up to read as long as she wanted, but I was strict about getting in bed on time.

She used to complain about having to get into bed so early. Eventually the complaining subsided. I think Aubrey realized she was getting better sleep when she was at my house because of the structure of bedtime.

She was mostly over wanting to cuddle or read in bed with me like she used to; however, on occasion she'd ask to read in bed with me. We'd both get into bed, me with my Kindle, her with her chapter book from school, reading in silence until she finally got sleepy.

She didn't ask tonight, but I still leaned over to kiss her on the forehead after she got in bed, something I always did. I can't express how much I love her, more than anything on this damn planet. I never wanted her to question that.

"That was a nice gourmet post for your Instagram account tonight. I love you."

"Thanks, I love you more."

"Goodnight, love."

"Goodnight, Mom."

I lingered outside her door a moment and sighed happily. Yep. Being a mom was totally enough.

As I got into bed that night, a little voice inside my head asked, *was it really… enough*?

Chapter 7: Nothin' But A Good Time

The truth was that being a mom filled *some* of the void I felt in my life. I could keep myself busy with cooking dinners, helping with homework, and running errands. However, I could never entirely avoid that ache of loneliness that caught up with me in the silent moments. While waiting in line at the store or whenever I was home alone. These moments piled up on me.

Let's be honest, single parents have needs in many areas due to not having a spouse as a support. Sometimes I found myself missing 24, I know it might be hard to believe with how difficult our relationship was, but I missed the comfort of lying in bed with my partner after a difficult day. I missed the closeness of another person to remind me that I wasn't entirely alone. I missed being able to talk to someone about my challenging day or about Aubrey's complicated world as a pre-teen.

It was Friday night again and Aubrey was at her dad's house.

I fidgeted on the couch and ran my hands through my hair. I tugged at my tank top needing some distraction from the heat that seemed to suffocate me. God was it hot in here. I got up and pulled open the door to the porch to get some fresh air.

I could hear my neighbor's chatting on theirs.

I could see myself walking over to their house and joining the chat. They would ask about Aubrey and it would only remind me that my daughter wouldn't be back for another three days. I lay back on the couch hoping for a breeze to visit me.

The desperate need for human touch and connection, to feel a man's arms wrapped around my body. Not for sex, but just connection—that's what I was longing for.

And damn, I needed it like oxygen. The longer I went without it, the more frantic the feeling inside me grew. I was a woman, goddammit, it wasn't wrong to have needs.

I grabbed my phone and laptop then sat back down on the couch.

Okay. There were ways other than dating apps to find men.

A few months ago, I'd sat on an interview panel with Raul, a hot as fuck cop. Raul was so good looking that the local police department he worked at used him as the model for their community outreach ads. I'd literally seen Raul's face plastered on billboards around town and on the back of public transit busses.

Raul and I spent the whole day together for the interview panel. Our down time between interviews was filled with chatting. Despite his professionalism, he let a compliment slip here and there, which led me to believe there was mutual interest. We exchanged numbers and I brought Aubrey to visit him at the police station a few weeks later.

When we left the station, I asked Aubrey what her favorite thing was and she replied, "Raul." I laughed knowing Raul was my favorite part of the field trip as well. Raul friended me on Facebook and Instagram. We touched base every once in a while, but nothing serious happened. Nor did he try to seek me out.

As I transitioned into this "self-discovery" phase in my life, I was feeling much bolder and confident. So, on this particularly lonely night, I texted Raul. A man I knew I'd feel safe with. This was someone I had history with. I respected his profession and the way he conducted himself. If I was going to let myself seek out the physical connection that I so desperately needed again, it was only going to be with someone like Raul. I trusted my gut instinct on this. It would be nothing like my last experience.

I quickly texted out my message to him, then took a deep breath as I waited for Raul to answer.

Me: HI. HOW ARE YOU DOING?

Raul: GREAT. HOW ARE YOU?

Me: I'M GOOD. I'M SORRY IF THIS IS TOO FORWARD, BUT I'VE BEEN HORMONAL AS FUCK LATELY AND WANTED TO SEE IF YOU ARE INTERESTED IN HAVING SEX. IF NOT, I TOTALLY UNDERSTAND AND I HOPE MY FORWARDNESS DOESN'T UPSET YOU.

After hitting send, I felt a little surprised by myself. I was known for being forward, but this was one of the most forward things I'd ever done.

Raul responded a few minutes later.

Raul: I LIKE YOUR STYLE AND YOUR FORWARDNESS DEFINITELY DOESN'T BOTHER ME. IT'S FUCKING HOT. WHAT EXACTLY ARE YOU LOOKING FOR?

Me: I'D LOVE SOMEONE TO HAVE SEX WITH ONCE IN A WHILE. SOMEONE I CAN BRING INTO MY HOME AND TRUST. I'VE ALWAYS BEEN ATTRACTED TO YOU AND HAVE WANTED TO SLEEP WITH YOU SINCE THE DAY I MET YOU, SO I FIGURED I HAVE NOTHING TO LOSE BY ASKING.

Raul: TRUST ME, I'D LOVE TO. WHEN AND WHERE?

Me: I'M FREE THIS WEEKEND OR MONDAY AND TUESDAY NIGHTS.

Raul: LET'S DO NEXT MONDAY. IT'S MY FIRST DAY OFF THAT I DON'T HAVE PLANS.

Me: SOUNDS GOOD. I'LL PLAN ON IT.

Raul: I DEFINITELY WILL TOO.

The day for Raul and me to meet came and passed. I never heard from him. I decided against texting him as I didn't feel like dealing with the blatant rejection I'd felt so many times before. So, I assumed he wasn't interested. Maybe it just wasn't a good time. I opened up my laptop to see if he'd be online tonight then I'd know he was available. If he was on Facebook, maybe I could message him?

I went on Facebook and looked him up. Immediately, I saw pictures posted of him smiling with his arms around a woman—who was obviously his girlfriend.

Son of a—I slammed the lid of the laptop shut and tossed it onto the couch.

I thought Raul was a good guy. I felt so disheartened and distrustful of men, again. Not to mention the feelings of insecurity and self-doubt. Did he even really want to sleep with me or was he just telling me what he thought I wanted to hear?

And so the justification began. I guess it wouldn't be soooo bad if I reinstalled Bumble. After all, Raul proved to be no different than any of the men I'd met online, despite my belief that he would be. I thought he'd be more mature and respectful, like how he'd presented himself at work and on the interview panel.

I was still terrified after what had happened with Zack, but I didn't want to think about it. I tried to reason with myself. I hadn't spent as much time getting to know Zack as I had with Thomas. We had only texted back and forth before the coffee date. I would be more careful this time and be absolutely sure to avoid men like Zack.

A little bit of texting and a 15-minute coffee date hadn't allowed me to get to know him and determine if he'd be capable of sexual assault.

I would be smarter this time. Take things slower like I did with the other men I had slept with before Zack.

I searched in the app store for Bumble. Before I could think better of it, I hit the green *Install* button.

***

Joey was one of the first new matches that I connected with. He came from a close-knit Italian family. Prior to us even facetiming, I stalked his Instagram account and saw that he was very close with his family and friends. All of his posts were from family events or outings with friends.

That had to be a good sign. Guys into assaulting and murdering women in their homes weren't close with their mothers or so I convinced myself. I thought back to Zack and how he must have treated all women—like objects rather than people.

Joey worked as a real estate appraiser in the Denver area, but he drove from Colorado Springs to Boulder on jobs. He earned his degree from CU Boulder and spent his college days partying, but not really having much sex, apparently.

Joey informed me that I would be only the eighth person he had slept with. I was taken aback, especially because he was so cute. I assumed all twenty-five-year-olds were getting laid every weekend, much like the men I had met before.

Breaking my own rules of being more cautious, I met Joey at his small gray Nissan truck in my guest parking lot. I could immediately tell he was nervous. We got to know each other on FaceTime so I felt comfortable giving him my home address. Joey showed up with a flask of whiskey. He shook the flask. "Need a little liquid courage."

I laughed. It helped to calm some of my worries to see he had his own. Clearly, Joey was neither a player nor a murderer.

He had a slight social awkwardness which displayed itself in the frequent uncomfortable movements he made, like looking down at the ground and rarely making eye contact. When he did, it was quick, and he seemed bashful.

I caught on right away that Joey's sense of humor was to make a comment then immediately follow it up with a comment under his breath, which always ended up being even more hysterical.

"Did you eat dinner already? It's still a little early."

"Yeah, I had chicken and pasta just before I left the house."

"That sounds yummy. You cook?"

"My mom does. I live at home."

Joey lowered his voice. "Does wonders for my sex life."

I laughed out loud. Joey was cracking me up right away. I had a good feeling about this.

I was instantaneously at ease with Joey. There was no hesitation inviting him inside. I could tell he was relatively shy and mildly awkward.

As we walked to my condo, Joey started telling me about his family. He lived at home with his parents in Lakewood, just outside of Denver.

It was interesting to me that the very next person I would run across on Bumble was the polar opposite to Zack. In retrospect, I can see that I needed to draw in the safest experience possible to be able to continue with my "sexual revelations." With that being said, Joey made me laugh so hard that night I nearly peed my pants several times.

"I ran into some issues coming here tonight," Joey began.

My heart stopped as I thought back to Raul and the girlfriend that likely kept him from coming to my house. "Oh… yeah…" I replied skeptically.

He gave me a grin. "Yeah my dad asked me where I was going. 'Hey son, where are you headed off to?' to which I replied, 'oh, well…this lady's house'." He'd deepened his voice making what I could only guess was an impression of his dad.

Joey winked. My heart rushed at the use of the term lady in reference to me. This couldn't be the kind of man who thought of women as disposable blow-up dolls.

"Well," Joey went on, "then he rose an eyebrow at me and asked 'Lady?' to which all I could reply was 'yeah, lady.' I will never live this one down, Lacie. He started asking all kinds of question about you: 'who is this lady, how does she have her own house…' all kinds of them, you would have thought I was stepping out on him."

I giggled. I could tell right then and there that Joey's sense of humor was going to be a turn on for me.

"That isn't the end of it either, I went to fill up my flask from the liquor cabinet and my mom went at me with a few questions! When I told her I was off to see a lady friend she was speechless."

I was hysterical at this point in the story. I could not believe it was so hard for Joey to get out of the house to come see me. I laughed harder wondering how his parents would react if they actually knew where their son was headed.

"Then, I finally got to the front door and my dad was standing there ready to continue interrogating me. He asked again where I was really headed off to. 'To a lady's house. I already told you'. My dad was beside himself at this point. 'Like that?' he asked me as he looked down and pointed to my beat-up slippers. I told him, 'yeah, like this.' And I walked out the door." Joey said with exasperation.

By the end of his story my stomach hurt from laughing. It was no wonder he needed to travel with a flask.

I looked down and saw his hunter green velour slippers and started laughing again—he must have left his house in a rush to avoid his parents.

After the comedic telling of his departure from home, he decided to come in for a hug, which I had no hesitation in accepting. He smelled fresh and soapy, like Irish Spring. I assumed he showered just before coming over. Nothing hotter than a man who wants to show up to a woman's house looking and smelling his best, even if that includes comfortable slippers and a flask full of courage.

I don't know what it was exactly, but Joey was doing it for me. I think it was the humor and the fact that his joking put me at ease and in a happy mood. We sat on the couch together. I was drawn to him almost solely due to his personality. He was handsome, but he seemed to lack self-confidence and self-esteem. It kinda reminded me of Mario in some ways, but Joey was much easier going. Don't get me wrong, he was adorable and funny as fuck. It was endearing and exactly what I needed. He felt *safe*.

As we sat on the couch chatting, I knew I was going to have to make the first move. Joey continued drinking from his shiny gold flask. I noticed he started loosening up and was making more eye contact. I put my hand on his forearm.

"You have such soft skin," I said.

"I know." Joey dipped his head while giving me a self-deprecating smile. "I need to roughen them up a little."

I started laughing. "What are you talking about? Why would you want to do that? Your skin is so soft, I don't want to stop feeling it."

"Because it's not manly! I used to have calloused hands. They were rough manly hands. Now, I work on a computer all day and have soft pussy hands. I need to go home tomorrow and dig holes for fence posts or something."

I laughed. Joey was one hundred percent serious while criticizing his smooth hands. I would never for a moment analyze the "manliness" of a man's hands, but I could tell this was something he had been ridiculed for or at a minimum felt insecure about. I decided I would refocus him on the humor I saw in him.

"Manliness shows up in many different ways." I said winking.

Even though I was laughing my ass off, he continued to plead his case as serious as could be.

"No woman wants a man with soft hands."

Joey was shaking his head. I could tell the alcohol from his flask was finally starting to kick in.

As we continued talking, our gazes caught for longer and longer periods of time. Finally, I stopped talking and stared into his eyes. He held my gaze but made no attempt to move.

"Kiss me," I said.

As if he'd been waiting for me to ask him all night, Joey melted into his seat. With his breath still catching up, he leaned forward slid his hand under my hair and kissed me.

Surprisingly, Joey was a great kisser. I predicted he'd be lackluster due to his inexperience, but I was wrong. He was very passionate. I could feel the emotion in his kiss. Another surprise.

Joey was great at placing his hands all over my body and rubbing in all the sensual places. His hands lustfully grabbed me as if it'd been a long time since he had touched a woman. His heavy breathing told me he was getting more and more aroused.

Unfortunately, I was not able to get fully aroused by our foreplay. Sure, it was passionate and I was turned on by Joey's arousal, but he didn't *feel* masculine. He didn't take charge or take part in leading our sexual encounter. Once we finally started having sex, I had to move us into different positions. I love taking turns fulfilling my partner's wants during sex, but I don't enjoy having to do all the work and directing by myself. It's fun to take turns while having sex, but Joey lacked that type of confidence and it was a turn-off.

As a result, our sex was disappointing, but Joey was a champ cuddler. He was warm and pressed his body up against mine from head to toe. I melted into his arms and lied there completely relaxed, eyes closed, enjoying the blissful moment.

Joey stayed all night. We had sex three more times. I never came. I tried. Trust me. I suggested highly stimulating positions and thought about sexual fantasies hoping to increase my arousal. Neither worked. We never really discussed my inability to have an orgasm and I'm not one to fake it, so I assumed Joey knew. He may or may not have been aware, but I didn't care. I was happy with the fun I was having and enjoyed his company.

Fun.

Companionship.

Touch.

Safety.

Joey was checking all the other boxes for me.

The next morning was a Monday but also a holiday. We were both off work, so we slept in. When we finally did get up, we went to the nearby bagel store then Starbucks for something to drink. I always felt slightly on edge going there after running into 24's family there, but we lived in the same zip code and I wasn't going to hide.

We brought everything back to my house to eat. As we ate, we chatted. I noticed it was mildly awkward since Joey's liquid courage had long since worn off.

"So, what are your plans for the day?"

"I'm going home to dig holes."

I laughed at his seriousness.

"What are you going to say to your parents? You didn't go home last night. Aren't they going to interrogate you again?"

"I messaged them last night and told them that I drank too much and couldn't drive."

"That's good. Hopefully they'll leave you alone then."

"I doubt that."

I laughed again knowing if Joey was going home to anything similar to what he experienced when he left, he was in for a lot of questions.

We finished eating, then had a nice goodbye hug and kiss. Joey headed out and I immediately started tackling my to-do list. I was going to take full advantage of my extra day off work.

I did end up texting Joey several times that week to see when we could hang out again. The sex might not have been great; but damn, I couldn't remember the last time I'd had so much *fun*.

Like Thomas and Colton, he never replied… why??? The lack of responsiveness was agonizing. The horrible communication was maddening. We'd had such a blast. I didn't think I was alone in feeling this way. Yet, here I was home alone again after being ghosted by a man whom I thought had a great night with me.

It was official, I did *not* understand men. At all.

Chapter 8: Save A Horse (Ride A Cowboy)

Matched! When those words popped up on my phone screen, I was giddy with excitement. Once in a while, I would come across a man's profile that I'd hope and pray to match with.

Billy was one of those men. When I swiped right for him, I was immediately hopeful. The comment section of Billy's profile was empty. He had no words, only pictures. Ones that might turn some women off, but those pictures were all I needed to know that I was interested in meeting Billy.

I was wildly attracted.

He was in hunting gear in one photo, holding up the giant rack of a deer he had killed. In another he was with his family at a Broncos game. The last one was at a rodeo with him roping steer. Billy was twenty-five when we matched, soon to turn twenty-six. He was tall with dirty blond hair, a thick beard, and ice blue eyes. He looked like a Nordic god.

He was a foreman for a large electric company that took him all over Colorado. He was a bit on the thinner side when I met him, probably from being on the road a lot and usually skipping lunch to stay on top of the crews.

I messaged him after we matched.

Me: HI! HOW ARE YOU DOING TODAY?

Him: GREAT. HOW ABOUT YOURSELF?

Me: I'M DOING GREAT AS WELL. I'M SORRY FOR BEING SO FORWARD, BUT YOU ARE FUCKING HOT AND I WAS VERY HAPPY WHEN WE MATCHED!

Him: THANKS. YOU'RE PRETTY FUCKING HOT YOURSELF AND I WAS HOPING WE'D MATCH, TOO.

These were the words (or pretty damn close) that started an on and off relationship (of sorts) that would last for the next year to come.

Billy was in town for work. I wasn't able to meet him that day when we matched because I had Aubrey. We decided to talk on the phone that night after she went to bed.

His voice was higher than I expected. It didn't match his rough and rugged exterior. We chatted for over an hour.

"Tell me about your family."

"We've lived in Steamboat Springs my whole life. I recently bought my grandparent's house. My sister is married and lives in town with her husband. My parents still live in the same house that I grew up in. They've been married for 30 years and it's kind of sickening because they still hold hands and kiss all the time."

"Why is that bad? It sounds to me like they love each other a lot and are great at showing it."

"Yeah, I guess, but it's not really what I want to see all the time."

I felt like I was learning a lot about Billy. As I laid in bed talking with him, I was reminded of talking all night on the phone with my high school boyfriend, not wanting to hang up. It was nice to feel a familiar sense of normalcy and openness in the bizarre world of online dating.

Before getting off the phone, we agreed that he would text me the next day, once he was off work, and I'd drive to the hotel he was staying at near the Stapleton Town Center, the site of the old Denver airport.

We texted on and off, all day, starting the next morning.

Billy was different and it thrilled me. He wanted to get to know me. Most of the other men I had been with were only looking to do the basic amount of communication to get themselves in the door. Billy seemed to really enjoy being on that "getting to know you" level of the relationship and kept our conversations going.

Apparently, I wasn't the only one who was excited for our date. Billy showed genuine interest and it felt great to finally feel a man show some curiosity about my life.

Billy: I'M REALLY EXCITED TO MEET YOU IN PERSON.

Me: ME TOO! HURRY UP AND GET OFF WORK ALREADY!

When Billy's text finally came saying he was ready, I hopped up and got dressed in leggings, a thick flannel jacket, and UGGs then headed out the door. It was freezing outside and I was in no mood to dress up just to freeze my ass off. Especially not when I had already come to realize that men really weren't looking for a perfectly put together woman. Not the men I was meeting at least. Even though Billy seemed different from the previous guys I'd met on Bumble, he had a natural and casual quality about him, I could tell he would also appreciate it in a woman.

There was horrible traffic on my way to pick him up. He wasn't able to meet in the middle or come to where I lived, because he was driving a company truck and its miles were monitored.

On a normal basis, I always make men come to me. I feel safer being in my own house with neighbors nearby. But as I said, Billy was different. We seemed to have immediate chemistry and an attraction to one another's personalities. Because of my excitement to meet him, I didn't even mind the horrendous traffic.

When I arrived at his hotel, I sent him a text. He must have been waiting for me, because as I walked into the lobby, the elevator door opened and he came out. We immediately made eye contact and greeted each other with huge smiles.

I had butterflies in my stomach. Freaking *butterflies!* Billy was just as hot in person as in his pictures. Although the other men I'd been with had been attractive, I felt drawn to Billy in a different way. The attraction I felt for him was intensely strong—on more of a cellular level. I couldn't put my finger on it yet, but I knew we were going to have a great time together. By the grin on his face, I sensed he felt the same.

I couldn't tell if it was his smile or the fact that he couldn't stop staring at me that I found most attractive about him. I had a strong sense that Billy felt the same instant attraction that I did. Every time I went to make eye contact with him, he was already looking back at me. We seemed drawn to each other.

Billy was wearing jeans, a North Face fleece jacket, and black Converse. He gave me a strong hug that lingered a little longer than most hugs. He was warm and I wanted him to stay close.

"Hi," I said. "How are you?"

"Great. How was the drive?"

"Lots of traffic but that's okay. Where do you want to go eat?"

"I was hoping you'd have suggestions. I haven't had many overnights here for work."

"Well, we can go grab pizza by the slice. There's a great place nearby."

"Sounds good to me."

"I have to use the restroom before we head out to dinner. Sitting in traffic does that to me." I said winking.

We checked with the front desk. There were no restrooms in the lobby, so Billy offered me the one in his room. Initially, there was an awkward silence as we entered the elevator.

In an attempt to break the silence, I said, "Well, do I look like my pictures?"

I wanted to know what he was thinking and felt it best to just come out and ask.

He laughed then said, "You look even better in person than in your pictures."

I smiled. "So do you."

The awkwardness didn't immediately go away. Billy was on the quiet side of shy and I was feeling bashful because of how insanely attracted I was to him. I walked into his bathroom and it was still steamy from a recent shower. Shaving cream was in the sink. Wet towels on the floor.

As I came out of the bathroom, I couldn't help glancing around the room. My eyes landed on the bed as we headed out the door together. Billy opened the door and we headed down to my car.

As we drove on to the main street of the Town Center, I tried to pull my SUV into a smaller than average parking spot. Billy looked a little apprehensive.

"Don't worry. I can park this thing anywhere."

I pulled into the spot and smiled at Billy. He smiled back, obviously amused. "I can't open my door. I thought you said you can park anywhere?"

"I can and did. I never said you would be able to get out."

We both laughed. I backed my car up far enough for him to be able to get out then parked again. We walked over to the pizza place. When we got there, Billy opened the door and allowed me to walk inside first. The smell of freshly baked pizza greeted us.

We ordered our slices and drinks. Billy immediately pulled his wallet out.

"I can pay for my own pizza."

"Absolutely not. You drove through all that traffic to see me. The least I can do is buy you dinner."

"You're very sweet but it's not necessary. I'm happy to pay for my own. I don't expect you to pay for my dinner."

"I'm paying for the pizza."

The tone with which Billy responded, told me to stop arguing. He was very well-mannered and was just trying to be a gentleman. I needed to let him.

I smiled at Billy, even more attracted to him in that moment.

"Thank you, I appreciate it."

It was September in Colorado, so you never know what you're going to get for weather, but my UGGs and flannel turned out to be perfect for the cool evening. We found a table outside and enjoyed the cool crisp evening air.

"This is a perfect. I prefer to be outside whenever possible" Billy said.

"There isn't a nicer place on earth than Colorado in autumn. Okay, maybe except for the beach anywhere else."

We both laughed.

As we continued to talk, I learned more about Billy. At only twenty-five, Billy already owned his own home. He was very motivated and hard-working. He often woke at three or four in the morning to get on the road. He was raised to work hard and would do so until the day he died. I would bet my life on that.

Billy and I would often make eye contact as we chatted with one another. Staring into each other's eyes for longer periods of time. It's interesting how, once you truly pay attention to eye contact, you realize how much of your daily conversations involve little of it. It feels very obvious and noticeable now but I was so struck by it. I valued it for how rare it was.

Billy was quiet and intense. Our chemistry and draw to each other seemed to match, yet Billy never attempted to touch me as we sat close to each other. I wanted very badly for him to make a move by holding my hand or putting his arm around me. I got the sense he wanted to touch me, as well, by the way his gaze lingered on me for long periods of time; but although I could feel all this, he still didn't.

We stayed for a while and chatted, just enjoying the evening. We were the only ones out. I decided to take him to a really good dessert place that had an amazing selection. I had every intention of buying since Billy had insisted on paying for dinner.

We arrived at the bakery and again, Billy opened the door for me. We decided on a slice of chocolate cream and key lime pies. I pulled my wallet out to pay and approached the register. Before I could get my card out, Billy was already in front of me handing his card to the cashier.

"Billy! I was going to pay for the dessert since you paid for dinner."

"Nope. I'm paying."

I stood speechless for a few seconds before deciding to not argue. I had already learned at dinner to give in when Billy insisted on paying. He wanted to treat me to dinner and dessert; what a turn on. Although it was unexpected, I let him.

"Well, thank you again. You're super sweet and well-mannered Billy. It is refreshing to see in this day and age."

He looked down and smiled. Only looking up again to take his card from the cashier.

"You want to take it back to the room and eat there?" I asked.

We shared another long moment of eye contact before he smiled and nodded. We grabbed our bag of dessert and headed back to his hotel.

There was nowhere to sit and eat in his room. There was only one chair and a king bed.

I glanced at the bed. "Do you mind if we eat on your bed?"

He shook his head, his eyes on me. "No, not at all."

We both removed our shoes and sat on the foot of the bed. I started taking everything out of the bag. Placing napkins on the bed in a makeshift paper table. We started eating the pie slices, trading boxes here and there so that we could try both pies. We put on the TV and found an Avalanche game.

I put the leftover pie in the refrigerator, then we both sat back resting against the headboard.

For close to an hour, we continued chatting while watching the game. I was beginning to become very aware of the time. I had a 45-minute drive home ahead of me and work in the morning.

Billy still hadn't attempted to touch me. I wanted him to so badly.

Billy was different than the other men I had met. This night was, too. He was shy and expressed how glad he was that we talked on the phone, because it had made him more comfortable. I knew I was going to have to make the first move at this point; so in my typical fashion, I didn't beat around the bush.

I picked up his hand and placed it on my thigh. "We've been sitting on this bed for an hour Billy. Are you ever going to kiss me?"

111

"I wanted to at the park."

"Why didn't you?"

"I don't know. I'm shy, I guess."

"Do you want to kiss me now?"

"Yes."

"Then kiss me."

Billy leaned over, grabbed my neck, then ran his fingers into my hair caressing my ear with his thumb and forefinger. I felt like a teenager, excited for a first kiss. Fireworks lit up inside of me as all the anticipation exploded within me. He finally kissed me. I could feel my stomach doing flip-flops and my muscles go weak. Oh God, *yes*! The tension building between us all night *finally* released in a flood.

Despite the fireworks, our initial kisses were somewhat awkward. We were sitting shoulder to shoulder on his bed and it was not a position conducive to making out. We both adjusted our bodies slightly so kissing became more comfortable. After this, our kissing became more and more passionate. Our hands started wandering around each other's bodies. Billy wrapped his arm around my back and pulled me closer to him.

Billy wasn't verbally expressive, but he wore his emotions on his sleeve. His breathing came in heated puffs against my skin. As he ran his hands down my legs.

His breath caught as he traced up my inner thigh and a moan burst from him, one that screamed arousal.

He was hungry for me and nothing could have turned me on more in that moment.

We slowly undressed each other. Enjoying every step in the process. I could feel that he was in no hurry and wanted to take his time. It was very refreshing to have slow drawn out

112

foreplay. Once I was naked, I got up quickly to get a hair tie and condom from my purse.

He teased me saying, "Did you already plan to have sex tonight or do you always carry condoms in your purse?"

I laughed. "Well, I just happen to have two condoms in my purse and no—I didn't plan on having sex with you tonight."

Lies. All lies. I'd been envisioning sleeping with him ever since I saw his pictures. The hour-long phone conversation and his consistent texting only created more desire.

As I walked back to the bed pulling my hair up, Billy blurted out, "You are sexy as fuck!"

I was taken aback and turned on all at the same time. Although Billy was expressive with his feelings over text, he hadn't really complimented me in person much after our initial meeting. Like I said, he was on the low end of the verbal expressiveness and compliments scale.

I walked over to the bed pressing my knee down on the edge. I used the knee to push forward arching my back as I rose over Billy, my nipples nearly brushing against his chest. I held his face in my hand as I began kissing him again. My lips moving up his neck to his ears. I gently sucked on his ear lobe then bit gently down.

Billy stiffened and inhaled deeply.

The chemistry that I'd felt while sitting in the park? Holy shit did it translate to the bedroom!

With me still hovering above him, he grabbed my face firmly with both hands and pulled me into a kiss. I could hear him breathing loudly as he kissed me and kissed me and kissed me. Billy had me so fired up. I continued kissing him, my hands caressing his back as I straddled his hips and watched as he slid himself into me.

Billy was passionate and I could tell he felt every touch. His moans surrounded me. Feeling and hearing how turned on Billy was fueled me even more. I could tell I was driving him wild and it was so fucking hot.

Billy groaned loudly then grabbed my hips and rolled me onto my back. He ground his whole body into mine as he fucked me. It was amazingly sexy the way Billy took charge.

After having raised one of my legs onto his shoulder, Billy finally lay down on top of me. He kissed me, moving up my neck then down to my breasts. It was all too much for me to handle and I exploded with a hugely satisfying orgasm. I felt my entire body light up. The kind of orgasm that remains in a woman for quite a while leading to her feeling numb and tingling.

"Holy fuck! That was incredible." I knew I couldn't make Billy wait too long to get his, but I had to take a few seconds to bask in the glory of that O.

My head still washed with sensation, I got onto my hands and knees then looked back at Billy with a smile. Billy flashed a broad smile then threw his head back and shook it from side to side. He grabbed my hip with one hand while he used his other to guide himself into me. He moved with purpose holding onto my hips.

Billy came fast. I could feel him cumming as his dick pulsed inside me. His groans and breathing were loud, I felt a sense of accomplishment knowing Billy was so turned on by me.

I loved that I could hear and feel Billy's orgasm. It's so anticlimactic when a man cums and I don't even know it.

After Billy pulled out, he cleaned up in the bathroom. I lay there on the bed catching my breath. That was great sex. The level of passion and emotional expression made it a thousand percent better.

Billy immediately cuddled up to me when he got back in bed. He was warm and his body felt amazing.

I relaxed against him. Every part of our bodies touched from head to toe. This. God, *this* was everything. He cuddled me so easily. So naturally. I didn't have to ask for it. I closed my eyes and soaked in the feeling.

However, me being me, my inner voice couldn't stay quiet for long. *Why did he think I looked so sexy when I walked over to grab a hair tie and condom earlier?* I was curious. "Aren't you used to seeing naked women walk around?"

"No. Are you kidding? Not at all." He sounded genuinely surprised by my assumption.

"Twenty-something-year-old women don't walk around naked?" I was legitimately surprised.

"Nope," he confirmed.

Wow. There's another benefit to maturity, I thought.

"What attracts you to older women?" I was curious to hear what Billy had to say.

"Well, for starters, older women are easier to talk to. They listen and engage on a higher-level, have mentally stimulating conversation. I don't want to talk about social media or famous people. None of that matters to me, but younger women tend to talk a lot about those topics and can't even take a photo without using filters or just not taking one at all."

"Wow, this is interesting. I always wondered what drew a younger man to an older woman, aside from the sex of course."

We both laughed.

Billy went on. "Most older women don't play games and are comfortable with telling you what they're wanting or needing. Getting straight answers from younger women isn't always easy. Of course, older women are more sexually experienced and there's just no match for that."

I'm not surprised the sex is better with a forty-three-year-old woman, but it shocked me to hear that younger women lacked the confidence to walk around naked. Young women have such beautiful bodies. They all look skinny and athletically fit to me, frequently walking around in leggings and crop tops.

In our society, we're programmed to believe thin is beautiful and I guess my viewpoint was aligned with this way of thinking. I'd think twenty-something-year-olds would walk around all day long naked in front of a man with the bodies like they have.

Shit, I did it at forty-three with stretch marks and a C-section scar. My body was far from perfect; but admittedly, I've been mostly comfortable with my body for as long as I can remember. I wondered if I felt the same insecurity when I was in my twenties. Unfortunately, I wasn't very sexually active back then and couldn't recall.

Billy fell asleep cuddling me. His face buried in my neck. I stayed like that for a while. I knew I needed to get going but couldn't bring myself to move. I could feel his warm breath on my neck. I didn't want to disturb him and honestly it had been ages since I had a man cuddle me like this. I was going to enjoy every moment.

After a while I sighed knowing that I really *did* have to get going. Especially, if I was going to be even semi-human at work tomorrow. I woke Billy. We both got up and got dressed. He sat on his bed in baggy gray sweats and a white t-shirt looking groggy. I grabbed my purse and a water bottle from the mini fridge then walked toward the bed.

Billy grabbed me by the hips and pulled me in between his legs. While I was standing with my legs pressed against the bed, he kissed me again.

His hands moved from my hips to my lower back then up under my shirt. He grabbed my breasts while we kissed and squeezed them firmly. My bra was in my purse. I had both hands full and could only stand there kissing him back while he fondled me. Our kissing became more and more passionate. Our breathing became louder and I felt my knees go weak. We both emitted little moans and sounds of pleasure.

I stopped and asked, "Are you going to let me leave?"

"No," he said, smiling.

I smiled back then walked over to the desk. I put my things down, took out the second condom, and slipped off my boots. I turned back to face him then walked back over to the bed.

I hadn't felt so wanted by a man since dating 24. It felt amazing to know that I turned him on so much that he wanted me again. That he didn't want to let me out of his grasp.

I stood in front of Billy as we continued to make out. He unbuttoned my top and undressed me for a second time that night. We had sex in my "go to" position—my legs closed lying on the bed with Billy on top of me as his knees straddled my legs—he fucked me this way until I came for the second time that night.

Billy took a little longer to cum and wanted to have sex doggy style. He spanked me occasionally as he nailed me from behind. Just like the first time, I knew exactly when he came. I could feel his larger than average dick pulsing inside of me and it felt amazing. He arched his back and moaned, one hand on my hip and the other on my shoulder.

"You're going to sleep good tonight," I said after we'd both caught our breath.

"If that doesn't do it, I don't know what will."

We both laughed then began to clean up.

Billy walked me to my car. It was midnight and I still had a long drive ahead of me with work the next morning. I gave him a peck on the lips before I got into the car.

As I drove home, I had a huge smile on my face. Billy, the fucking cowboy, just gave me one of the best nights of my life. I hoped I'd be seeing him again.

After my first few online dating adventures, I wasn't sure what to expect with Billy. Would he call or text? Would he be like the others and never make contact again? All I knew was that our chemistry and connection were different than those who came before him.

Everything about Billy felt different. He was well-mannered, opened every door for me, paid for dinner and dessert, and was beyond respectful as I sat on his bed for an hour not once attempting to touch me.

I don't know who texted who first—oh, who are we kidding, I can say with almost a hundred percent certainty that it was probably me—but Billy and I texted on and off for a week. I think I was great company for him on his off hours. He told me how lonely his job could get.

I couldn't wait to see him again.

I kept reliving that night over and over in my head. Our conversations. The sex. The feel of his body behind me, his strong arms curled around me. The rhythmic feel of his chest as it rose and fell with each breath as he slept.

I had a giddy feeling every time I saw a text from him.

I was crushing hard.

Two weeks later, I was online and saw that Billy was back in my neck of the woods.

He never texted me to tell me he was coming back, nor did he text while he was there. I kept waiting for it. All weekend. I watched the little dot on the app that showed he was only thirty minutes away.

The text never came.

My heart sank.

Chapter 9: Don't Stop Believing

I called up Claudia. She and I had been friends for twenty years. She was tall and slender—naturally gorgeous. Even when she claimed that she needed to lose weight, Claudia's body always presented as tall and thin.

She was originally from Argentina, but had lived in the United States since middle school. As a result, she still spoke with a beautiful Argentinian accent. She had dirty blond hair and was a natural beauty.

We met when we were both hired in the same human resources department at the same time. We helped each other learn the ropes. We had a lot of parallels in our lives, too. Our friendship continued through our marriages, the birth of our children, and also our divorces. Claudia and I could always lean on each other for anything.

I divorced first, so I was a few steps ahead of her in the healing process. What I gave her in divorce support, she gave back to me ten-fold in the form of dating advice. Claudia had men nailed down to a T. She was a woman who gave no second chances to men who were idiots.

I had a lot to learn from her.

"So, I officially don't understand men," I ranted over the phone. "I've had great sex a few times now with multiple men, only to not hear from them again. What does a girl gotta do to find some steady sex around here? What am I doing wrong?"

I didn't call her up to beat around the bush or to have her tell me what I wanted to hear. I called her up to get the cold hard truth that I was clearly too oblivious to see for myself.

"Stop reaching out to them. Don't text them. Let them come after you. Men like the chase. How do you think they got themselves to your house in the first place? I'm not suggesting you play games but play just a little bit hard to get. It's their language of desire."

I was genuinely surprised at what she was telling me. How many times had I heard the saying "play hard to get" and dismissed it? I valued open honest communication so much that I just assumed the best way to handle things was to text a man whenever I wanted more from him.

And how well was that working out for me? Well, up until this point it wasn't. At all.

"Holy shit, you're right. I need to stop texting them at all and let them come to me if they want to see me again." As I reflected back on the one guy to come back, Mario, I never actually reached out to him, he eventually came back around, wanting to hang out again.

This was not an ingenious strategy, yet I hadn't thought to put it into action before. It was all coming clear to me now. I guess I really needed to go through it a few times before I could make sense of the game of online dating.

This was not my usual M.O. With most things in life, I was a quick learner. But when it came to men, it was different.

"Claudia, you're awesome. I'm so glad I called you. I needed to hear that. I promise I will do that from here on out. How are things with you?"

Claudia and I were both using apps to meet men, however with very different intentions. I was solely looking to satisfy my sexual desires. Claudia was looking for the right man. She had been divorced for a couple years now and still hadn't even had sex yet. She just didn't feel secure with those she was dating.

I was hoping she'd get laid, since I know all too well how hard that first time can be after a divorce—it was for me. The thought of being intimate with another man after having been with the same man for numerous years, it was daunting to say the least.

"Well, you're going to be happy with me. I finally had sex and it was amazing. His name is Mitch and he was an incredible lover."

"Oh my God! I'm so happy for you. I told you the best was yet to come. I know it's hard to imagine when you're in the thick of things, but the experiences I've had post-divorce are far better than any I had with my ex-husband, that's for sure."

"You were right, as usual. The only shitty thing is... he lives in Arizona, so I won't be seeing him very often. Only occasionally when he's back here for work."

"When are you going to see him again?"

"I'm not sure. We haven't gotten that far yet."

"Definitely keep me posted. I'm dying to know where it goes. I told you, life would get better after divorce. You and I will both find amazing men one day, I'm confident."

"You may be right, my friend, but I know one thing for sure: I will never get married again. Ever."

I was somewhat surprised to hear this coming from Claudia.

"Really? I'm surprised you feel that way. I'm open to marriage again—with the right man."

"I don't know if any man will be right for me. I thought my marriage was forever. I thought my ex-husband *was* the right man. I went to counseling and provided so many solutions to fix things with him. In the end, he wasn't interested in doing any of them."

"I know and I'm so sorry, but not all men are like your ex-husband. I believe there are some really good men out there, just waiting for great women like us."

"I hope you're right because right now I have a hard time believing it."

I knew exactly where Claudia was coming from. For years after my divorce, the thought of opening myself up to another man was out of the question. Then one day I realized that if I had the mindset that finding a great man was impossible, I was essentially sentencing myself to a lifetime of solitude and loneliness in a self-fulfilling prophecy. And for me, that thought was out of the question.

I hoped with time, Claudia would continue healing and get to a place where she'd be willing to open her heart up to another man, even if the end result wasn't marriage.

After we got off the phone, I went back on Bumble in hopes of putting Claudia's advice into action. I was determined to not reach out to any man after spending time with him, even if my intention was still to hang out with him again. For the first time in my life, I was going to play hard to get.

Come hell or high water.

Chapter 10: Cheatin' Heart

It turned out that my next encounter wouldn't come from Bumble at all. When my birthday rolled around, Raul the hot cop texted me.

Raul: HAPPY BIRTHDAY BEAUTIFUL.

Me: THANKS! HOW ARE YOU DOING?

I wasn't going to lose an opportunity to flirt with Raul. Apparently, he was notified by Facebook that it was my birthday. He was out drinking that night with friends.

Me: ARE YOU GOING TO BE MY BIRTHDAY FUCK?

I presumed he had a girlfriend after checking out his Facebook (which made his text to me completely inappropriate), yet I was curious how he'd respond.

Raul: I CAN'T COME OVER, BUT TRUST ME, I WANT TO VERY BADLY

(Note to all men out there… if you are going to let a woman down, let her down nicely so she doesn't feel completely rejected. At least hearing that Raul wanted to sleep with me numbed the sting of rejection a little bit.)

Me: IF YOU CAN'T COME OVER AND HELP ME OUT, AT LEAST SEND ME ANOTHER MAN IN UNIFORM WHO CAN. HELP OUT A SINGLE MOM.

Raul: I'D DO ANYTHING TO HELP OUT A SINGLE MOM. I'LL SEE WHAT I CAN DO.

Raul texted me the next day with a picture of a police officer friend. He was super handsome, so I told Raul to give him my number.

And that was how Robert texted me. My birthday was on a Friday and Robert came over that Sunday morning after getting off work. Only a few minutes into hanging out, Robert asked if I smoked weed.

"Yea, I do occasionally. Do you?"

"Yes, I do. I brought some weed in case you smoked. I find that most people do nowadays with it being legal."

"Yes, I agree. When I first smoked weed a few years ago, I was hesitant because I was raised with the belief that drugs are bad. After I started smoking here and there, I came to find out that most people I encounter smoke weed to some degree. It was rather eye opening to say the least. I felt like I'd been living in the dark my whole life."

After finding out that I'd smoke weed with him, Robert pulled out a joint and a lighter. We sat on my patio and smoked together while getting to know each other some more.

Robert talked a lot about his family. Robert looked up to his mom as the strongest woman he knew. She was a single mom who struggled through a lot. I admired the respect and admiration that he had for his mother. He apparently had a soft spot for single moms, which worked out great for me.

Robert was one of the few men who displayed confidence around me and was able to make the first move. He was thirty-four and older than most men I had spent time with recently, so that was probably why. He was average height, in good shape but not overly muscular, and had brown hair and brown eyes. He showed up in shorts, a t-shirt, and a baseball cap turned backwards.

Gah! Why do men wear backwards baseball hats? Don't they realize that it makes them look like punks? I wished there was some way to tell Robert, but it didn't feel like the right moment. We did just meet and I wasn't sure how he'd take it. I'm fully aware my forwardness is not for everyone.

The first two times we hung out, we had amazing chemistry. However, Robert struggled with erectile dysfunction. We could barely have sex due to his dick repeatedly going soft. It was a problem. Robert was a great lover though and made sure to make me orgasm with his hands and mouth.

A week or so after his visit, Robert texted.

Robert: HEY, I'M NOT GOING TO BE ABLE TO HANG OUT ANYMORE. I STARTED DATING SOMEONE.

Me: NO PROBLEM I APPRECIATE YOU LETTING ME KNOW.

Honestly, I wasn't that disappointed because even though we had a great emotional connection as well as kissing chemistry, our sex had left a lot to be desired.

I was surprised a few months later to get a text from Robert at 1 am. He wanted to know if I was up and if he could come over. I completely forgot about him seeing someone a few months earlier and never thought to ask if he was single then. I assumed he was if he was reaching out. So naïve.

Robert arrived at 2. I opened the door wearing lace panties and a tank top (my typical sleeping attire). He walked in and grabbed me like he wanted me. I was taken aback and lost my breath by Robert's clear display of hunger for me.

Robert started kissing me. His breath tasted of alcohol, but it wasn't a turn off. The opposite. God, the way he confidently took me in his arms—it was a highly erotic moment. My hand fumbled in the air trying to push the door shut. I could barely grasp onto the front door as I was breathless from kissing.

I stumbled backwards slightly as he came at me with a forceful desire. His hand cupped my face as he continued kissing me. I stumbled back again. He caught me with his other arm then quickly wrapped it around my waist. I tried to gain my balance. Robert never missed a beat. He pulled me close so that our bodies were pressed against each other. I could feel his erection poking into my belly.

Holy shit! This was hot and so unexpected. Especially considering the last encounter we had. I scrambled, my hands still behind my back, holding onto the door. I shivered from the cool night air that was flooding my house.

I managed to finally get the door closed. It slammed shut with a loud bang. Robert picked me up, walked over to the kitchen table, and placed me on top of it. He never stopped kissing me. I sat on the edge of the table with Robert between my legs, as we continued making out.

My body was lighting up like crazy. Robert had his hands all over me. They were moving around my body, grabbing my breasts, squeezing my ass, pulling me closer to him.

The smell of alcohol was strong and he seemed more expressive than before, letting out sighs and moaning loudly. Robert was drunk and I could tell he was insanely turned on.

He shoved the vase and candles on the table out of the way and lay me down so that my legs were dangling off the edge. Never taking his eyes off me, he leaned over and pressed our lips together.

I could not believe this was the same man that I had mediocre sex with before. A man who had to please me with his mouth because he was unable to any other way.

What the fuck had happened to Robert? I didn't know, but I liked it.

He moved my panties to the side and began fingering me.

"Shit, you're wet." He sounded in awe like he had never had this effect on a woman before.

This whole scene was so intensely erotic, that when he spoke those words, it was mind blowing.

He was right. I was wet. As his fingers kept working, I couldn't help moaning as my arousal kicked up another notch. The more he touched me, the more I wanted to have sex.

His fingers left me. I nearly screamed in frustration. I was ready for him to enter me and he did the last thing I wanted by leaving my legs open without him between them.

He pressed his hand on my stomach as he knelt down before me. Then I felt the light touch of his tongue on my clit. I truly lost all control and screamed. *God* did this man knows how to please a woman. He was driving me absolutely insane with his mouth. I placed my hand on the top of his head and ran my fingers through his hair.

"Oh my God. Oh my God." My fingers clenched in his hair. I couldn't stop saying it. "Oh my God. Oh my *Goooooooood*."

I was so turned on. I was begging Robert to fuck me. He lifted me off the table and carried me to the couch. When he sat down, I immediately straddled him. I needed more of his mouth. I kissed him as I started undressing him, slowly moving down his body and onto my knees in front of him.

He just rocked my world and I was going to show him my appreciation. I pulled his pants off and was pleasantly surprised to find his dick was rock hard. Clearly, he had fixed his problem. I started giving him head, relieved by how hard he was.

After a few minutes, he burst out, "Oh my God, you can suck a dick!" I laughed a little even though my mouth was full.

One of Robert's amazing sexual moves was that he would let me give him head until he was roaring to go, but he would always stop me before he would cum, thus lengthening our sexual encounter.

Robert wasn't just looking to get off. Robert was looking to fuck. He was looking for the whole experience from beginning to end—and he wanted it to last. This was another quality about Robert that made him so much better in bed then other men, especially since some men I'd encountered would cum first making it harder for me to have an orgasm. It is much easier for a woman to have an orgasm when a man is fully erect. After a man cums and goes soft it's sometimes impossible for me to cum.

Robert was an animal.

He literally picked me up, turned me around, and placed me on the couch. He was on top of me instantly. Robert's masculinity was so fucking sexy. I think his ability to achieve a full erection changed his confidence and allowed him to fuck me the way he'd been wanting to.

He started kissing me and fingering me. I was ready but unlike other men, he wanted me more than just ready. He wanted me desperate for him. Robert brought me up to the same level of horniness he was at. He knew that the sex would be even better if we were both roaring to go and he was right.

He made me beg for it.

And beg I did.

"Please fuck me, Robert. Please!" I pleaded.

Robert waited until I was wild with arousal, begging him to fuck me, grabbing his body hungrily, before he finally stuck his dick inside me. He felt amazing. He was so hard. Robert fucked me on the couch in missionary position then turned me onto my hands and knees.

He fucked the shit out of me in a way I never guessed he'd be able.

Then we moved to the bedroom.

Robert was not interested in starting over from the beginning. He picked me up and put me down on the bed, the headboard hitting the wall from the weight of my body. I couldn't even change my position before he was already on top of me, inside me again.

We fucked in every position that night. I don't know if there is a position that we didn't enjoy. When I was finally ready to cum, I said, "Please let me close my legs."

Robert was on top of me. He straddled my legs and let me bring them together. He leaned down and started kissing me.

I could feel my body explode, throbbing and pulsing. My body shook and twitched from the truly epic orgasm.

Robert shifted his weight. I was reminded that he was still inside me. My clit was hypersensitive. I quickly opened my legs and pushed him off me. I turned over onto my hands and knees to assume the position that I knew was very stimulating for men. I had my orgasm and wanted Robert to have his, sooner rather than later. Robert grabbed my hips and slid himself into me.

I still could not believe how hard Robert was and what mind-blowing sex we were having. Talk about raising the bar. Robert just moved my bar up a bunch of notches. This was definitely in the top three sexual encounters of my life. No questions asked.

Robert came quickly after we changed positions. His control was amazing. He pulled out, holding the condom onto himself and headed for the bathroom to clean up.

Lying in bed afterwards, I was reminded that Robert didn't want to cuddle the first time we met. He was a good sport though and gave me a fairly decent cuddle before he got up to leave. As we were walking out, we stopped in the kitchen.

While I smoked more weed (there isn't a better way to get to sleep), he stood in the kitchen and chatted with me. By now it was 3:30. It was odd how he wasn't in a hurry to leave. We chatted for another half hour. Robert enjoyed a piece of chocolate-chocolate-chip cake that Aubrey and I had baked. He devoured the cake then eventually left around 4 am.

Robert texted me every three to four weeks to say hi and ask how I was doing. He was definitely good at keeping his foot in the door. Every time I'd tell him that I was free or ask when I'd see him again, he'd string me along by making promises but never plans. My first missed red flag; Robert's actions and words didn't align. Unfortunately, I'd spent my life accepting this subpar behavior. I didn't know different. But finally, at forty-three-years old, I was becoming more aware and slowly deciding I wasn't ok accepting these misaligned and deceptive practices.

Six weeks after we hung out, I was out of town and woke up to find a text from Robert with a 2 am time stamp.

Robert: ARE YOU AWAKE?

In other words: are you up and can I come over to fuck?

Me: GOOD MORNING. SORRY, I JUST SAW THIS. I WAS ASLEEP LAST NIGHT WHEN YOU TEXTED AND I'M OUT OF TOWN. I'LL BE CHILD FREE NEXT WEEKEND.

Robert: NO WORRIES. HAVE A FUN TRIP.

Me: THANKS.

Two weeks later, I had an epiphany. I was hanging out with Chloe and a business client of hers named Gus. Chloe and I had been close friends for the last ten years. We had bonded from being single full-time moms and navigating the dating scene.

131

Chloe got up to get something to drink as Gus and I sat on the porch smoking. I watched as Chloe flitted through my living room toward the kitchen. We were both small and had to stand on our tip toes to reach the cabinet, but there was something so cute about her. She walked that fine line of comfort and casual. She was petite and wearing leggings in place of pants while still looking professional.

I was hosting this little get together because Chloe and Gus were very much into smoking weed, but they couldn't do so at her house. Chloe worked from home and lived with her dad, so she was always anxious about smoking at home.

She had worked hard starting her own business and was driving two hours away to meet a client near me. I had them over because Chloe wanted me to meet him, so we naturally all smoked weed together. Chloe's ex was out of the picture which meant she had her daughter all the time. Any time she had alone was treasured.

As we chatted, the topic of men came up.

"Sometimes, I feel like I will never understand men and their actions." I openly admitted.

Chloe chimed in, "Yeah, it seems as if interpretation is always needed. Why can't men be easier to read and understand?"

"Here's a thought, how about not having to read or interpret at all. How about if men were just more communicative?" This was the kind of man that I was hoping for since day one.

"Yes!" Chloe agreed.

"I find it interesting that you ladies feel this way since it is the exact way most men feel about women." Gus began, "Most men just wish women would speak up, be honest, and open with their thoughts and feelings. We feel like we're always reading between the lines or trying to interpret what a woman is saying."

We all laughed. Chloe and I had heard this before, but had felt we weren't in this group. We were both communicative and couldn't relate.

"Help us understand men, Gus."

"Sure, what do you want to know?"

I decided to share my confusion around Robert. "I've been sleeping with this guy named Robert. He texts me here and there, unlike the other guys that I've slept with, yet I haven't seen him in several weeks. That guy, he waits so long between our encounters that I think I will never see him again. Then poof, out of nowhere, he wants to come over at 2 am."

"You're his booty call," Gus said. "He has a wife or girlfriend. He can't see you any more often than that or she'll figure it out."

My eyebrows shot up in surprise. "You're saying that he's had a girlfriend this whole time while he's been sleeping with me?"

Gus nodded. "I'd bet my life on it."

I decided to text Robert right then and there to find out. Chloe and Gus waited anxiously beside me.

Me: DO YOU HAVE A GIRLFRIEND?

Robert: YEAH.

Well hot damn. What a dick!

Me: THANKS FOR YOUR HONESTY. I'M NOT GOING TO TEXT YOU ANYMORE. THANKS FOR THE FUN AND TAKE CARE.

Robert: OK. WHERE DID ALL THIS COME FROM? I TOLD YOU I HAD A GIRLFRIEND.

Me: DON'T MAKE ME A BAD WOMAN. WHEN YOU CAME BACK AROUND, I ASSUMED THAT RELATIONSHIP WAS OVER. I

DIDN'T THINK YOU WOULD BE THE TYPE TO SLEEP AROUND WHILE YOU'RE IN A RELATIONSHIP. I'M BETTER THAN BEING SOMEONE'S OTHER WOMAN.

Robert: I WON'T. YOU AREN'T. I TOLD YOU.

Me: THANKS FOR THAT. GOODNIGHT.

Robert: YOU SEEM MAD.

Me: I'M NOT MAD.

Robert: GOODNIGHT.

With this knowledge in mind, I now had a hunch that he was with his girlfriend the last time he texted me, so I decided to ask.

Me: WERE YOU WITH YOUR GIRLFRIEND A FEW WEEKS AGO WHEN YOU WERE TEXTING ME?

Robert never replied. I wasn't surprised. I caught him at his game and he didn't have anything to say for himself. I was surprised that he was honest when I confronted him about it. I was pretty sure he had a girlfriend the last time we fucked. Why else would so much time lapse between his visits? Robert was trying to act like he was being forthright and honest, yet he probably had a girlfriend this entire time. I was guilty for assuming he didn't.

I will never understand why men will stay in a committed relationship and continue to sleep with other women. Why wouldn't they just stay single then settle down when they're ready to be with one woman? Why have a girlfriend and continue to come sleep with me?

Because he could—I guess.

I sat on the couch with Gus and Chloe, they both looked anxiously at one another. I was fuming.

Could he not keep it in his pants? Stay committed to his relationship and not sleep around. I believed in my heart that it was possible for men to be respectful to their partners, but my own experience didn't speak to this. All I could think about was all the horrible experiences that I had with men most recently. I was stewing in it.

Three weeks later, Robert texted on a Sunday morning. I had deleted his contact number but recalled his area code. I was fairly confident it was him texting me, but I wasn't a hundred percent sure, so I replied coyly.

Robert: HI.

Me: WHAT'S UP?

Robert: HOW ARE YOU DOING?

Me: I'M GOOD.

Robert proceeded to send a picture of his dick—in hand, fully erect. Not the biggest turn on for a woman, but at least I knew for sure it was him. He had sent me this picture before.

Robert: WANT SOME OF THIS?

I decided to ignore the dick pic.

Me: DO YOU HAVE A GIRLFRIEND?

Robert: NO.

Me: WHAT HAPPENED?

Robert: I JUST WASN'T INTO IT.

Me: CLEARLY, IF YOU WERE STILL WANTING TO FUCK ME.

Robert: CAN I COME OVER?

I read Robert's text over and over. I was tired of feeling used by men; but at the same time, the loneliness I had felt was formidable. I didn't respond and busied myself around the house, starting laundry and tidying up. I was still contemplating Robert's question and thought about how I'd answer.

After 20 minutes, he texted again.

Robert: CAN I COME OVER? LET'S HANG OUT.

Against my better judgment I said yes. Notice any patterns forming? Loneliness and making good decisions do not go hand in hand.

Me: SURE. LET ME KNOW WHEN YOU'RE ON YOUR WAY, SO I CAN SLIDE MY HAND DOWN MY PANTIES AND WARM MYSELF UP.

I knew exactly what Robert wanted to hear.

Robert: FUCK YEAH.

Truth be told, I was thinking about our last time together and I really wanted more sex like that.

The sex I had with Robert, when he barged through my door and carried me to the kitchen table was the best kind of sex there is. Spontaneous. Passionate. Completely satisfying. The kind of sex that you can't stop thinking about. I was long overdue for some grade A sex like that. Now that I knew Robert had the capacity to give it to me—I wanted it.

At this point, I'm not that naïve anymore. I knew it was possible that he still had a girlfriend. Admittedly, in that moment of desperate loneliness and having not been touched by a man in weeks, I didn't care. I was tired of feeling like all men did was take and take and take. I wanted my own needs met. I wanted a man to give to me. A man who'd cuddle me. The way I saw it, the less I knew about Robert the better. In my defense, I did ask him outright. I made the choice to believe what he told me, rather than going with my gut that said his (hopefully ex) girlfriend knew nothing about his late night I.

Ten minutes later, Robert texted saying he was on his way. I had a few things to do before he got to my house. I needed to get a move on, I only had about fifteen minutes until he showed up at my door.

I grabbed a robe from my closet and put on slippers. I put Chewie's leash on and ran him outside to potty—yes, in my robe!

After Chewie did his business, we ran back inside. I threw on some music and rushed into my bathroom to freshen up. It was only about 9 am and I hadn't even gotten up to brush my teeth yet.

I quickly did just that. I put on deodorant and squirted a spritz of perfume over my head. I opened my bedroom window to let some fresh air into my room, since it was still stuffy from last night's sleep.

My house was feeling fresh and well aired out. I packed a fresh bowl since my pipe was sitting out on the counter. I only smoked when Aubrey was away and would leave my paraphernalia out knowing that I was the only one home for the weekend. I took two hits to relax myself a little. I started feeling light-headed from the weed. I hung my robe in my closet and removed my tank top so that I was only wearing navy-colored lace panties.

I went back to the kitchen to take two more hits.

Then it struck me, I said I'd warm myself up.

Robert would arrive any minute and I hadn't gotten myself going yet. Shit! I didn't have much time.

I sat on the couch sliding my hand down my panties. Honestly, I wasn't feeling horny at that moment. I was definitely excited to hang out with Robert. He was a great fuck; but otherwise, I really didn't feel into it. I did it anyway.

Think sexy thoughts. Think sexy thoughts.

I yawned. God, it was 9 am and I was sitting on my couch touching myself. Did I even feed Chewie?

No, dammit, think sexy *thoughts! He'll be here any minute.*

After a few minutes of dedicated rubbing, I was finally able to get myself there. I thought about the last time with Robert. How he'd lifted me up and carried me around like I weighed little more than a feather.

His hungry mouth all over my body…

My breath hitched as my fingers became slick from my own wetness. I was sure to spread it all over myself so that when Robert slid his hand down there, he'd see how I had gotten myself ready for him. I got even wetter by the thought of him.

My phone pinged, I hopped up to check the message. Robert was here and heading towards my front door. I cracked open the door to my porch so he could get in. I couldn't exactly open the front door as I had neighbors in the condos facing it.

Chewie started barking his head off, so I knew Robert was here.

"It's open," I called. "Come in."

Robert stepped into the house and pushed the door closed behind him. He came right up to me and grabbed my breasts in both hands before leaning down to kiss me.

"Holy fuck, you are sexy," he murmured. "Oh my God." He continued fondling me and kissing me.

Robert was charged up and ready. He grabbed me firmly, his hands moving down to my waist. He pulled me closer and kissed me deep.

I was in ecstasy. I could tell by his kiss that we were going to have amazing sex again.

He stopped kissing and grabbed my hand. "Come here."

Robert led me to the couch. He pulled off his pants and underwear then sat down. I pushed the coffee table out of the way and crouched in between his legs.

Robert was soft which was surprising. The last time we hung out, he came over already rock hard.

No! Please no! I was reminded of his past struggle with erectile dysfunction.

I grabbed Robert's limp dick and placed it in my mouth. *Oh God!* I agonized silently.

It really isn't much fun having to get a man hard. I much prefer when he's already excited and ready to go. It takes a little more effort to start with a soft dick. I quickly realized that I wasn't a fan. Not to mention it was awkward as hell, flopping around like a fish out of water. A hard dick I can work with, but this?

Robert got fully hard after a few minutes of me working his shaft and balls with my mouth and hands. I knew he loved my head, so I was sure to spend a little extra time down there.

I stood up and removed Robert's shirt. After his shirt was off, he leaned forward and grabbed my breasts. He slid his dick in between my tits, squeezing them tightly together. Robert fucked my breasts like that while I stuck out my tongue, licking the head of his dick each time it popped out from between them. I ran my hand through Robert's hair while he fucked me like this. He exhaled loudly, closing his eyes as he rolled his head to one side. Robert was in heaven and I loved being able to take credit for it.

After a few more minutes, I was ready to have sex.

"I want you to fuck me," I begged. "Do you want to go to my bed?"

Robert stood up. "Yes."

As I walked naked down the hallway to my bed, Robert didn't immediately follow me. He was grabbing a condom from his pants that were on the floor.

Robert got into my room with two condoms in hand and placed them on the nightstand.

"If it's ok, can we use my condoms? They're latex free."

"For sure." Robert didn't give a shit. He was just ready to get it on.

He lay back on a pillow that was propped up against the headboard. I crawled onto the bed after him. Laying between his legs, I kissed his thighs alternating sides all the way up to his dick. I took Robert's balls into my mouth and sucked gently before releasing each one. I licked his dick up and down. Robert went wild.

"Suck my dick, baby," he managed to say in a tone that was rough and commanding.

I did just that. I took his dick into my mouth, trying to take him as far down as I could.

"I can feel the back of your throat. You feel fucking amazing, baby."

I continued sucking Robert until I was ready to fuck him.

"Put a condom on. I want you to fuck me," I commanded.

I grabbed a condom from the nightstand and handed it to Robert. He put it on and rolled over on top of me. He spread my legs open then held the back of each thigh up as he slid himself inside me. He felt great sliding into me. He was hard. Thank God!

"Holy fuck you feel great," I gasped as he filled me up.

"You like my dick?"

"I fucking love your dick, baby." It was the first time we had both used the term baby and it was slightly uncomfortable for me. I rarely use a term of endearment with a man, unless I'm in a relationship with him. Yet, with Robert, I did. I wasn't quite sure why. Was there a stronger emotional connection because the sex was so great? Or was I just too in my head about it. Either way, I said it back even though it felt somewhat forced.

Robert fucked me. His dick getting harder and bigger as he went.

He already knew how I liked to cum, so as he saw my arousal level growing, he immediately straddled my legs, allowing me to close my legs for my orgasm.

He continued fucking me and it felt great.

"Slow, slow, and deep baby. Please."

Robert slowed it down immediately and rammed his dick as far into me as it would go. Feeling him so deep inside me, those slow thrust giving me the final stimulation I needed to have an orgasm. At the last minute, Robert pinned my hands behind my head so I couldn't scratch his back.

I came immediately screaming, "Fuck yes!"

Robert tried to continue fucking me in that same position after I came.

I squirmed and stopped him immediately, not being able to handle the sensitivity.

I laughed. "You can't fuck me like that anymore. It's too sensitive. Let me get on my knees for you."

Robert turned me over onto my hands and knees then slid his dick back into me. He fucked me doggy style. I reached my hand between my legs to grab his balls. Robert's balls had retreated up near his dick. I ended up just barely being able to grab his sack, so I pulled on it a little. At the mere touch of my fingers, Robert moaned loudly, "Oh my God!"

I was done having sex and wanted Robert to cum. There was nothing worse than fucking forever after you've already cum.

"I want to feel you cum in me, baby. I want to feel your dick pulsing inside me," I lied, trying my best to turn him on and make him cum.

Robert moaned and arched his back. He felt insanely hard which was uncomfortable and over-stimulating to my clit. I hoped he was going to cum soon.

"I want you to come in my mouth. I want to suck you until you cum in my mouth then lick your dick clean. Tell me you'll cum in my mouth." I continued to tell Robert what I knew he'd love to hear. From my past experiences, I knew men loved when a woman talked dirty to them. I was done and had no intention of doing any of that. I just wanted Robert to finish and was using all the tricks in my bag.

"Fuck yeah! I'll cum in your mouth, baby."

He stopped fucking me and lay back. I reluctantly moved between his legs.

I kneeled frozen for a few long seconds. I had hoped the mere thought of it would make him cum, but Robert had something else in mind. He wanted me to fulfill the little fantasy that I had just put into his head.

Well that backfired!

His dick was wet. It was easy to get started giving him head without missing a beat. I took his whole dick into my mouth and down my throat as far as I could handle. I stroked his dick from top to bottom in one long continuous motion, gripping firmer than usual in hopes of making him finish faster. Robert put his hand on my head, not putting pressure, but just feeling my head moving up and down.

Two minutes later, Robert declared he was going to cum. I felt I should live up to the fantasy so I kept my mouth around his dick. I could feel him pulsing in my hand. Warm cum filled the condom. I pulled him out of my mouth immediately for fear the cum would start leaking everywhere, namely into my mouth. Because I had an empty stomach, the taste of the condom was not sitting well with me. I rushed to the sink to rinse my mouth out and drink some water.

The water helped settle my stomach and I returned to bed. Robert immediately got up and went into the bathroom. He washed his hands and used the restroom.

I was lying on the bed watching that perfect physique of his. Fuck, Robert was so hot. I could look at him all day long. He walked out of the bathroom and stood in the doorway. The light was still on. His eyes scanned the room for his clothes. I watched as he realized they were all in the living room.

"Please tell me you're going to cuddle me?" I practically begged.

"I can't."

"What?" I was shocked. "Are you kidding me?"

I made no effort to hide my annoyance.

He cuddled me every time we were together, because I wanted and needed it—he respected that need. He had never left me high and dry before. I was genuinely surprised that he wasn't going to this time.

My surprise turned to anger.

"If you aren't going to cuddle me, this is going to be the last time that we hang out."

"I understand. I'm sorry."

I was surprised that Robert genuinely seemed to feel bad. He was looking down at the floor and appeared to be sincere.

"Don't be sorry," I said. "I like sex with you, Robert, but this time was different. You won't even lay with me after... I feel used. I don't want to feel this again."

"I understand and I'm really sorry. I just don't feel comfortable."

"It's fine." I was miffed and he knew it.

"Are you going to hate me now?"

"No. I'm just disappointed." Let's be honest. I *was* disappointed. Not really because of missing out on cuddling. I was disappointed because I knew our time had come to an end—I meant what I said—I didn't want it to but it had to be over. I was not okay having him leave now, right after sex, but he didn't care—so the only thing to do was end it.

Robert finished putting his shoes on. I opened the front door. Before walking out, Robert leaned over and hugged me. He exhaled loudly as he leaned over me. The sigh sounded emotional like he was about to cry. It was a very strange moment.

"I'm sorry, Lacie."

"No worries, Robert. Take care."

"You too."

Robert walked out the door. I watched him leave.

I knew he was still with his girlfriend, despite telling me that he wasn't. Why else would he not cuddle me like the times before? I set myself up for that one. Why would I believe anything he had to say? The fact of the matter is that I didn't want to know, so I made the choice to believe him. It was the only way I could go through with having sex with him.

I was over these bullshit encounters. I wanted something real. I was tired of casual sex. It didn't meet any need except my sexual ones—and even that was a crap shoot.

I didn't know it at the time but ending things with Robert was my first step toward self-empowerment. It was also my first step toward creating expectations and boundaries that I had gone far too long without. I finally stood up for myself and for my needs. When Robert was not willing to give me what I needed, I sent him packing. I felt a little bit stronger that day. A little more capable of standing up for myself.

I crawled back into bed, folding my arms around myself, and curling my legs up to my chest. Somewhat soothed, I drifted back to sleep.

Chapter 11: You're My Best Friend

Aubrey was with her dad for the holidays that year, so I traveled to Boulder to see my friend Claudia. We were going out for New Year's Eve and I planned to stay through the next day, as well.

Claudia and I relaxed on her couch in sweats and under blankets checking out guys on Bumble.

I mean, come on, we were both on the app. I was curious to see what guys were in her area.

Also, I knew if she changed her age range to twenty-five, Billy would come up in her mileage setting. I wanted to stalk him a little and see where he was spending his holiday.

I had unmatched with him long ago and hadn't seen hide nor hair of him. But it didn't mean that I wasn't still curious.

Was he still online? Would he want to match with Claudia? Okay, duh—of course he would, she was drop dead gorgeous with amazing sharp features. This wasn't me being insecure, Claudia was just a shiny beautiful blond and her body was rocking for a woman in her mid-forties. Any living, breathing man would swipe right for Claudia.

After a few minutes of swiping, she came across Billy's profile.

"Man, he's cute!" Claudia exclaimed.

"I told you."

"Let's fuck with him." Claudia swiped right.

As we started cleaning up, Claudia's phone pinged. She had matched with Billy.

146

I immediately spoke up. "I kind of have a crush on him. Please don't be too flirtatious."

"Don't worry—I won't."

Claudia messaged back and forth with him for a few minutes.

"What are you saying? What's he saying?" I reached for the phone.

Claudia grinned and pulled it out of my grasp. "Just where we live and what we're doing to ring in the New Year. Now, I'm going to tell him that we have a mutual friend. Let's see how he responds to that."

My heart did a little skip.

"Did he text back yet?" I reached for the phone again.

Claudia grinned. Still holding the phone out of my reach, she read aloud his text: *"Oh yeah? Who is that?"*

She had piqued his interest.

Claudia didn't reply on the app. Instead, I gave her Billy's phone number and she texted him her response. He immediately asked who the friend was. We decided to play twenty questions.

Billy: DOES SHE LIVE IN THE FT. COLLINS AREA?

Claudia: No.

"Well, now, we know he's fucking a woman in Ft. Collins." My tone was slightly irritated from the ping of jealousy I felt.

I was so naïve. Of course, Billy was fucking other women. He was hot and online. It didn't feel good to think about it though, being that our sexual chemistry and connection had seemed somewhat extraordinary. I didn't want to believe that he'd experienced that with everyone. At least for my ego's sake, I told myself that he didn't. I admit that my jealousy was silly—of course, I'd continued dating since him, too.

Claudia agreed then said, "Yes, I'd say Ft. Collins is a for sure."

Billy: IS SHE A COUGAR?

Claudia: YES.

Billy: DOES SHE LIVE NEAR DENVER?

Claudia didn't respond.

"Well, he knows it's you. He guessed that pretty fast."

I laughed, "Yes, he did. I guess it's safe to say that he's not sleeping with any other women, at least in the Denver area."

We laughed knowing Billy probably had other women strewn out across his work area.

Did I just play a game to get my foot in the door with this man again? Yes, I did.

Did Claudia and I have a ton of fun while doing it? Yes, we did.

I truly wanted to spend time with a man who wanted me. Billy wasn't coming after me; but damn, I wanted him badly. So, I went after him. It's not an approach that I'd recommend by any means.

Since the cat was out of the bag and he knew it was me, I started texting him from my phone while Claudia got into the shower.

WOW, YOU'RE GOOD AT 20 QUESTIONS. I texted Billy from my phone.

Billy: LOL. YEAH, IT WASN'T THAT HARD. I HAVEN'T SLEPT WITH ANY OTHER COUGARS SINCE YOU. HAVE YOU SLEPT WITH ANY OTHER 25-YEAR-OLDS?

Me: YES, I HAVE.

I think it's so funny when men call me MILF or cougar. For me, who I choose to spend time with doesn't come with a label. It's just what I've enjoyed doing in this phase of my life. For men in their twenties, I think it comes with bragging rights. They puff their chests out and talk about their "cougar" or "MILF".

I could tell, Billy didn't like that answer. Oh well, he shouldn't have asked. Billy told me that he would be drinking beer all night at a friend's house. I told him that we were going out dancing at a bar in Boulder.

Billy: BY THE WAY, IT WOULD BE MY GREATEST FANTASY IF I COULD BE WITH YOU AND YOUR FRIEND.

I laughed out loud.

Me: THERE'S NO WAY YOU CAN HANDLE THE BOTH OF US.

Claudia heard me laughing and asked what we were discussing.

"He wants the both of us. I told him he couldn't handle it," I laughed.

Claudia agreed and laughed too.

I explained to Billy that it would never happen. Although Claudia and I were both on the higher end of the horniness scale, we both agreed there are some things friends don't share. Men being one of them. Billy expressed his disappointment. He could tell I meant what I said.

Billy: WHY HAVEN'T I HEARD FROM YOU? HAVE YOU BEEN UP AT YOUR PARENTS?

One of the other connections we had discovered, back when we were getting to know each other, was that Billy lived in the neighboring town near my parents. We had even discussed meeting up sometime when Aubrey and I were there to visit. After our first meeting, I was even more excited to see him in his home setting, but I never heard from him again.

Me: I'LL BE OVER THERE FOR THE FEBRUARY BREAK TO SKI. I TEXTED YOU A WHILE BACK AND YOU NEVER REPLIED. I DON'T KEEP TEXTING MEN WHO DON'T RESPOND TO ME.

Billy: I'M BUSY. I WORK 60-70 HOURS A WEEK. IF I DIDN'T GET BACK TO YOU IT'S BECAUSE I'M BUSY AS FUCK.

I could sense the irritation in his text.

I didn't care. I shot back.

Me: THAT DOESN'T MATTER. YOU CAN STILL TEXT SOMEONE TO SAY THAT YOU'RE BUSY OR THAT YOU'LL GET BACK TO THEM. IT'S RUDE AND SHOWS A LACK OF INTEREST.

Billy: LOL. HAHA

He completely laughed off my advice-rant. He asked me to text him when I was up at my parent's house in February. I said that I'd see.

He already knew I would.

We wished each other goodnight and I turned my attention back to Claudia

Claudia and I finished getting ready to go out for New Year's Eve. We took a few selfies in front of the Christmas tree and made obligatory Instagram and Facebook posts. Then, off we went to downtown Boulder.

The bar we went to had three distinct areas. There was a live cover band tearing it up in one room, playing the best dance music for patrons our age. Claudia and I danced until we were sweating then headed to the closed in patio to cool down and check things out.

Outside was a huge wrap around patio bar and an outdoor seating area for the warmer weather. At this time of year, they had it tented with sections of clear partitions so you could see the winter wonderland outside, plus they had plenty of space heaters. We grabbed drinks and cooled down out there, while we talked about what a good New Year's this was turning out to be.

After relaxing, Claudia showed me another area of the bar. It was on the opposite side of the patio, there was a DJ playing rap music. We went in there as well. There were sooo many people dancing. Everyone was crammed together and sweating bullets. The energy was amazing.

Claudia and I slid into the crowd and danced. We always had so much fun together. We smiled and laughed, while we sang and danced to the music. Dancing makes me feel so sexy and I could see it did the same for her. There's something about moving my body, that's just so sensual, depending on both the music and setting.

While we were crammed in with a bunch of drunk people, Claudia and I would point out to each other any particularly funny drunks. Some rolled over people like a bowling ball, completely oblivious of the damage left in their wake. Other drunks would spill their drinks all over people, also clueless.

Then there were those men, the ones who were always creeping up. We couldn't seem to lose them. Stalkers!

Finally, there were a few couples who were practically having sex on the dance floor. Gross!

Dancing with a bunch of drunks on New Year's was a blast. Needless to say, we did a lot of laughing that night.

As it neared midnight, we made our way back to the patio area to find the New Year's hats and noisemakers set out alongside some much-needed fresh air.

Claudia was intent on getting a kiss at midnight and she had told me so. I, on the other hand, couldn't care less about kissing a drunk stranger, especially being that I was completely sober.

Claudia pensively looked around the patio. "Everyone looks paired up. There's no one to kiss."

I looked around and saw that she was right. There was a sea of couples around us and there didn't appear to be any lone men.

Phew! I was relieved. I had no desire to have some shit-faced stranger slobbering all over me. No thanks!

The partygoers counted down. Ten, nine, eight, seven, six, five, four, three, two, one...

Happy New Year! The noisemakers were deafening. Claudia and I hugged surrounded by kissing couples.

"Happy New Year, my friend!" Claudia cried.

"Happy New Year, Bonita!" I gave her a squeeze before letting go.

After a momentary hiatus, the partying resumed. Claudia turned to walk back inside. I followed her.

From behind, someone grabbed my arm. I stopped walking and turned around to see a young man in his twenties.

"I wanted to ask if you'd be my midnight kiss. You're beautiful and I'd love to kiss you." I was surprised at the balls this guy had, considering we were standing in the middle of the patio and people were all around us. He didn't seem drunk. He was polite—cute even.

I smiled. "You're so sweet. Of course, I'll kiss you. You have to do me a favor though. Can you please kiss my friend as well? She really wanted a New Year's kiss."

His face lit up. "Fuck yeah, I can do that."

He leaned down and kissed me. I kissed him for longer than was normal. I figured, why not, since he had the courage to come right up to me and ask. Hell, he was a good kisser, to boot!

I stopped the kiss. It was bordering on making out and I had no desire to join the other couples nearby. I pointed to Claudia who was walking towards the band. "Go give her a New Year's kiss too, please."

The young guy walked up to Claudia, clearly explained what was going on. He was pointing to me. I watched them as they kissed. I started laughing. I was so happy that Claudia got her New Year's kiss. I was also happy that this guy got to kiss both of us that night. He deserved it for having the balls to ask.

Claudia came over to me, throwing her arms around me, and giving me a sloppy kiss on the cheek. "Happy New Years, gorgeous!"

I laughed as I hugged her back. We heard fireworks going off, welcoming us into the New Year. I felt in my bones it was going to be a good one. I just hoped I was right.

Chapter 12: Back In The Saddle Again

Before I headed up to my parent's house for our annual ski trip, I texted Billy to let him know what days I'd be there. He texted me the following Friday afternoon saying he had a three-hour drive home from work and would love my company once he got back.

Me: ARE YOU GOING TO BE SHY WITH ME TONIGHT?

Billy: PROBABLY, BUT JUST A LITTLE.

Cute and honest… I liked it.

Me: JUST SO YOU KNOW, I'M NOT MAKING THE FIRST MOVE THIS TIME. IF YOU WANT ME TONIGHT, YOU'LL HAVE TO COME AND GET ME.

Billy: HAHAHA. DON'T WORRY, I WILL. I WON'T BE ABLE TO KEEP MY HANDS OFF YOU.

Billy had a going away party that night for a friend, he asked if I wanted to hang out for a couple of hours before the party. I agreed then told my mom that I'd be home for a late dinner. There was snow everywhere and my car was buried under it. I had to dig it out. Not the best start to my visit with Billy, but nothing was going to hold me back.

When I parked in Billy's driveway, he immediately came out of his house. He was wearing familiar looking sweats, a t-shirt, and baseball cap. As soon as he came outside, he looked toward my car. He had the biggest smile on his face. That amazing contagious smile. I felt myself smiling back as he walked over.

I got out and met him. We hugged right in front of his walkway.

"Long time no see," I teased.

"Yea how come you're always so busy?" he teased back.

"Oh fuck, don't get me started!" I warned. I looked up from him and noticed his house. It had large windows overlooking the mountains. "You must have an amazing view from inside!"

Billy's house sat within a direct view of the mountains. The sun was setting and there were only a few sparse homes below. His porch was in the front of his house. A small tattered outdoor couch and fire pit filled most of it. He probably spent many nights out there with a beer, just enjoying his view. At least that's what I'd be doing if I lived there—minus the beer.

Billy opened the door and gestured for me to walk inside. I smiled then strode past him.

Billy's house was exactly what you'd expect a twenty-five-year-old's house to be... at least one like Billy. There was green carpet that had to be nearly as old as him, a run-down couch, a couple of deer heads on the wall, and a loaded shotgun leaning against the wall in a corner.

After showing me around his house, we sat on the couch. Our legs touching. We turned so that we could face each other and chatted for a few minutes. Sports Center was on in the background.

Billy leaned over to grab my face and kissed me.

Based on our texting, I had thought he would come at me hard and heavy. Hungry even.

To my surprise, though, Billy kissed me slow and gently. The kind of kissing that makes your stomach drop out from under you and causes you to catch your breath.

God, *yes*. This was why I got butterflies in my stomach whenever I thought of him. This connection. It was what I was missing from all of the other men. Tender and passionate, slow kissing which felt more like the start to making love, rather than just fucking.

I straddled him. Sitting on a man's lap was a comfortable position for making out and put us perfectly face to face. I could feel through his sweats that Billy was already as hard as a rock. As we continued to kiss, I started moving my hips, grinding on his erection.

Billy stiffened and caught his breath. He pulled off my top then grabbed both of my breasts and started sucking on my nipples. I ran a hand through his hair as I sat on his lap. I relaxed and allowed myself to enjoy his attention. He looked up at me. I smiled a coy closed-lip smile.

"God, you are so sexy!" he burst out.

"So are you!" I said emphatically as my eyes widened. He was so nonverbal. I cherished every compliment he gave me.

I started kissing and sucking on his earlobe. I moved downward kissing his neck and chest. Sucking on his nipples. I kissed all the way down Billy's body until I got to the top of his waistband.

I teased him. Kissing along his waistband and grabbing his dick through his sweats. Billy was moaning and squirming with arousal. I slid onto my knees. Pulled off his clothes and dropped them onto the floor. Billy opened his legs wider.

I placed a kiss on Billy's inner thigh. Starting on his left leg, I worked my way up. I'd been around long enough to know that if you found this kind of connection, you linger in it and fan the flames for as long as you can.

I'd planned to torture Billy a little tonight.

When I reached his balls, I moved back. Away from him. Then repeated the same slow kissing down his other thigh. This time, I took one ball into my mouth and sucked gently before moving to the other. I licked the base of Billy's dick. All the way up the shaft until I reached the head.

By the time I started giving Billy head, he was dying from anticipation. He stiffened arching his back as I took him into my mouth. He moaned grabbing my long hair in his hand tightly. I had no intention of making him cum—yet. I got up from my knees and we moved to the bedroom.

We toppled onto the bed. He rose over me. The next thing I knew, he had a condom on and was fucking me. *Hard.* Grabbing my hair and mashing his mouth to mine in a way unlike how he'd been the first time we were together.

Before we were making love. Now we were just fucking. He was fucking.

Billy no longer gave. He never touched me other than to seek out my kiss or grab my hair. He was much rougher and more dominating—not in the way I liked at all. It was a turn off.

Although I managed to get off, he was a very selfish lover this time. He fucked me until *he* came. No thought of my needs.

When he laid down next to me, he made no move to cuddle.

I lay there stunned.

"I'm sure you fuck men all the time," he said, sounding almost angry.

I was completely taken aback. I wanted to enjoy our time together and thought he wanted to do the same. Instead he was bringing up my sleeping with other men. What the hell? This wasn't what I came here for. What was going on?

I looked over at him. His arms were crossed and he was looking away. I could see immediately what was really going on. Billy was trying his best to guard himself. To push me

157

away. He was doing a great job. I chose to completely disengage from the conversation, treat his question as if it was rhetorical, and quite simply not respond. Although his actions were meant to protect himself, they felt hurtful. He was rejecting me to save his own feelings and it didn't feel good.

A few uncomfortable minutes later, I got up from his bed. My mind set on getting ready to leave. As I did, I looked up to the most beautiful sunset. A bright red color lit up the sky. I stood naked in front of his bedroom window.

"Oh Billy! Look. Your view is amazing. You are so blessed. If I lived here, I would sit and watch the sunset every day." I was truly mesmerized by the beauty of it.

"Yeah I know. It's beautiful." His monotone voice was still cold and detached.

I didn't look back at him. I threw on my clothes, grabbed my purse, and walked to the door. Billy was already there, ready to open it for me.

He had gotten his quickie and was done.

What a bad taste he had left in my mouth.

I had no intention of ever seeing him again. I felt like I had been used by Billy and it was something that I didn't want to feel again.

It's one thing to be used for sex. It was completely different to *feel* used. I left Billy's house that night feeling like I had been used then disposed of.

There is nothing worse than a man who gets his and does nothing to please a woman. I'd built Billy up in my head to be the man I knew from that first time. But tonight… I wasn't even sure what had happened to that man or who I had slept with before—he certainly wasn't the same. Nothing could have turned me off more from a man than the way Billy treated me that night. I was so much better than this. I deserved better.

As I drove home down the windy mountain roads, I asked myself. *Why the fuck are you doing this, Lacie? Is the anger, frustration, and rejection worth the occasional sexual satisfaction?*

I scolded myself the entire drive.

I knew what I wanted and deserved in a partner. Why was I having such a hard time attracting the right type of men? Why weren't my standards higher?

Shortly after my divorce, I was hopelessly lost and desperate for any ounce of male attention. Now that I was years into being single, I couldn't figure out what work I still needed to do to finally achieve emotional healing and self-love. Why did I need validation from twenty-five-year-old strangers?

Why could I not draw a line in the sand and stick to it? With every man I had met, I erased that line and moved it down, lowering my expectations for the hope I might have— something. With some men, I'd erased the line altogether and never redraw it. Why couldn't I see that I was deserving of much more than the crumbs these men gave me?

I was very capable of setting boundaries when it came to female friendships. Why did it not translate over to my dealings with men?

I've had a few friendships in my adult life that needed to come to an end. I felt at complete peace and never looked back, because letting those relationships go was the best decision for me. Why did it matter so much to let go of some of the men I'd encountered? Especially when they gave me great reasons to leave them in the dust.

Why did I cling to them when they gave me close to nothing?

A beautiful, smart, independent, and hard-working woman didn't need any of this shit. I can say proudly that I'm resilient when I look at what challenges I've faced and where I stand now.

I survived my ex-husband leaving me only a few days after being inseminated with another child. I lived through finding out that he was involved with my best friend, the maid of honor in our wedding. It may sound strong to use the word survived; but after the level of pain and heartache I endured, survive is exactly what I did. I not only lost my husband and best friend, but also my home and half of the time I had to raise Aubrey. The losses I endured through that experience were the most devastating in my life and I'd vowed to heal and ultimately thrive rather than let them destroy or define me.

Was it possible I hadn't fully healed from these events? If I truly loved myself then why did I allow men to treat me less than what I deserved?

I didn't come up with any answers at the time—only a bunch of questions. I was beginning to feel numb and jaded toward men. I didn't have much Bumbling left in me. Regardless, I decided to keep trying to find a real relationship—only hanging out with younger men when I was really lonely and horny. Only when I needed the sex.

Both of these emotions, unfortunately, always seemed to be prevalent in my life during those months—fueling me like a locomotive.

Chapter 13: Heartbreaker

After Billy, I felt a little older, a little wiser, and much more reflective about the men I met online. Some men didn't have the emotional maturity to handle being with a woman in an honest way. I saw that firsthand. Other men would withdraw for a time then come back in a few weeks or even months later, sometimes even after I deleted their numbers.

This was all turning out so very different from how I'd envisioned it in the beginning. I thought it would be so easy to find one man to have regular sex with. Boy—was I wrong. Very wrong.

However, I was starting to learn the game. As much as I still wished that we could all just be grown-ups about this and tell each other what we wanted—avoid jumping through all these hoops…this was just part of the rule book of online dating.

Jeremy, my latest match, was a total nature freak. He was living in the small town of Eagle way up in the Rockies. We did the usual: texting, talking, and facetiming which was now my standard procedure before agreeing to meet. He seemed like a genuinely nice guy.

He drove over two hours to meet me. I offered to buy dinner and let him pick the place as a thank you for his effort. I figured any guy who lived in Eagle (I looked it up on Google maps and yep it was there, just barely.) would enjoy some variety that the big city could provide.

He didn't let me down. He chose Thai. My favorite. Two points for Jeremy and the date had only just begun.

I didn't have a lot of expectations going in. I'd been at this for a while now, I knew this guy probably wasn't going to be Mr. Forever. But that didn't mean we couldn't have a fun night out on the town. Even though Billy had left me feeling a little jaded, this evening was full of possibilities that were enough to get my heartbeat racing a little.

Jeremy showed up right on time. He had brown hair with a hairline that was already a bit thin. He was more than a foot taller than me. I knew from the app that he was twenty-eight and unlike a lot of the guys I'd gone on dates with lately... Jeremy felt more... real. Like Billy had when we first met, he was raised and lived in a small town. He seemed more interested in getting to know me on a personal level, rather than jumping straight into bed.

He texted when he was almost to my house. I met him out in the parking lot and caught him as he was just getting out of his truck.

Jeremy looked at me and smiled. "Hi," he said cheerfully.

"Hi. How was the drive?" I asked.

"Not bad at all. I'm used to it. I'm so glad to meet you."

I smiled. "Likewise. I'm hungry, I'm sure you are too after that long drive. Let's go eat."

Things with Jeremy were just so *easy*. You know how sometimes you meet a person and it feels like you've been friends for years—that's how it was with Jeremy.

We were seated at a small table, just enough room for two, looking over the menu.

"What do you usually order?" Jeremy asked. "I'm not sure what to get."

He let me choose everything we ordered. He was excited to try new dishes. I ordered yellow curry chicken, red curry prawns, pad Thai, and brown rice.

162

We were engaged in conversation during the entire meal. Totally unaware of what was going on around us. I was surprised by how outgoing and confident Jeremy was. I could see confidence in the way he held his body. Jeremy sat up straight and held eye contact as we talked. Something about his posture spoke to his being engaged by our conversation.

I also loved how he was soaking up every opportunity to converse with an older, educated woman. It felt nice to have a conversation with someone so interested in what I had to offer beyond the physical. Jeremy never looked around while we were talking. He gave me his full attention and it was noticeable.

"I'm excited to eat Thai food. There aren't any Thai restaurants where I live."

"I was glad when you chose this place, it's one of my favorite restaurants."

"I was glad when you mentioned it, I don't get a lot of opportunities to eat out and when I do most places are pretty much all the same."

"I guess you have to come off the mountain to get a hold of some really great food! In truth, I was worried that you may not be interested in this place."

"Why is that?"

"Well, small towns can kinda be a little less open-minded—it was a worry I had. It's great you're so open-minded. From my experience, there are a lot of people from small towns who aren't. I remember taking a friend out to this restaurant and she refused to eat anything but steamed vegetables and rice. She thought the curry would make her sick—of all things—although she had never had it, so she couldn't know how the food would settle with her. Food can be so important to culture and she was phobic of it because someone told her curry makes you sick. If only she had more exposure and interaction, she'd realize what a great place the world is, how everyone has their own unique contribution to make. Plus, I am a huge fan of curries!"

"You're very intelligent," he said, eyeing me with appreciation. Jeremy was really comfortable with eye contact and held mine for long periods of time throughout that night. He had a knowingness in his gaze that felt a little uncomfortable to me at first. I wasn't used to people seeking out that depth of connection.

As I eased into getting to know Jeremy, it started to feel like the most natural thing for me to do. Why didn't more guys let themselves be vulnerable enough to look a woman in the eyes? To ask them probing questions and consider their responses, rather than speaking about themselves. I always liked listening to the men I dated, but to have someone listen to me made me realize I liked it as well.

"I could talk to you all night," he said, reaching out and touching my hand. "It's nice to spend time with someone so smart."

I smiled. I couldn't help it. I loved genuine compliments that were geared towards character traits. I'd much rather be complimented on my intelligence. So far, the men I had met focused on my looks and it only worked to make me feel more used in our interactions, in this too, Jeremy was different.

"Thank you. I appreciate you telling me. It's very flattering."

Jeremy loved the food choices. He ate quickly. We both had seconds of our dishes and happily packed up the leftovers.

"You can take the red curry shrimp home," I told him. "It was too spicy for me, but I'd love to keep the yellow curry if that's ok with you."

"You paid and should take it all home." But then he grinned. "If the shrimp will just go to waste, though—I'd love to take it."

I paid the bill and we hopped back into my car.

There was no question that I wanted the night to continue after dinner. We stopped at the liquor store to pick up some beer for Jeremy then continued back to my house. Ten minutes later we were sitting on my patio, Jeremy with his beer and me with my pipe.

He looked completely at home in my condo and on my patio. The ease from the restaurant continued to flow. We chatted and chatted. There was never a lull in our conversation. Partly due to the fact that I could talk enough to hold conversations with inanimate objects.

After an hour, we moved into the living room. Jeremy's confidence followed him to the couch. Almost immediately he started kissing me. By the way he grabbed me, I'm guessing that he'd wanted to kiss me for quite some time.

Jeremy and I had similar kissing styles. Once we started kissing, Jeremy didn't want to stop.

"Man, you're a great kisser." Jeremy took a break from kissing me just to tell me.

I smiled. "Thanks, you are too."

Jeremy wasn't afraid to touch me everywhere. His hands moved down my back, around my waist, and up to my breasts. It was as if he was feeling every outline of my body and memorizing it with his hands. It was a huge turn on. He was exhaling and inhaling rapidly as his hands moved over me. Everything about this experience felt so right, especially this guy.

I pulled his shirt off and ran my hands over Jeremy's chest. Occasionally, I slid my hand along his jawline while we kissed. Every time I did this, Jeremy would catch his breath. The simple gesture drove him wild. My hand made its way down his body to his dick. I was completely shocked to discover that he was huge. I couldn't stop the words that escaped me.

"Holy shit Jeremy, you're hung!"

Jeremy laughed and said, "Yeah, I do ok."

I was so turned on as my hand ran over the length and girth of him.

No way. No way!

In addition to everything else I liked about him, Jeremy was a two-fister!

Claudia was never going to believe this.

I dropped to my knees. I wanted to see him up close. Some things you just have to experience that way. I couldn't get all of him in my mouth. I took him as far into my throat as I could, but there was still a good three-quarters of it left. I stroked the rest of the length.

"Oh my God!" The muscles in his legs tensed. "Oh my God!" His groans only encouraged me to work harder. Jeremy put his hand on my shoulder to stop me then pulled me up to him.

"I want to fuck the shit out of you." He spoke to my lips then kissed me.

I was on board with that. "Ok. Let's go."

I took his hand and led him to my bedroom.

The connection we established in our conversation translated into our sex. We teased each other playfully once we got onto my bed. I could tell Jeremy wanted to find out what turned me on. He'd touch me then he'd ask, "Do you like that?" or "Do you want this?" I tried to mirror his communication and would check in every now and then to see if my actions were pleasing to him.

He had me on edge. Literally and otherwise, he knelt down between my spread legs and returned the favor. Taking his time to kiss and finger me. I didn't think of it at the time, but he was getting my body warmed up enough to take him. Either way, Jeremy was a considerate lover and definitely enjoyed giving as much as receiving.

"Do you like when I do that?" Jeremy asked as he slid his finger in and out of me.

"Oh my God, yes! Please fuck me," I begged.

At last, he knelt in front of me and slid on a condom. I was so ready, I all but dragged him down on top of me.

Jeremy kissed me tenderly as he slowly slid himself into me. I don't know if he was simply used to having to go slow due to his size or if the tenderness was part of his game. Whatever the reason, it created so much anticipation and excitement for me.

I was dying for him to start fucking me in earnest.

How did he know exactly where I like to be touched? Just where I loved the pressure? I loved long, drawn out foreplay. I loved being fingered, but not all men know how to warm a woman up the right way. Jeremy seemed to know exactly what I wanted. It felt like we'd been having sex for years. It was incredible and I let him know it.

"You turn me on Jeremy. I love how you touch my body. You make me so horny for you."

Jeremy smiled and said, "Good." I just told him exactly what he wanted to hear.

He finally slid all the way inside, I groaned as I felt him. He froze. I dug my nails into his shoulder communicating to him how much I liked it.

We quickly progressed from hot and heavy to downright combustible. "Jeremy—I'm going to cum!" I nearly screamed as I felt sparks light up my body as he fucked me slow and deep.

"What do you need?" he asked.

I could barely speak, but I closed my legs. "Fuck me, fuck me like this."

Jeremy slid his hands under my ass and squeezed while he fucked me.

It felt amazing. I hadn't had sex like this in a long time.

I came quickly after closing my legs. My nails scratched down his back, leaving long red marks from his shoulders to his waist. Jeremy arched his back and moaned loudly. My scratching must have turned him on.

He immediately flipped me over. He pulled me up onto my knees and slid into me from behind. Jeremy fucked me and didn't hold back.

There were a few times when I wanted to say ouch, but I bit my tongue and let him enjoy himself. I didn't want to ruin the mood and I wanted him to be able to fuck me in a way that felt great to him. So, I endured the mild discomfort, knowing I'd speak up if I got too uncomfortable.

I reached down between his legs and started playing with his balls. I needed him to be able to come soon as I was getting sore from his size. He came almost immediately and let out a loud moan. His body stiffened and his back arched. His hands held my waist tightly. I could feel him throbbing violently inside me.

We both collapsed beside each other breathing heavily.

Both exclaiming *holy shit*!

"That was fucking incredible!"

We breathed hard in the aftermath. When we cleaned up and got back together in bed, he cuddled me on his side—without me even asking.

I put on a movie as he dozed off.

After about thirty minutes, Jeremy was up and had his hands all over me again. We fucked another time that night, then again in the morning right before I had to get up for work.

Each time we had sex, it was electric. Even better than the first time. Which I hadn't thought was possible.

While I showered and got ready for work, Jeremy went to the nearby bagel store and Starbucks for breakfast. We sat at the kitchen table and ate breakfast together.

Jeremy planned to do some city exploring while he was in town. We left at the same time.

He walked me to my car then hugged and kissed me before leaving.

It had all been just... *perfect*.

Too perfect, I was sure.

He'll be like all the others, I thought. He won't call or text. It was one perfect—fantastical night. And that was all it would be. And I was starting to become okay with that.

I thought I was, anyway.

But then on Sunday, he texted asking if he could come back again on Tuesday

My fingers stumbled over themselves as I quickly messaged back: YES PLEASE!

Shit! Did that sound too eager? Screw it. I was tired of overthinking what I should or shouldn't say to men. I'm a very straightforward woman and beating around the bush just didn't feel natural to me. I wanted Jeremy to come any time he could.

When Tuesday rolled around, I knew I had a few hours after work before Jeremy would arrive. We agreed on a menu the night before, I wanted to cook this time. (I was happy to do these things for Jeremy, considering the amount of effort he was putting in to coming see me.) He chose schnitzel, pineapple rice, and parmesan roasted cauliflower. It had been a long time since I had cooked for a man and it was something I loved doing. I was in my element in the kitchen and entertaining was something I dearly missed post-divorce.

When I was married, we entertained often, whether it was appetizers for football games on Sundays, baby showers for our married friends, or big birthday parties for Aubrey. I loved entertaining and cooking; however, now that we were living in a 900-square-foot condo, it didn't lend well to entertaining as much. I'd still throw great birthday parties for Aubrey, but they were on a much smaller scale.

I had dinner nearly ready when Jeremy arrived. He showed up at my door dressed casually and wearing a backpack. I imagined he packed to stay the night and felt a jolt of joy from this.

He leaned down to give me a little kiss, but it quickly turned to a full blown make out. He walked me backwards to the couch. Gently pushing me onto it, he got on top of me. Jeremy's hand grasped onto my thighs spanning their width. He began settling himself between them.

"Let's go to my bedroom," I barely managed to gasp out.

Jeremy readily agreed.

I turned off the oven and hoped we wouldn't cause the cauliflower to overcook. Not that I really cared, but I did take my cooking fairly seriously, enough to check on it.

I then walked to my bedroom with Jeremy trailing behind. Once we were inside, Jeremy walked over to me. He grabbed me and started kissing me where I stood.

He was bubbling over with passion and desire—it was intensely hot. We frantically took off each other's clothes, dropping them all over my floor.

Once we were naked, Jeremy turned me and gently pushed me onto the bed. I bounced down on the mattress then quickly scooted up and spread my legs open for him. Jeremy rolled a condom on in one continuous motion, hopped onto his knees, and lay on top of me. He slammed his dick into me.

"Holy shit!" I yelled in total ecstasy.

Our sex was just as electric and satisfying as the first time. Jeremy remembered exactly how to please me and encouraged me to close my legs while he grabbed my ass in his hands again. Jeremy didn't have to fuck me for very long like that before I was ready to cum. This time, he came almost immediately after me. There's a lot to be said for anticipation—the build-up of desire. Achieving an orgasm is much easier and happens quicker when you've had some time to think about it.

Afterwards we dressed. I went into the kitchen to finish dinner while he sat at a barstool keeping me company while I cooked.

"That was fucking incredible!" Jeremy exclaimed, his head nodding back towards the bedroom. "It was even better than last time and I didn't think that could be possible."

I laughed. "I couldn't agree more. We have insane chemistry."

"Fuck yeah we do!"

I put the finishing touches on dinner. Pulling the cauliflower out of the oven, putting the plate of schnitzel on the table, and grabbing two waters.

Jeremy loved it. He ate more than I had seen any man eat in quite some time. I loved watching him enjoy my cooking. I could never date or marry a man who didn't love the meals I made.

Jeremy might have lived over two hours away, but if he was willing to make the drive, I was more than eager to keep spending time with him. After all, two hours wasn't that far considering the caliber of chemistry and sex we were having.

The way he kept talking, he didn't sound eager to break this off anytime soon.

"I really like hanging out with you," he said, giving me that intense eye contact of his again. "I'm going to try and come see you as often as I can."

I grinned as we cleared the table. We did the dishes together then moved out to the patio. Maybe, just maybe—I had found the friends with benefits that I was looking for. As we sat on the patio enjoying the crisp night air, I smoked while he drank a beer. We talked for a long time on the patio about our careers, life, and our childhoods.

Jeremy volunteered at his local public library, he taught kids about nature and the animals that could be found in the forest surrounding their town.

"I have to create some lessons and activities. I'm not sure what to do. They're little kids, I want it to be educational, but also engaging for them."

"Well, I taught preschool in college, maybe I can come up with some suggestions. It's great for children to have tactile experiences. Maybe bring in leaves, acorns, and a variety of other flora from the forest for them to touch. They can make collages and rubbings with crayons. For the older children, you can have them label various parts of the rubbings."

"Wow! Those are great ideas. I'm going to use your suggestions for sure." Jeremy shook his head. "You're a great person Lacie. You don't have to cook dinner for me. Especially when you have a full plate, caring for your daughter. I can tell you're a really good person."

"Aw, thank you so much Jeremy. You're sweet for saying those things. I can't believe you came to see me from where you live. The least I can do is make you dinner. I don't want you to feel like you have to come see me every week. It's far—so just when you're up for the drive."

I didn't want to feel like a burden, but I was thrilled when he kept on talking about visiting regularly.

"But I *want* to come see you, Lacie."

I leaned in. "Well that's good because I want to see you too."

Jeremy grinned. "Are we going to get bagels and Starbucks in the morning—like last time?"

All sorts of little firecrackers were going off inside my belly. "That would be awesome. Especially if you don't mind getting them while I get ready."

"Absolutely!"

After talking and smoking weed, it was late. We brushed our teeth, got ready for bed, and turned on a movie. It felt a little strange to be getting ready for bed with a man. Oddly enough, it felt as if we were an old married couple who had been doing it for years. I wondered if Jeremy felt it too.

We cuddled and watched our movie for a while. Jeremy's hands were between my legs. His thumb would circle the sensitive skin of my inner thigh every now and then. It was getting me so aroused. I turned my head from where it rested on his chest to look at his face. He started down at me for a few beats then grabbed my face with his hand and kissed me.

We had sex again and a third time at around 4 am.

I fell asleep completely sated and absolutely happy to have Jeremy in my bed by my side.

I woke up the next morning.

He wasn't in bed.

"Jeremy?" I called. I sat up and stretched languidly. "Jer?"

No response.

Hmmm… maybe he left to get bagels?

I got up and saw that the bathroom was empty. I walked into the living room. Jeremy's backpack was gone. There was nothing of his in my house. I fell onto the couch.

What was going on? Why would he take his backpack to go get bagels?

Bewildered, I picked up my phone and texted him.

It sent, but never said it was delivered.

I called. I got a message stating the phone was not in service.

Not in service—

A cold knot of dread pitted itself into my stomach as I logged on to Instagram and Facebook. I couldn't find Jeremy when I searched his name.

He ran.

I opened the dating app. We were still connected. I could see that he was in Golden, a small town about 30 miles away.

He hadn't gone for bagels. He'd dumped me in the worst possible way. He literally up and disappeared in the middle of the night.

I sat up. My purse! My wallet! I went straight to my purse and grabbed my wallet. Phew! My credit cards and personal things were still there. At least he hadn't robbed me on his way out the door. As I looked around my apartment, I saw that he had locked the handles of the screen and front door when he left.

This was oddly strange to me. He ghosted me yet he still made sure I was safe. Go figure.

The sick feeling in my stomach merged with anger as I messaged him over the app.

Me: WHERE ARE YOU? WHY DID YOU LEAVE? I DIDN'T DESERVE THIS.

Jeremy unmatched with me immediately. His face disappeared from my screen. I watched it.

I stood in my living room in only my underwear, utterly shocked. How could I go from having an amazing night with Jeremey to this? A night where he says he will get breakfast in the morning, but leaves before I wake up. A night where he talked about visiting me again, but blocks me the next day?

I was so confused and couldn't understand what would drive someone to do that. I *am* a good person. He saw that. How could he treat me this way?

I hadn't been the one pressing him to come back. He kept saying that *he* wanted to come back. He was planning to visit me on a longer-term basis. Why would he do that? Why get my expectations up only to leave once I was asleep?

A few hours into the day, with the shock worn off and the depression setting in, I asked myself an all too familiar question: *Why the fuck are you doing this, Lacie?*

The bottom line was that it just wasn't worth it anymore. Feeling like a piece of discarded trash after a night of bliss, it just wasn't worth this horribly painful feeling.

I texted Claudia.

Me: I FEEL LIKE SHIT. WHY THE FUCK WOULD HE DO THAT? HE COULD'VE LIED. IT WOULD HAVE BEEN SO MUCH EASIER ON ME.

Claudia: I AGREE, BUT LACIE, YOU HAVE TO REMEMBER THAT THE MEN YOU ARE CHOOSING TO SPEND TIME WITH ARE IMMATURE. THEY DON'T KNOW HOW TO COMMUNICATE. HE CLEARLY JUST RAN, FOR WHATEVER REASON. THAT IS ALL HE COULD THINK TO DO.

Me: I KNOW YOU'RE RIGHT, BUT IT STILL HURTS. I FEEL LIKE SHIT.

Claudia: I KNOW YOU DO AND I'M SORRY HON. YOU OF ALL PEOPLE DON'T DESERVE THIS.

I texted my other friends to tell them what had happened and to get some more comfort and advice. If this is what it was like having fun with twenty-something year-olds, I wanted nothing to do with it. *This* felt like shit.

When I got home from work that day, I went to my neighbor's house for support. She encouraged me to call him from her landline and leave a message. Normally, I'm not the kind of person who would need the last word, but I hadn't felt so betrayed and let down by a man since my divorce. My approach was to talk in a sad, shocked, and hurt tone.

He probably never even listened to the first word. Wimp.

Still, it gave me the smallest sense of closure.

"Hi Jeremy, it's Lacie. I wanted to let you know that what you did was very hurtful. I have been nothing but kind to you and I never deserved what you did to me." I took a deep breath before continuing. "You could've told me anything. Literally anything. That you wanted an early start on your long drive home. That the two-hour drive to come see me was too much. Any other way you could've handled it would've been better than what you did. I beg you to never do this to another woman ever again—goodbye Jeremy."

Leaving Jeremy that voicemail was the second step I took to empowering myself. I didn't know the baby steps that I was taking back then. Standing up to men, putting my foot down when they didn't treat me right, and slowly raising my expectations. This was getting me closer to being more confident and in control of my own life.

For a very long time, it felt like I had no control and could only just weather the storm. Shared custody, selling my beautiful home, losing my best friend and husband within weeks of each other. These were just a few of my struggles. They were enough to drive someone to drink—only I didn't like alcohol.

Sure, the casual sex, I was having helped boost my ego. I had never felt this sexy or beautiful. But, at what cost?

Being ghosted by Jeremy hurt me to my core. I felt ashamed for letting him have such a big impact on my emotional well-being. I was allowing a man with intimacy issues push me down when all I wanted to do was rebuild myself. Enough was enough. I was ready to stand up for myself.

Chapter 14: Girls Just Want To Have Fun

It felt stupid to let what had happened with Jeremy get to me so badly—but it did. I felt such a strong connection with him. I thought it was reciprocated—but he was using me. Just like all the other men. Lying the entire time we were together. What was *wrong* with people? I wanted to have some fun and escape from my loneliness—but if this was the outcome, I'd rather just stay at home with my popcorn, binging Netflix—thank you very much.

I was packing my bags while talking on the phone with Claudia, who was doing the same. As I looked at my empty suitcase, I made a silent prayer to leave my emotional baggage at home.

"I'll pay for the plane tickets with my points and I'll cover the room," Claudia assured me. "You buy the food this weekend."

We were leaving soon for our annual seaside trip and I was still arguing with her over costs.

I frowned at my bathing suit. "Ok, but it won't be even. I'll still owe you money at the end of our trip."

Claudia and I had so many parallels in our lives, but our financial situations were complete opposites. She received an insane amount of child support every month in addition to her salary. I, on the other hand, lived paycheck to paycheck and got a very small amount of child support every three months when my ex-husband received his miniscule bonuses.

"I don't want your money. I just want to see you. I miss your face!"

I smiled while putting a hand to my forehead. It really had been too long since I'd had myself some good quality Claudia time. "Do you want to invite anyone else or just have it be us?"

"I just want it to be us."

"Ok. That sounds amazing actually."

Claudia booked a room at a seaside resort near Santa Cruz, California. The resort was on a bluff overlooking the ocean. All the rooms faced the water.

After checking in, we talked to the concierge. Claudia booked a bonfire for us that night. I guess she wanted to lift my spirits. Bonfires might be my most favorite activity in the world—aside from having sex of course. Feeling the warmth of the fire and listening to the sound of the ocean, it has to be the most relaxing setting that I can possibly think of.

"God, Claudia, you don't know how much I needed this."

"I've always got your back." She bumped her shoulder into mine. I smiled.

"Look at this view!" I said while opening the sliding doors and walking out onto the patio.

It was a beautiful day—in the mid-70s. It couldn't have been more perfect. I leaned against the balcony. The ocean was as far as the eye could see. I could enjoy this view all day long.

"Let's explore the grounds," Claudia suggested.

We grabbed our room key and cell phones then walked out the door. We walked to the edge of the bluff and sat on a bench that over-looked the ocean. It was beautiful watching the waves crashing onto the sand and rolling backwards out to sea.

"So how are you doing? Really?"

I shrugged, still looking out at the waves. "A little off-kilter from the whole Jeremy thing, I guess."

"I told you, that asshole was just young and wanting to spread his seed. Guys his age want to fuck with no strings attached. They don't have the mental ability to even have a causal relationship. I think in order to not develop feelings, they'd rather fuck a woman and move on to the next, regardless of how great it was."

I nodded. "I know. I know!" I waved a hand. "It's not even him—not that much. It's just unfathomable to me that he wouldn't want to come back and have sex again. Just sex. I could have that every day."

Claudia laughed. "Of course, you could! You're forty-three and horny as fuck. Sex is like air for you"

That cracked me up. Claudia got me too well.

We sat there enjoying the view in comfortable silence, before venturing off to the other side of the resort. We spent some time on the beach that afternoon and ate dinner at a nearby restaurant.

I ordered truffle gnocchi with gorgonzola cream sauce. The gnocchi were like fluffy little pillows. The best I'd ever had. Claudia ordered a pasta dish topped with filet mignon. The meat cut like butter, red and tender.

This was the life! Relaxing and feeling pampered with all this amazing food—without a worry about calories or anything else. God, I had so needed this respite from all the bullshit!

After dinner, we headed back to the resort and changed into more comfortable clothes for the bonfire.

Just before 9 pm there was a knock on the door. I opened it to be greeted by a young man in his twenties, dressed in black slacks and a collar-shirt.

180

"Hi, I'm Rob. I'm here to take you to the bonfire."

"Hi Rob!" I said with a smile. He was young and adorable. "How are you tonight?"

"Not too bad. How about yourself?"

"I'm great. Can't wait for the bonfire. I love bonfires and am so ready to make some s'mores."

Rob laughed. "Yeah, s'mores are pretty good."

Claudia came out shortly after. We all walked over to the golf cart that would take us down to the beach.

"Can I drive?" I tried to wheedle. "Please, I'll be careful. I promise."

Rob laughed and responded a little uncomfortably, "Uhhh… no. I'd get into trouble."

Of course, that made sense. "I get it. No problem." I hopped into the passenger seat. "When are you off? Come join us at our bonfire later."

Rob laughed again. "Really? I don't think anyone has ever invited me to their bonfire before."

"Are you kidding? They're all assholes! We're fun and just looking to have a good time." I blinked at him owlishly as I realized how that sounded. "Not in the inappropriate sense, but the very literal sense."

Rob laughed. "I'll see what I can do. Are you having a bonfire tomorrow?"

"I'm not sure yet. They're fucking expensive."

"I know. It's crazy," Rob said. "I get off earlier tomorrow and could probably join you then."

"Ok. We may not have a bonfire tomorrow, but we still plan to lite up!" I joked. One of the bonuses of vacationing in California.

Rob's laugh was even louder this time. "I don't smoke, but that's good to know."

We made it to the bottom of the hill. Rob introduced us to Mario, another hotel staff member, who manned the bonfire area. Mario set up all the bonfires and got everything ready for guests. He also added wood to the pits as they died down to ensure that guests could keep partying into the late hours.

"How are you ladies this evening?" Mario greeted us with the utmost respect.

Claudia responded, "We're great. How are you?"

"I have a view of the ocean and I'm surrounded by bonfires, I couldn't be better."

"Yeah, plus unlimited s'mores. You definitely have a dream job."

Mario showed us to our bonfire. There were bottles of water on our chairs and a white box. I opened it and found graham crackers, chocolate bars, and a bag full of large marshmallows.

"Oh my God. This is amazing. We have enough to feed an army."

Mario laughed. "Yes, you do and I'm happy to bring you more if you need it."

Claudia and my eyes widened.

"If we eat more than what's in this box, you'll have to roll us home."

"I'm sure that we can get you home safely, ma'am."

We all laughed.

Mario was eighteen; but you never would have guessed it, he was mature beyond his years. He was the most respectful young man I had ever met. He always said 'yes ma'am' in reply to everything we asked. Claudia and I were smitten with him. We gave him life advice and encouraged him to go to college.

We quickly became two unofficial mothers—something Mario probably never wanted.

"Come hang out at our bonfire with us," I cajoled. For once it felt nice to hang out with a member of the opposite sex—just for fun without looking for anything else.

A novel idea, I know.

"Yes ma'am," Mario said smiling. "I have to check on all the other guests, but I'll be right back."

Mario zoomed off in his own golf cart, stopping at each fire before coming back to ours. He parked his cart and turned it off. He pulled out a white plastic chair from the back of his cart and joined us. We chatted with Mario for a long time. He loved us. We could both tell by the way he spent so much time with us and kept coming back to chat after helping the other guests.

"So, what brings you ladies to California? Are you on vacation?"

"Yes, we are. We needed some relaxation and this is just the place." Claudia replied.

"What about you?" I asked. "Are you from here?"

"Yes, I've lived in the Santa Cruz area my whole life. I graduated from high school last year and I'm attending a community college for now. I work here a few nights a week."

"Good for you!" we both chimed.

"Stay in school. Trust me. An education is the greatest thing that you can do for yourself. It will open doors that would otherwise be closed."

"Yes, ma'am. I intend to keep going and to finish."

"Good for you Mario," Claudia encouraged.

I pulled out my pipe, packed it, and took a hit.

After exhaling, I asked Mario if he wanted a hit.

"No ma'am. I don't smoke. Plus, I'm working."

"Good for you, Mario," Claudia said. "You are so responsible. Stay that way."

"Yes ma'am."

We laughed. We loved being called ma'am. Mario was so endearing.

After twenty minutes, Mario drove around to check on all of the bonfires again. Some people were ready to head up to their rooms. Mario radioed in for their rides.

After all of the other guests had left, he returned to sit with us at our bonfire. A few minutes later, Rob drove down with his cart and parked near us as well.

I shouted out to him, "Rob! You made it! Come have a hit and some s'more."

"No thank you," Rob said while holding up his hands. "I've had too many s'mores. I'm sick of them. And I'm working so can't smoke cither."

"Oh, that's right. Well, I'd feel rude not offering."

We laughed and chatted, enjoying the bonfire until well after the 10 pm curfew. It was a great time. Rob gave us a ride back and thanked us for inviting him out.

"I'll see you tomorrow?" Rob asked as we got out.

"Yes! We can't wait to have another bonfire." I was high and overly enthusiastic for the next day.

"Goodnight ladies."

"Goodnight," we said in unison.

As I went to sleep that night, my head a little spacey and my body relaxed from the weed, I thought—yes, this is what I'd been looking for—a bit of *fun*.

We'd had a great time with Rob and Mario. There'd been no expectations, no one using anyone else, no hidden agendas.

Was it because there had been no sex or even attraction involved with this encounter? Did sex always complicate things and make them so messy? Or had I somehow been approaching all this wrong?

I thought about the fact that I wasn't looking for a relationship; but was I being honest with myself about this, did I really think that it would be enough? I got upset when guys didn't respond to my texts or ghosted me after we spent the night together. Maybe I was still taking it all too seriously, maybe I was contextualizing these encounters like someone seeking out a relationship. Instead of this, maybe I should embrace playing the game. But I just wasn't much of a game player. I told it to people straight and expected the same courtesy in return.

But I wanted to have more nights like tonight, genuinely fun with absolutely zero expectations or rules. Well… you know, adding in some sexy times and occasionally some very happy endings.

I went to bed that night with a better frame of mind. And not just because of all the weed.

Claudia and I spent the next day at the beach. We dressed in our bathing suits after breakfast, grabbed some beach towels and a portable speaker then headed out. We chose to walk down the path onto the beach instead of taking the golf cart—to get some exercise. We waved and said hello every time a golf cart filled with passengers would pass us.

We laid out on the beach for hours. A couple of guys came by and hung out, flirting and smoking weed with us. They were cute enough, but we were ready to ditch them after a couple of hours. We both wanted the weekend to be about just the two of us.

We excused ourselves then went back to the walkway to pick up the phone there and call for a ride. A new chauffer greeted us introducing himself as Tyler. We got into the cart.

"You must be the ladies I've heard so much about."

We laughed out loud. "Our reputation precedes us! Please, do tell us what you've heard."

"Well, the guys were talking about you two after our staff meeting."

"Really?" Claudia asked tickled pink. "What did they say?"

"They said there are two hella cool ladies staying here—beautiful and fun."

"Aww," we said simultaneously. How sweet these guys were.

Given that we made such a splash, it had to mean that most resort visitors weren't giving these guys the time of day. Which was just a shame. Claudia and I were truly just looking to have fun with whomever was around—regardless of their status or age. The only requirement was not to be a douche.

Life is what you make of it. In the end, you can either choose to remain in your bubble or live. Claudia and I chose the second.

Tyler stopped by the bar so Claudia could grab a Bloody Mary. When she returned, drink in hand, he drove us the rest of the way back to our room.

"Come join us at the bonfire tonight—if you're still around," I said. "Mario and Rob will probably hang out with us too."

Tyler smiled. "I definitely will. It isn't every day that we get invited to a bonfire with two beautiful women."

Adorable. We both loved the attention and so, it seemed, did these young men.

After dinner, Rob picked us up and we headed down to the beach. When we got down there, Mario drove us over to our pit. S'mores and other supplies were waiting for us. Mario was a rock star! Not only did we get a free bonfire that night, but he hooked us up with s'mores to boot! I had forty dollars in my pocket that we wanted to tip him at the end of the night. Claudia and I were beyond grateful to be saving money. Not being charged for the second bonfire was great.

Mario left us to get settled and returned after checking on the other guests. He stayed with us on and off for the rest of the night then finally settled down after everyone else left. Rob and Tyler came down to our bonfire as well. We all sat chatting and laughing for another half hour.

When it was time for them to clean up, Tyler drove us back to our room.

"Are you ladies checking out tomorrow?"

"Yes, unfortunately. We don't want to leave. We agreed that we'd try to come here every year for a weekend getaway, just the two of us. So, hopefully we will see you next year.

"Most definitely. Goodnight ladies. Have a safe trip home."

"Goodnight Tyler."

We sat on our patio for a while listening to the ocean and just relaxing.

I held out my arms and felt the sea breeze brush past my body. This. Fucking *this*. This was the life I wanted. A big, full, happy life.

All my realizations from the night before felt reinforced in this moment. I wasn't going to let anyone make me miserable, not anymore. Certainly not a man—that's for damn sure. I was done trying to look for Mr. Right or even Mr. Right Now.

I'd been investing too much of myself into online dating. The past two days were absolutely effortlessly fun. I wanted more of that.

Finding a regular fuck buddy was obviously not going to happen. For whatever reason, it just wasn't the way these guys worked.

I could accept that. Right then and there, I did accept it. I was going to have fun and live my life, dammit. Maybe that was continuing to see guys, maybe it wasn't.

Through all of my encounters this past year, I had been learning who I was and rediscovering my true self. I was becoming empowered and gaining my confidence back. I was done feeling out of control—that was for damn sure!

Chapter 15: Can't Get You Off My Mind

After I let a little time pass, I found that I was hesitant to get back into the dating game; but when I did, I knew this time it was going to be different. So, when a familiar face showed up among my matches—Billy, still handsome as ever in his cowboy hat and wranglers—I didn't hold back.

I read his message.

Billy: HEY. HOW ARE YOU DOING? I WANT TO SEE YOU AGAIN. I'VE HAD A LONG DAY AT WORK AND COULD USE A GOOD FUCK.

I had gotten to the point that I ignored stupid text messages or asinine behaviors from Bumble guys like this. Yet this time, I was going to speak my mind. After my revelation while on vacation with Claudia, I was done taking shit from anyone, especially Billy. I was ready to push back.

I messaged Billy on the Bumble app—the same way he connected with me this time.

Me: HI BILLY. SEEMS LIKE YOU KEEP POPPING UP WHEN I LEAST EXPECT IT. IF YOU HAVE ANY INTENTION IN MEETING WITH ME IN THE FUTURE, I SUGGEST YOU NEVER TREAT ME LIKE YOU DID THE LAST TIME WE MET. I DON'T DESERVE IT AND I WON'T TOLERATE IT. I'M NOT GOING TO DEAL WITH MEN WHO CAN'T PLEASE ME OR THOSE WHO MAKE ME FEEL USED. IS THAT ALL YOU SEE ME AS, 'A GOOD FUCK'?

Billy: I UNDERSTAND AND I WON'T. I PROMISE. I STAND CORRECTED, YOU'RE A GREAT FUCK, LACIE.

I rolled my eyes and shook my head after reading his reply. I didn't respond. I wasn't going to be the fish at the end of Billy's hook. I felt different and I planned to act differently.

Twenty minutes later, Billy messaged me again.

Billy: WHEN CAN I SEE YOU? WHEN WILL YOU BE BACK UP TO YOUR PARENT'S?

I made Billy wait another hour before I replied. Partly because I wanted him to wait and partly because I was trying hard to *play the game*.

Me: IN A FEW WEEKS.

Billy: TEXT ME SO WE CAN GET TOGETHER.

Me: MAYBE. I THINK YOU LIKE ME BILLY. YOU LIKE TO ACT LIKE YOU DON'T, BUT YOU KEEP COMING AROUND AND SURE SEEM TO LIKE CHATTING WITH ME.

Billy: HA HA! I LIKE FUCKING YOU.

I didn't reply.

Unfortunately, I wasn't meeting with Billy the cowboy that night. I had made plans with someone new.

I was scheduled to meet up with Napoleon.

And as per my new dating philosophy, I was simply out for a good time with no expectations.

And believe me, I was having fun.

We went back to my place after meeting up at Starbucks. Napoleon was very comfortable and walked into my house with ease. He had been seeking out touch and physical connection throughout our coffee date. Several times as we passed or were in close proximity, he would take the opportunity to touch me, so I knew he was attracted.

We sat out on my patio.

"Do you mind if I smoke?" I asked while taking out my supplies.

Napoleon lifted a brow at me then pulled out a sandwich bag of weed. We laughed and packed a bowl to smoke.

190

"God, you're so sexy." he said as he placed his left hand behind my shoulder. Direct skin to skin contact. He placed the other hand on my thigh while we smoked. He began running his fingers down my arm and touching my back. The hand at my thigh a steady firm touch.

He impressed me. The majority of the time—with younger men, I was the one who had to make the first move.

At twenty-eight, Napoleon was a man who knew how to connect with a woman. This was working for me on every level. His physical contact was great, it helped break the ice and open me up to more of his touch.

His confidence and masculinity were abounding. It was turning me on. I felt myself making eye contact more and for longer periods of time. I wanted to take him in, see and be seen. When Napoleon offered me the pipe, I stared into his eyes as I lit and inhaled.

With *38 Special* playing in the background, I had made up my mind. I was ready to get down and dirty.

It was time to reciprocate those touches and reward him for his confidence. I put my hand behind his neck and ran my fingers through his hair while pulling his lips to mine.

I gave him what had to be the sexiest shotgun of his life. It was most definitely in the top three for me. He opened his mouth immediately inhaling my hit and ending it with a gentle kiss on my lips. When we separated, I left my hand behind his head. Looking up at him, I smiled. We moved to the couch and continued our conversation.

We made small talk for a few minutes. I had no interest in what Napoleon was saying and it showed.

"I grew up in Texas and moved to Colorado when I was in high school. I love it here. Did you grow up here?"

My phone beeped. I reached for it without thinking. Billy texted.

Billy: I WON'T. I PROMISE. I WANT TO SEE YOU AGAIN.

His words rang in my head as I tried to bring my attention back to Napoleon.

"Did you hear me?" Napoleon asked, clearly aware I was distracted.

"Oh, I'm sorry. No, I didn't. What did you say again?"

"I asked if you grew up here."

I felt like it was obvious to Napoleon that I was disengaged. I was checking my phone and not always following our conversation, so I decided to be completely honest with him.

"Hey, I'm sorry but I feel very distracted. I had a conversation with someone earlier today and I just keep fixating on it. Would it bother you if I talked to you about another man?"

What did I have to lose? My past experiences told me that I'd probably never see this guy again. At that moment in time, what I really wanted was a man's interpretation and advice, so I went for it.

Napoleon didn't look surprised. He was unfazed and his voice was even when he said, "No, not at all."

I explained to Napoleon how I connected with Billy twice in the past nine months and that we had reconnected earlier that day. That I foolishly agreed to hang out with him one more time, knowing full well that we don't seem capable of any sort of functioning relationship (physical or otherwise).

I told Napoleon everything from the text exchange earlier that day to our prior meetings. He nodded along listening intently as I went.

"I really don't understand why I can't just tell him to fuck off…"

"Well, he sounds like a dick," Napoleon said succinctly. "My advice is to never talk to him again. But also, you need to ask yourself why you are drawn to him. Is it the sex? Or something else?"

Silence fell over the room. Damn, good one, Napoleon.

I had no idea what kept drawing me back to Billy. It definitely wasn't the sex. Although our first encounter was amazing, I'd had far better sex with other men since then.

So, if it wasn't the sex, what was it about Billy? Why was I allowing him to be a dick, when I would never tolerate his behavior from other men? Or would I? Billy was one of the few men to use me then come back for seconds. Was it just Billy that I would tolerate or was it because he was the only guy to connect with me again?

Honestly, I had no idea how to respond to Napoleon's questions.

"It definitely isn't the sex. I honestly have no idea, but I guess that gives me something to think about. You're very perceptive, Napoleon."

I put Billy out of my mind and focused back on Napoleon. (Fucking weed! Try focusing on more than one thing while high. It's impossible.)

We moved beyond the conversation part of the evening and Napoleon couldn't keep his hands off me. Like other men, he went straight for my breasts.

Actually, Napoleon went straight into the top of my dress, sliding his hand inside my bra, cupping his hand around and under my breast then freeing it. He immediately leaned over and gently sucked on my nipple.

We hadn't even really kissed yet, aside from his perfect ending to my shotgun. Mind blowing right? A twenty-eight-year-old guy who has confidence like that? Damn.

Although, I guess the signs were there from the beginning, given that from the moment he sat down next to me at Starbucks, he stared at me in a way that screamed: I want to fuck the shit out of you!

I watched his face as he caressed my breasts. His eyes moved from my chest to my face then back to my chest again. Napoleon thoroughly enjoyed my body and it felt good to enjoy the moment and feel the arousal that emitted from him.

"I like the feel of your hands," I said in a relaxed way that only weed can inspire. "I want to lie back, close my eyes, and just enjoy your touch. Let's go to bed, I have some massage oil. You can feel every inch of me."

"Let's do it!" was his enthusiastic reply. "I'd love to touch every inch of your body."

At this point, I feel it prudent to mention that I was on day one of my period. Something Napoleon and I previously discussed.

I'd already told him. "We can meet up and hang out, but we won't be having sex. I started my period today and having sex on day one of my period is not enjoyable at all."

"No problem," he'd said. "I totally understand and wouldn't want to have sex while you're on your period anyway. Let's just meet and hang out. See if we're interested in each other."

"Perfect!"

So, even though we knew sex was off the table, we were both so mutually aroused I knew we'd do everything but.

Napoleon doused me in massage oil. And I do mean doused. Apparently, his vision isn't so great. That combined

194

with dim mood lighting wasn't a good combo when determining a proper amount of massage oil. I didn't care. I was going to use those sheets as "sex sheets" anyway. That was totally a thing, right?

Sacrificing the sheets was worth it, let me tell you. Napoleon gave me an amazingly sensual massage.

He slowly rubbed the puddle of oil around my back, I could feel the warm oil dripping down my sides. Napoleon quickly caught some of it with his hands. He moved his hands in circular motions around my back and up onto my shoulders. There was an abundance of oil, so he rubbed his hands down my arms to my hands then back up to my shoulders and all the way down around my waist. My skin started to feel warm from his touch.

Napoleon continued rubbing my back, shoulders, and arms. He teased me by occasionally rubbing around my waist and down to the top of my butt.

Was he going to slide his hands between my legs? Or go for the side route around my waist, diving his hands into my panties? Due to Aunt Flo, Napoleon went with option A, grasping my waist and moving down to my ass.

He moved his hands from my ass back up to my hips then flipped me over onto my back. He put more oil in his hands. (It was too late for me to tell him that he really didn't need more.)

Napoleon proceeded to massage the front of my body, just as skillfully as he did the back. He started with a hand on each breast, simultaneously massaging them with oil. He slid his hands down my legs rubbing my inner thighs. He did a slow mountain lion crawl up to my face and began kissing me.

Oh, damn was he a great kisser! He laid down on my left side and positioned his body so that his dick was exposed. I reached down between his legs and grabbed his testicles firmly, drawing them up towards his body.

Napoleon reacted exactly the way all men do. His body stiffened, his back arched slightly, and he inhaled slow and deep. Most men usually shout out in the form of an "Oh my God" or "Fuck" or "Holy shit". (For the record, my favorite is "Oh my God!" I quite frankly can't think of a higher compliment). I wondered how Napoleon would express himself.

As I slid my hand onto the base of his dick, I could feel how hard he was. I moved my hand upward. I was surprised to find that Napoleon was much larger than I had anticipated. A huge smile spread slowly across my face. Apparently, all the talk of small men and small penis sizes was just an urban legend.

Instinctively, I grabbed a condom from my nightstand and put it on Napoleon. Time to have some fun.

I gave Napoleon head that night. Twice. What can I say? I'm a giver. Unfortunately, I didn't have my happy ending; but I was okay with that, being that I had cramps. Also, I was a royal mess down there.

Some men cum within a minute, some take longer. Napoleon definitely took more effort than most. In the end, I pulled it off. The first time, I finished him off with my hand. Napoleon wasn't vocal when orgasming like I thought he might be.

I looked up at him and smiled.

"Fuck!" he said. "You give great fucking head!"

A big smile spread over my face. I thought, *"Oh I know, Napoleon, I know."*

After we cleaned up, we returned to my bed to cuddle. Napoleon was a great cuddler and I could tell he enjoyed holding me. He made sure every inch of our bodies were touching and didn't make an attempt to break our closeness. We started chatting as we lay spooning.

"I'm glad you're so insistent on using protection. I have a two-year old son who was the result of an unplanned pregnancy. Using protection is important to me and I won't sleep with a woman if she isn't insistent on using it."

"I totally understand. I'm very adamant about using it. The way I see it, if a man wants to have sex with me without using a condom, he's doing the same thing with every other woman he sleeps with. I've never had an STD and I never want one."

"Yeah, don't get me wrong, my son is the greatest joy in my life. I just don't want another child at this age and co-parenting with someone you're not in a relationship with really sucks."

"Trust me, I feel your pain." As we chatted, my mind returned to Billy. What the fuck was I supposed to get out of my experiences with him? We clearly had unfinished business and quite frankly, I wanted to get it taken care of. We both needed to move on.

I immediately thought of Billy's Instagram page. Yes, it's public—and no, I do not nor have I ever followed him. Because... there's no need, his account has always been public. I recall all of his trophies. Deer, fish, turkeys, guns, bows, and beer.

Billy was a hunter. Even though I had always seen him as a cowboy. The primal fact of the matter is that Billy needed the chase.

I had historically been chasing Billy.

So, starting tonight, I would be the prey.

Don't worry... I hadn't forgotten about Napoleon. I was lying on his chest with my leg draped over his. How could I forget?

I turned my attention back to him and his abundant body hair.

"I fucking love body hair. I love that you don't shave."

"Really? Most women don't. Most women hate body hair."

"Not me. I don't understand why a man would want to shave his body hair. I think it's so manly."

"I agree. Most women shave and it makes them look like little girls. I don't find it appealing at all."

(I'll stop there as reading multiple paragraphs about my preferences on body hair might be none too appealing for you, although I can go on indefinitely.)

I continued to play with Napoleon's chest hair while we cuddled. God, it was nice to find someone who didn't mind cuddling.

Napoleon pretty much never moved his hands from my breasts the entire time we talked and cuddled. Smart man that Napoleon. He was very well aware of the fact that it's not every night he's lying next to a pair of genuine, God-given triple D's. He made sure to enjoy every moment with my body while I did the same with him.

Our fondling resulted in Napoleon getting another erection. I'm not one to waste an erection, so I started stroking his dick with my hand then gave him head for the second time.

I made sure to moan and pull out every last trick since this was his second blow job in about thirty minutes. (Between you and me, my jaw was still hurting from the first one and I wanted to get this over quick.)

198

After a few minutes, I lifted his hand from the bed and asked him to take over. I was more than willing to continue, but my jaw was screaming, no more!

I'm guessing he'd never masturbated in front of a woman before, because he was reluctant and somewhat shy about grabbing his dick. He got over that right away when I positioned myself in between his legs and slowly started taking each of his testicles into my mouth.

This was the first time I had ever gotten into a rhythm while sucking on a man's balls. Gently sucking, releasing, pulling in the next on, then sucking, releasing, and so forth.

It was new for me and Napoleon seemed to approve. He moaned and stiffened from my erotic rhythm. As he continued to masturbate, I crouched above him so that his hand and dick were now moving back and forth between my breasts, causing them to bounce around. Napoleon came fast after that.

We both got up and started getting dressed. I walked Napoleon to the door.

"Are you free this weekend?" I asked (aka, after Flo left town).

"Yes. I'll come back over this weekend then?"

"Sounds great! We're going to have great sex! If you liked my head, you're going to love fucking me."

He knew what I said was true. He smiled then shook his head in disbelief, kissed me, and finally said, "See you this weekend."

As soon as he left, it hit me. Billy was in my life to teach me how to be hunted, how to be pursued. He was going to teach me how to play hard to get.

Maybe it was weird to think about Billy after having been with Napoleon, but Billy had been on my mind all night.

I have no problem initiating conversation and physical contact—especially with men who are in their twenties, possess zero body fat, and have a great face. Unfortunately, most men want to be the pursuer and I had a hard time letting them.

Billy was going to get a whole new me the next time he texted. (Fuck let's hope. Pray for me. Keep your fingers crossed.)

If Billy texted again, I wouldn't be replying so quickly. He was definitely going to have to work for me.

As unnatural as it was, I had learned to play the game.

Chapter 16: Cowboy Casanova

The night eventually presented itself for Billy and me to get together again. It was a warm Saturday in August. I'm proud to say I never once reached out to him. Instead, He called at 11:30 pm—drunk. He was in Castlerock for a rodeo. He wanted to see me.

And the truth was I wanted to see him. In the last few months, I had done as I'd sworn to do.

I didn't immediately text back. I took my time responding. I'll admit it, I had always been drawn to him. That first night we'd spent together had been so amazing, our connection so intense. Admittedly, I was more attracted to him than most of the men I had met.

So, on that warm summer night, I said yes.

He took an Uber to my house and I met him outside in the parking lot. Aside from being a little too drunk, Billy stepped out of the Prius looking hot as fuck!

He had on a white cowboy hat, wrangler jeans, a huge shiny belt buckle, a plaid button up shirt that looked brand new, and dirty worn cowboy boots.

We made eye contact and smiled broadly at each other. The butterflies were as fresh as ever in my stomach. Billy was dressed in full blown cowboy gear, still dirty from rodeoing earlier that day—he was a fantasy. Just looking at him was enough to turn me on. I wanted him to grab me then and there, but we instead walked to my house in near silence.

As was par for the course, the initial awkwardness between us extended past my doormat. Instead of walking into my front door and grabbing me like I'd hoped, he strolled over to my kitchen and started reading aloud the notes I kept on my table.

"Grandma's surgery on the 10th of August and dinner plans with the girls tomorrow. I see you keep busy, Lacie."

Even drunk, Billy lacked confidence. I opened a beer for him. I don't normally have alcohol in my refrigerator; but on this night, I had leftover beer from a family dinner.

Once Billy drank some beer, he came up behind me and wrapped his arms around me then started kissing my neck. I turned around to face him and we kissed.

Okay, that was more like it.

But we only kissed for a little bit then he pulled away. He leaned against the counter next to me and started chatting. Random things.

I could barely hear a word he said. Chewie wouldn't stop barking at him. My latest attempt at dog training was to bang two metal utensils together to warn him to quiet down. But not even that was working tonight. I hoped getting Billy out of sight might do the trick.

"Would you mind going down the hall to my bedroom? You can sit on the bed and wait for me there."

Billy nodded but there was a slightly odd look on his face. I didn't pay him much attention as he walked down the hall. That was why I was struck dumb when he called out over his shoulder, "Will you tell me I'm stupid, a dumb fuck, and a worthless piece of shit while you're fucking me?"

Wait. *What?* I was shocked at what he was saying.

"Absolutely not!"

"I'm the guy that you make a mistake with at a bar, right?"

I was beyond astonished. "You're the man at the bar that I would choose every single time. Plus, you know I don't drink." Clearly, Billy didn't think too highly of himself.

I dealt with Chewie and headed into the bedroom. I turned on the light. Billy had been sitting in the dark on the far corner of my bed. I moved Billy to the center edge of the bed where I could stand in front of him and continue our discussion.

"I bet it disappoints you that I have a small dick."

I was completely shocked at the direction he was taking our conversation.

"Why would you say something like that? You don't even have a small dick. You have a larger than average dick. You know I can't lie about anything."

"I've seen plenty of dicks and know mine is small."

"Where are you seeing all these dicks? Porn? Locker rooms?"

"Both!" he snapped.

"Well, stop watching porn. It's unhealthy and unrealistic. Most men don't have dicks like that. Your dick is perfect."

I changed the subject and asked if it was ok if I turned off the lights. I didn't want to have to get back up to turn them off if things started to heat up.

"No, I want to see you. If I don't see you, it could be anyone under there. I want to see while I fuck you."

As Billy sat on the edge of the bed, I moved in and stood between his legs. We kissed and he slid his hands under my dress. He moved my panties to the side and started fingering me.

Despite the fact that I was previously not aroused by our conversation, his now forward behavior aroused me instantly.

I unbuttoned his shirt and removed it so I could see him in just his jeans, boots, and belt. People always talk about how visual men are. I can honestly say that women in their forties may be just as visual as men.

I wanted that snapshot of cowboy Billy—shirtless on my bed. After a few minutes of making out, he leaned back and propped himself up on his elbows.

"I can't get a hard on. I'm twenty-six years old and my dick won't get hard. Not even when I'm sober."

Billy was a very reserved man and shared very little when it came to his thoughts and feelings. I was shocked that he felt comfortable enough to tell me about his erectile dysfunction issues.

"You're drunk right now. That's normal."

"No, you don't understand. I can't get an erection, even when I'm sober. I don't know what's wrong with me."

I sat beside him on the bed. "Well for starters, you put up a wall between yourself and the women you're sleeping with. That wall may be there to stop you from getting too attached or developing feelings, but it also stops you from having any feelings in general." I ran my hand through his hair. He leaned into the touch. "Maybe casual sex isn't for you. I'm guessing you've had your heart broken before and don't want to go through that pain again?"

"Once."

"Well, you've gotta start letting yourself feel when you're having sex. It's an emotional block that you've got to fix."

"Yeah, my friend said the same thing."

I went to my medicine cabinet and grabbed a small pill box. I offered Billy a Viagra that I had been saving for a while. A friend had given it to me to help when I'd been sleeping with Robert. I never had a chance to use it with him.

"Fuck yeah," Billy said. "I want to try it."

"Ok. Do you want to try a half or a whole?"

"Give me a whole pill. I want to fuck the shit out of you tonight."

I laughed and gave Billy the Viagra. He took it.

"So, why do you have a Viagra anyway?"

I laughed.

"That's a great question. A while back I was sleeping with a man who had erectile dysfunction. My friend gave it to me so I could see if he'd be willing to try it. The problem corrected itself, so it was never used—"

Billy interrupted and said, "Are we going to talk about my dick all night or are we going to fuck?"

I cracked up and said, "Let's fuck!"

Billy was different from beginning to end. His kissing lacked passion. We were going through the usual motions, but the emotional connection I originally had with him was gone.

He had closed himself in and locked all the doors. I told him I wanted him to make love to me the way he did the first time we had sex. I couldn't remember the last time a man had made love to me. Billy was always good at listening and doing whatever I asked. He'd made himself vulnerable with me that night and I thought maybe we could break through some of his walls.

After just a few minutes of making out and touching, it became apparent that Billy had forgotten how to make love to a woman. He was so busy fucking women that he lost the very thing about himself that set him apart from the rest—his passion and emotion. I wanted so badly to tell him, but Billy didn't always appreciate unsolicited advice, so I kept my thoughts to myself.

Billy was lying on his back. I inched my way down between his legs, grabbed his dick, and started giving him head.

"Flip your body around and let me taste that pussy."

I did as Billy asked and was in ecstasy as Billy pleased me orally. The more aroused Billy got me, the more effort I put into giving him head.

After both of us became so aroused that we were on the verge of cumming, we switched positions to make it last longer.

Billy was most turned on by face to face sex, so we moved into missionary position. While Billy fucked me, I told him that his dick felt fucking amazing. It did or I wouldn't have said it. Plus, I figured he could use all the positive encouragement I could give him that night.

We changed positions again. I turned to my side while he remained on his knees. He slid one of my legs up onto his shoulder without missing a beat.

"I want to make you cum. How do you want it?"

"Let me lie on my back. Straddle me with your legs."

Billy did as I instructed and drove his dick (which was rock hard from the Viagra) into me. I told him that I like it slow and deep. This time, he did just as I asked and made me cum quicker than most men.

I scratched down Billy's back then grabbed his ass hard. Billy could tell by my physical reaction that he was driving me wild.

"You like that? Does that turn you on?"

"Fuck yeah I like that. You're going to make me cum."

"Cum for me then."

At that, my body exploded, I orgasmed as Billy continued to thrust himself into me.

After I came, Billy rolled over so that he was lying next to me with his body touching mine.

"It's your turn. How do you want me?" I asked.

He mumbled something inaudible. His breathing heavy. Billy was passing out without finishing. I heard his breathing grow heavier. I removed his condom and went into the bathroom.

As I sat on the toilet, I could see Billy sleeping on the bed partially curled up into a loose ball.

For the first time, I didn't see Billy as the strong masculine man from before. I saw him as a broken man who lacked self-esteem and confidence. I looked at Billy and felt sadness for him.

The way I felt about Billy changed in that moment. From the first time I'd hung out with him, I had always had a little crush. Now, my crush had dissipated and what was left were feelings of wanting to help him. I saw him now as a flawed human being rather than the fantasy I'd built him up to be. As I sat looking at him, I hoped that he would be open to fixing himself. But from my experience, very few men were—especially at his age.

I returned to bed. Billy was nearly asleep. He cuddled up to me as soon as I laid down next to him.

At 5:15, we both woke up. Billy was significantly different in the morning.

He rolled over and cuddled up to me like the first night we met. His face was buried in my neck. I could feel his breath in my hair. Every inch of our bodies was touching.

I could feel and see that highly emotional side of Billy return. The side of him I saw on our first night together. The side he had tried so hard to repress. After a few minutes of cuddling, I got up to use the restroom and brush my teeth. I found a new toothbrush for him so he could brush his teeth as well.

I don't know if it was morning wood or the aftermath of the Viagra, but Billy was hard as a rock when he returned to bed from washing up. I anticipated more foreplay to get things going, but Billy crawled on top of me and slid his dick right inside me.

Billy finally got his wish and fucked the shit out of me that morning. My focus was on him to cum since he hadn't before. I wanted to be sure he left satisfied. Billy fucked me in missionary, then from behind. He lifted me up and sat me on his lap then buried his face in my breasts and began fucking me once again.

I knew he really liked me on my side with my leg up over his shoulder, so I moved into that position. He came fast, pulling out, tugging off the condom, and exploding all over me. Not all men shoot cum out like a rocket but Billy did. He was kneeling between my legs and managed to shoot cum onto my face and hair as well as all the way down my chest and belly.

"Holy shit! How long have you been saving that load?"

"Since the last time I fucked you."

I laughed out loud. "I doubt that."

I cleaned up and used the restroom. Billy remained in bed falling asleep once again. I laid down on his chest and put my leg up onto his. He had one arm stretched out onto the bed while the other was resting on his chest.

"Touch me."

At my request, Billy wrapped his arm around me and rested his hand on mine. One thing I have always tried to teach men is that a man's hands should never leave a woman's body. It isn't every night you have a woman lying in

208

bed next to you, so you should treat it as a gift. Why wouldn't a man want to feel a woman's body while lying with her?

Billy fell back asleep.

Five minutes before we needed to be up, I woke him and asked him to cuddle me for the last few minutes. Billy immediately rolled over and cuddled up for not only the last five minutes, but an additional five. We got up at 6:20 am, so that I could drive him back. He had another event to compete in and needed to be at his hotel early.

"Do you want to take your toothbrush with you?" I asked.

"Hold onto it."

"I'm going to throw it out if you don't want it."

"That's rude!"

I arched an eyebrow. "How would you respond if a woman asked you to hold onto a toothbrush for her at your house?"

"I'd hold onto it for her. "

"Ok, well if you really want me to hold onto your toothbrush, I will."

I slipped the toothbrush into a cup containing my makeup brushes and other random things. (Funny how no string attached sex led to Billy's toothbrush residing in my bathroom.)

As much as we finally connected that morning, Billy, in his typical style, started pushing me away as I drove him back to Castlerock.

"I can't believe I spent forty dollars last night on an Uber to your house. Do you have other cougar friends I can fuck?

I knew what Billy was doing and it was hurtful. Rather than get angry, I answered his questions.

"None of my other friends sleep with younger men. I'm the only one. So, sorry but no, I don't have other friends you can sleep with. And I'm sorry you regret spending forty dollars to spend the night with me."

"That's ok. I know plenty of other older women who do."

Again, my tone was not angry but matter of fact.

"Well, I guess you can reach out to them the next time you're looking for a good fuck."

"Will do," he said staring out the window.

He used all of his tricks and none of them worked. I saw right through his defense mechanisms and didn't take the bait. One thing I did do was reprimand him for complaining about the money he had spent to come and see me.

"Was last night really not worth the forty dollars that you spent to come and see me? You make tons of money and do nothing but work. I wasn't worth forty dollars?"

"I was just kidding. Don't go getting crazy on me."

I swiped a hand down my face. "6:30 is too early in the morning to joke about that, especially after you just spent the night with me."

I wonder if Billy was even aware of the things that he did to push me away. Despite the fact that it was a huge turn off, I didn't let it bother me. Now I knew what he was doing. I just felt sad for him and his inability to deal with his feelings.

Sometimes I asked myself why I wasted my time with someone like Billy. All of his actions truly pointed to him being a dick and unable to process emotions. Not to mention, his inability to communicate them. I guess I could see through all of that. I also had a bit of an addiction to helping people. As you may have already noticed, I like feeling needed.

I knew I couldn't really help or fix everyone; it was something only they could do for themselves, but I also believe that everyone crosses our path for a reason.

When I thought of Billy's brokenness, it reminded me of the times in my life when I had felt truly broken. All of those occasions were the result of a failed relationship with a man and my inability to process the overwhelming emotions which go hand in hand with a breakup.

Billy had mentioned a woman who he loved. Someone who *once* broke his heart.

I wondered if this was the reason for his brokenness. I started thinking about the parallels between Billy and me.

Both of us were very successful, strong, and confident in all areas of our lives, except when it came to the opposite sex. We'd both mastered our jobs and other hobbies well. Both of us had experienced brokenness as a result of heartache. I worked hard to overcome my brokenness and to learn to process emotions. I hoped Billy would one day, too.

A week later, I caved and initiated contact with Billy. I texted him saying, I'VE THOUGHT ABOUT FUCKING YOU EVERY SINGLE DAY THIS WEEK.

After two days, he never replied. I unmatched with him on Bumble, deleted him from my phone, and threw out his toothbrush.

Just because I could understand Billy's brokenness didn't mean I would put up with being treated like a disposable fuck. I was finally learning to stand up for myself when it came to men and how I handled Billy was no different.

A month later I had an epiphany that softened my heart towards him. I believed I was special to Billy, just as he was to me, which is why he seemed to swing from being affectionate to a grade A dick when we spent time together. When he was a dick to me, I truly believed it was because he didn't know what else to do after being so vulnerable in front of me. Claudia was right. Billy couldn't handle that type of intimacy. He didn't know what to do or say. He didn't know how to reply to my texts. I kept thinking about Billy for a couple days after that.

Then one night when I had smoked some fireball weed, I messaged Billy on his public Instagram account: I MISS YOU HOT STUFF. I WISH YOU WEREN'T SUCH A DICK.

Billy replied the next morning. This was out of character. He typically ignored my messages completely or replied days later.

BILLY: I MISS YOU TOO.

My heart was warmed by reading Billy's message.

Whatever it was about Billy, he had that *it* factor. He was the only man I had slept with since 24 who had it. I had a hard time getting Billy out of my mind. Thank God he was a dick or I'd have probably developed feelings for him.

I thought it was funny how Billy completely ignored the dick comment. Billy knew what he was. I wasn't the first woman to tell him so.

I had him figured out. Insecure and really in need of someone to talk to. He was gun shy. He'd been burned before and was too afraid to get hurt again so he built walls and reinforced them with insensitive and hurtful comments.

I hoped he'd figure it out in time and have the strength to fix himself or else picking up random women in bars would likely be how he'd spend the rest of his life.

Now that he was deleted from my phone, I intended to release Billy from my mind—for good this time.

Chapter 17: It's Raining Men

I might have had a new lease on life, but that didn't mean things always went according to plan. Some of my encounters were far from satisfying, but they did offer entertainment value for my friends. Case in point: Sebastian and the shopping center boner.

Sebastian and I got to know each other through text conversations. I had let it slip to him that I had a fantasy of being picked up at a bar since it's something that has never happened to me before.

Sebastian: LET'S ACT OUT YOUR BAR FANTASY.

Me: I'M NOT SURE HOW WELL I'LL DO AT PRETENDING BUT LET'S GO FOR IT.

Sebastian lived in Longmont, a long drive from Colorado Springs. He was twenty-eight and very eager to help me out with my fantasy, so I figured why not let him?

We agreed to meet at a bar within walking distance of my house. That way I could smoke a little weed and loosen up a bit before heading over. I got there before he did, so I sat at the bar.

I ordered water. I'm not much for soda—so alas, there aren't many options for me at a bar.

I saw Sebastian as soon as he walked in. I was nervous. The thing was, as hot as the idea of playing out a fantasy was, I was horrible at acting. The second I saw him, I knew I couldn't do it.

He walked up to the bar and ordered a drink then looked over at me and smiled. I laughed a little when I saw him. It was hilarious, him pretending to not know who I was. He came over to me.

"Hi, how are you doing?" I asked awkwardly. "How was your drive?"

He leaned in and whispered, "You're totally breaking character."

I laughed.

"I know. I'm sorry. I'm really bad at acting. I told you that I couldn't do it. I need it to happen naturally, organically. Sorry."

"It's fine but I was really trying."

"I know you were. I appreciate your effort and taking the time to drive so far."

"It's not a problem at all. You're beautiful by the way. Way better in person than in your pictures."

I smiled shyly. "Thanks."

Sebastian was a handsome man. He was still dressed in slacks and a dress shirt for work. He looked nice. We chatted at the bar for a little while. I was much more comfortable in my own house and I wanted to get going.

"Once you finish your drink, do you want to head back to my house?"

"Yes. Let me just drink it up."

He guzzled his drink and I hopped off the bar stool. I looked over at Sebastian and froze.

He had a raging erection. Causing the front of his Dockers to bulge out.

I whispered, "Oh my God, are you going to take care of that?" I was completely mortified.

"Nope."

What did he mean, *nope*? I started walking in front of him. Maybe in a few seconds, he'd calm himself down.

I looked back.

He was walking behind me. His raging boner sticking out. Oh my God, how quickly can I get out of this bar? I could feel my cheeks flaming with embarrassment.

Once we got outside there was the bouncer and some other patrons standing around smoking. I hurried out as quickly as I could. I didn't want them to know I was with him or that the huge pole in the front of his pants was meant for me. Dear God.

"Hey, wait up."

Was he serious?

"You're embarrassing me!" I hissed back at him. "I live around here. I come to this shopping center all the time. I might see people that I know. You have to fix that fucking thing."

Sebastian laughed and said, "What do you want me to do?"

"I'm not a man. I don't have a dick. Maybe tuck it in your waistband?"

Sebastian rearranged himself a little. When I saw that his dick was no longer protruding, I slowed down and let him catch up to me.

"Geez. You turn me on."

"Well that's nice and all, but I don't need everyone in the bar or out on the street seeing your hard on."

Sebastian laughed. Apparently, he thought all this was funny; meanwhile, I was dying inside. His little display was a major turn off and got him absolutely nowhere with me.

Once out of earshot of the bouncer, I informed him that I'd be going home… alone.

***

Then there was Sam. Oh, *Sam*. Sigh.

Sam was also twenty-eight. He was cute with dark features just the way I like. He had a good career as an engineer. All the confidence in the world to boot. He made consistent eye contact and as soon as we got back to my place, his hands were on me within a few minutes of sitting down.

Ding ding ding!

Finally, a man who knew how to take control.

But then the other shoe dropped. A few minutes later, Sam moved on to kissing.

He was a horrible kisser.

Robotic and stiff. His movements didn't feel fluid or full of feeling. Kissing him felt passionless. It was just awful.

But he was so cute! Surely, I could still salvage the night.

Just without any more kissing. It was seriously turning me off. I started sucking on his ear lobes and kissing down his neck.

I lifted his shirt over his head. He attempted to kiss me again, so I pecked his lips then began kissing down his chest. If there was one thing that could distract any man...

I kissed all the way down to his pants then looked up at him as I grabbed his dick through his pants. I wanted to see the look on his face when I grabbed him for the first time. He didn't disappoint.

He loved it. The look of ecstasy on his face and the way he threw his head back was all I needed to know. Now we were back on track. I started rubbing his dick firmly over his jeans. I traced the feel of him and quickly realized—whoa, it kept going down the side of his leg.

He was seriously packing. His nerdy engineer vibe had given me the wrong impression.

Don't ever judge a book by its cover, Lacie, I told myself. He was definitely a two-fister.

Eventually we made our way back to the bedroom. We were both eager by this point.

After the condom was on, I lay on my back next to Sam. He rose up on top of me and teased me with his huge dick. He rubbed it around between my legs, spreading my wetness all over it.

"I want to feel you inside me," I said. "Please fuck me."

Sam didn't even reply. He exhaled suddenly and slid himself into me.

"Oh my God!" I moaned. "I knew you were going to feel fucking amazing."

"You are so wet. I can't believe it."

Sam was a surprisingly great lover. My kissing rule was definitely wrong about him. I knew his dick would feel great as soon as I saw it, but I was a little worried our sex would be lackluster. Luckily for me, that wasn't the case. Here was one grand exception!

Sam fucked me in missionary. He sat back onto his knees, while I put both legs onto his shoulders. He loved this position. It allowed him to grab onto both of my breasts. Sam felt great and I was quickly ready to cum.

"I want to cum," I said. "Can you put your legs over mine?"

Sam moved his body just the way I told him to. He was straddling me while my legs were closed. His dick felt incredible. He made me cum faster than most men. That dick. Oh my God, that dick!

I screamed, "Oh my God!" as I came, scratching the shit out of Sam's back. He was very turned on by it. He squirmed with pleasure and kept repeating the phrase, "Oh my God. Oh my God." I could tell he was using every ounce of will-power to not cum. He had stopped kissing me and was trying his best to not stimulate himself any more than he was already doing.

When I was done, Sam turned me over onto my hands and knees. I felt a little weak and tired. I wanted to just lie there basking in the glory of my orgasm but knew that it wouldn't be fair.

Sam slid in from behind and boy did he feel bigger than ever. Rather than being on all fours, I leaned up to grab my headboard with both hands. I was kneeling upright. Sam held onto my hips with both hands and fucked me until he came.

To date, Sam was the loudest man I have ever heard cum, *ever*.

It's funny how men love a woman to be loud. I guess it strokes their ego—they're making their woman scream in ecstasy. I didn't really feel the same way about Sam screaming out. I was on the verge of telling him to be quiet. I was genuinely fearful the neighbors would hear. A man screaming like that just wasn't normal. At least to me.

After he let the world know he had just orgasmed, Sam headed to the bathroom to remove the condom and clean up. He left the door open and I could see his head shaking back and forth. Another one of those "Oh my God" moments that he didn't verbalize out loud? Most likely.

He was a cuddler. A cherry on top of a massive sundae. Well—okay, I got the feeling that while he didn't hate cuddling and may have been doing it for me; but after past experience, I wasn't complaining.

It felt so nice to feel his body wrapped around mine. He was warm and comforting. Knowing he was doing it just to please me made it all the more special.

When he finally got ready to go, he paused by the door and said, "I'd like to see you again."

"Sounds good." And it did. The sex had been incredible. "Just let me know when. I'm free Mondays, Tuesdays, and every other weekend."

"Ok. I will text you. Thanks for a great time."

"Thank *you*!"

Sam hugged me and then, right before he left out the door, he paused to lean down and give me a sloppy wet kiss. It was awful.

He was smiling as he left, but I was hiding a grimace.

Oh God, how had I forgotten? The kissing! I could not handle another night of Sam kissing me like that. Something had to be done about it!

If I was going to continue hanging out with this man, he had to give me good reason to—or at least work on the kissing. A great dick was just not enough. Kissing is huge in foreplay. I hadn't even realized how much until that night. It's probably the most important thing. I tried to imagine sex without kissing, it was like swimming without water.

Right then and there, I decided that I was going to try and help Sam become a better kisser. Hopefully he'd be open to it.

If not, there were other bees on Bumble.

Sam texted me the next morning. Confirmation that I'd actually see him again.

Sam: I HAD A GREAT TIME LAST NIGHT.

Me: ME TOO! THANK YOU FOR TELLING ME.

Sam: OF COURSE. I'LL BE IN NEW MEXICO THIS WEEKEND BUT WILL BE HOME SUNDAY. ARE YOU INTERESTED IN HANGING OUT AGAIN, THIS MONDAY OR TUESDAY WHEN YOU DON'T HAVE YOUR DAUGHTER?

(I fucking loved a man who could remember things that I had told him. He was a planner. Sam was actually listening

219

when we were getting to know each other. What a major turn on. Bonus points for Sam!)

Me: ABSOLUTELY! I'D LOVE TO HANG OUT AGAIN. JUST MESSAGE ME WHEN YOU'RE BACK IN TOWN.

Sam: OK. HAVE A GREAT WEEKEND.

Me: YOU TOO AND HAVE A GREAT TRIP TO NEW MEXICO.

I pondered whether Sam would be a man who liked to text every couple of days. He wasn't. I didn't hear from Sam again until Sunday night. Again, I was proud of myself for not reaching out to him. I know it may sound cheesy, but it was truly a challenge for me.

Sam: HEY, HOW ARE YOU?

Me: HI! I'M GREAT. HOW WAS YOUR TRIP?

Sam: IT WAS REALLY FUN. ARE YOU FREE THIS MONDAY OR TUESDAY?

Me: YES. EITHER DAY WORKS FOR ME.

Sam: OK. HOW ABOUT TOMORROW THEN? ABOUT 8?

Me: PERFECT. PLEASE TEXT ME WHEN YOU'RE ON YOUR WAY.

Sam: OK.

I pondered again after texting with him. Was he the kind of guy who knew that foreplay begins first thing in the morning?

Yes, he did!

The next morning Sam texted me at around ten.

Sam: I'M LOOKING FORWARD TO SEEING YOU AGAIN.

Me: I CAN'T WAIT TO SEE YOU TOO.

Sam: LAST WEEK WAS AMAZING. I CAN'T WAIT FOR MORE.

Me: SAME HERE. IS IT 8 YET?

Sam: I KNOW, RIGHT? HAVE A GREAT DAY AT WORK!

Me: YOU TOO!

It was nice to start the day and I had a perma-smile on my face. It felt good to know that Sam was thinking about me. It also got me thinking about having sex with him. I was anxious to see him. Sam may have been a shitty kisser, but he was smart enough to know that foreplay begins long before he's in the presence of a woman.

Around 4 pm, Sam texted again.

Sam: I'VE BEEN THINKING ABOUT TAKING YOU FROM BEHIND ALL DAY. I HAVE A HARD ON AT WORK.

Me: OMG! THAT IS SO FUCKING HOT. I GOT IMMEDIATELY WET WHEN I READ YOUR TEXT. HOLY SHIT! I WANT YOU BADLY.

Sam: TRUST ME, THE FEELING IS MUTUAL.

ME: SAM, YOU'VE MADE ME BLUSH.

Boy, Sam sure knew how to get a woman going. He probably googled it or did research on it—or something. Was it bad that I was doubtful that it came naturally to him?

Around 7:30 pm, Sam texted that he was on his way.

Me: OK. SEE YOU SOON!

Sam arrived at my door a little before 8. He was coming from Denver and smart enough to leave after the commuter traffic died down.

When he arrived, I opened the door and he stepped inside.

"Hey Sam, come in, I was just—"

He grabbed me immediately and cut me off with a kiss. Okay, the boldness was definitely hot, but I didn't know whether to finish my sentence or open my mouth for his tongue. (Answer: Open my mouth for his tongue. Honestly, who cares what I was about to say anyway?)

My feet weren't firmly planted, I had to catch myself a little. It definitely didn't go as smoothly as it could have, but it was a great way to start our evening together, nonetheless.

Sam had no interest in standing in my living room making out. Almost immediately, he started walking me backward towards my bedroom. Never stopping our kiss.

He was so in command. A trigger that turned me on big time. So much so that it took until he'd gotten me to my bedroom and backed me up against the side of the bed before I realized just how bad the kissing still was. Sam was a very wet messy kisser. My lips and the area surrounding them were wet. A couple times he came at me so hard our teeth clanked. Sam and I did not kiss the same, at all.

Why?!? He was so good at everything else. The whole situation was so hot. How he'd come barging in—so in control. How he'd kept up regular text communication. How he was currently pulling my tank top over my head and dropping it onto the end of the bed.

Except for the fact that he continued kissing me the whole time.

I grabbed his shirt and pulled it off, dropping it onto the floor. Sam ran his hands all over my body.

I interrupted him.

"Hey, can we try something?" I asked.

"Sure."

"I want you to copy me exactly as I kiss you. If I kiss softly, you kiss softly. If I give more tongue, you give more tongue. Got it?"

"Yeah, but why?"

Oh my God, he was completely serious. He had no clue.

Now, dear reader, here is how to handle the delicate male ego… tread carefully in practice.

I said, "Kissing is super important to me and I don't feel like we kiss the same. I want to see if we can create better chemistry. Sorry, but is that ok?"

Sam laughed and said, "Sure, whatever you want." I could tell he still didn't get it.

I started kissing Sam slowly. He might've tried but my gut said no. He was still kissing me exactly the same. His lips hard against mine rather than soft and fluid.

I tried to change things up a bit to see if he would change too. I started giving him more tongue, kissing him firmly like I was horny as fuck for him. Sam continued kissing the same way he always did, wet, messy, and way too hard.

What the fuck? I stopped kissing him.

"Do exactly what I do." I tried to keep the exasperation out of my voice. "Copy me."

"I am," he said blankly.

I started kissing him again. This whole thing probably sucked from his perspective. He clearly couldn't or wouldn't change how he kissed—so fuck it. I was done trying.

I grabbed his hips and moved him to a sitting position on the bed. I stood in front of him and continued kissing him, pushing on his chest.

"Sit up with your back against the headboard."

Sam did exactly as I asked. I crawled towards him and started kissing his inner thighs. Sam moaned loudly as soon as my lips touched his skin. I'd forgotten how loud he was and how over the top it felt.

What the fuck was I doing?

Why was I wasting time with a subpar lover whose mannerisms turned me off? I've had men who didn't need me to teach them a damn thing!

I needed to be putting my time and effort into men who knocked my socks off. Men who made my head spin.

Not men who couldn't even kiss or know how to hide their boners in public. I needed a change.

Chapter 18: One Step At A Time

Just when I was long overdue for a break from dating twenty-something-year-old men, I spent a weekend night with Emily. She was a long-time friend of Chloe's and we connected through her.

Emily was much younger than Chloe and me. She was thirty to be exact and had just gotten married. She was still glowing from her wedding as it had just taken place only a few weeks prior to our get together.

Emily lived in Evergreen and her main hobby was riding horses. She was very sweet, down to earth, and sharp as a tack. Emily and I were friends, but we only hung out when Chloe was involved. However, on this weekend, Emily had an early flight to catch and asked to stay at my house so it would be a shorter drive to the airport. I was happy to oblige.

At this point in my life, my friends (and probably some of their other friends) knew very well the crazy life I was living. Needless to say, I wasn't surprised when Emily asked about my sexcapades.

"So Lacie, Chloe tells me that you're having a lot of fun in your free time."

I laughed knowing exactly what Emily was referring to.

"Yes, you could say that." I smiled broadly at her.

Emily laughed.

"I don't know how you have the confidence to sleep with hot younger men. I'm in awe how you have the self-assurance to put yourself out there."

"Well, there were definitely times when I had to fake it. I had to pull myself out of the gutter after my divorce; but for the most part, I'm loving my life and having a ton of fun."

"Yeah... I have a very low sex drive. I feel kind of bad for my husband. Once we start getting it on, I get aroused but I have no desire to initiate. I wish he'd do more to get me in the mood."

I wasn't surprised at all by what Emily was telling me. I'd encountered lots of friends who felt the same. I've met many women who appear to have low sex drives. Honestly, I try hard to relate but I really can't. My sex drive had always been on the higher end, especially when I'm actively dating a man. During this year of my sexcapades, my sex drive was nearly insatiable.

I felt happy that Emily was comfortable confiding in me and I wanted to help her. I knew I could give her all the advice in the world, but she had to be the one to act in order to change her situation.

"Why do you think your sex drive is so low?"

"I was raised my whole life to be wholesome and innocent—to save myself for marriage. When I finally had sex with a boyfriend after high school, I felt so guilty and ashamed. I always associated sexual gratification with those negative feelings. Not only that, but my boyfriend was only in it for himself and made no effort to please me. So, sex always became an act of men taking and never giving. I had no real motivation to have sex; because from my experience, there was nothing in it for me."

"Wow! I totally get that. Now that you're married though, you can make it what you want it to be. Surprise your husband by wearing only an apron when he gets home one night or wear some lingerie to bed."

225

"But that's just it Lacie, I don't have the confidence to make it what I want. I don't feel comfortable even wanting it. I wish I had the confidence you have."

It was surprising to me that Emily didn't feel confident dressing up for her husband. She was beautiful with a great figure and huge natural breasts. I could totally see her looking great in something sexy. I could see the sexy in her, but Emily couldn't see it in herself.

I was accustomed to my friends coming to me for advice, but I wasn't sure how I could help Emily find her sexy. I could tell her lots of sexual acts that would blow her husband's mind or how to dress up for him, but I knew Emily would have to find her sexiness and self-confidence on her own.

So, I focused on offering her some strategies I had learned with younger men during the last year.

"Sometimes, I have trouble getting into the mood, too. When that happens, I find more foreplay helps. Men want to jump into having sex too quickly for my liking. I NEED good foreplay—well unless I happen to be off the charts horny."

"Yes, I need that too. I also wish my husband would do more to get me into the mood."

"Yeah, but how about getting yourself into the mood? Or, you can tell him the things you wish he would do. Men aren't mind readers. They just want to know how to please us. I'll bet your husband has no idea what you're needing. You need to tell him!"

"I know you're right, I just don't see myself taking charge and making the first move. I know my husband would love it though."

"He absolutely *would* love it. The only way to make changes in your sex life is to just do it. You have to try to make changes or your sex life will stay at status quo. It sounds to me like you're not one hundred percent happy with the way things are right now."

"Yeah, I know you're right."

I could tell Emily needed to take baby steps. I'd grown accustomed in my life to acknowledging that not everyone is like me. I must've heard my mom say it a million times, yet it took until I was in my mid-forties to fully embrace that concept. I'm a woman who charges full speed ahead, that is my natural way to think, but now I finally realize not all people tackle life the same way.

So, I opted to suggest a few baby steps for Emily to ease herself into finding her sexy.

"When do you feel the most beautiful? What specific items or actions are adding to this feeling?"

"I don't like talking about things like this."

I laughed out loud. Duh!

"I know. My goal is to help you change that."

"Fine—I feel most beautiful when my heels make me taller, my bra straps are for once NOT showing, I'm wearing a top that is flattering to my figure, and my hair is up in a bun." She said this all in a rush of words like she was confessing to a crime.

"Emily, that's great! I'm so happy you can articulate what makes you feel beautiful. I think it's important to know, especially as a woman. Some days women can be very hormonal and feel down in the dumps, physically and mentally. I think it's important for us to know what will give us a boost on days like those." She nodded, so I continued, "I also think it's imperative to look at yourself in the mirror on the days you are feeling your most beautiful and tell yourself—'I am beautiful'— I know it seems awkward and downright weird to talk to yourself like this, but changing that internal negative voice is the most important change you can make right now."

"Yeah, I can see that too."

"Also, I think it would be great for you to plan a surprise date night for you and your husband, where you can try to use some of these things to have a positive sexual experience." She frowned a little at this. "For example, tell him you're planning a date so he knows it's coming. Plan for something that would turn you on. Maybe dancing or a bonfire at the beach. Whatever you know will feel romantic and give you those warm fuzzies in all the right places."

"Ok, I can try that but what else? I feel like you're expecting more than that."

I laughed out loud.

"You're damn right I am! Wear your heels, get a strapless bra. I have triple D's so I feel your pain, but there are great high-quality bras out there. I have one that works great so I know you can find one too. Put your hair up in a high bun and do what it takes to feel sexy and beautiful. Plan a date that will do it for you and focus on making physical contact with your husband. It doesn't have to be sexual. I'm talking about holding hands, put your arm around his waist, any way that you would naturally touch him in an affectionate manner. Just connect."

"Ok, I can do all of these things." she said with cautious excitement.

"Great! I can't wait to hear how it goes. I'm not expecting you to just grab his dick, I'm asking for you to plan a night where you can feel sexy and beautiful with him."

Little did she know, I'd be expecting her to grab his dick in the relatively near future. Ha!

I wanted so badly to help Emily. I knew she would need to move slow regarding my advice. I was going to have to try my best to be patient. I say try because I know damn well that patience is one of those virtues most challenging for me to grasp.

Emily needed to work on small changes to increase her self-confidence, before I could give her advice pertaining to sex. I hoped and prayed that she'd reject the pattern of sexual repression she'd fallen into. She needed to step up and wholeheartedly take a risk and ask specifically for what she wanted.

I knew she'd be infinitely happier if she did.

Forever is a very long time to have the same boring, monotonous, and infrequent sex.

I believed in Emily. I knew firsthand the power and strength I've felt when others believed in me. I felt invincible and I wanted Emily to feel the same sense of empowerment.

Thinking back on this conversation with Emily, I had a little bit of an epiphany. *Was this another unexpected outcome from my sexcapades? Could I actually help other women find their sexy and learn to ask for what they wanted, too?*

It struck me how natural it felt to take on this mentor role with Emily. Her personality was totally different than mine—with the exception of her strength of character and desire to improve her relationships. I had to take what I knew were the answers to improve her sex life and put them into her language.

Don't get me wrong, I have no desire to be a sex therapist. What I want to do is change the way women hold themselves back from getting what they want just because that is all they have seen or been taught.

I had clearly taken the bull by the horns on this issue and felt the benefits in the best way possible. Maybe… just maybe I could help other women do the same. Perhaps even help them avoid some of the pitfalls that I fell into.

Either way, this period of my life was really starting to make sense to me.

Chapter 19: Hit The Road Jack

Okay, so there was no way I was sleeping with this guy. Ray.

The conversation had been stilted since we met at the coffee shop. I hoped that once we got back to my condo, he'd finally loosen up.

No such luck.

Ray kept droning on about his ex-girlfriend. Specifically, how crazy she was. As he continued talking, I was able to witness more of his mannerisms. He didn't give off a masculine vibe. I was becoming less and less interested in Ray with every word that came out of his mouth.

"My ex won't leave me alone. If I don't answer her texts, she goes crazy and starts calling."

"That sucks." I replied with a complete lack of interest.

I really didn't know how to respond to Ray. Our conversation about his ex was boring me.

To make matters worse, I couldn't stop glancing down at his hands. They were super small. Possibly the same size as mine or even *smaller*.

Looking at his short stature, small hands, and yep—small feet, his boring personality and lack of masculine energy all lead to one thing: I was not interested in Ray.

Sorry my friend. Please don't judge me. I was going through the horniest time in my life. I was looking for masculine with a side of hotness and Ray wasn't fitting the bill.

Yet, there he sat in my living room.

Dear God, how was I going to get this man out of my house? There was no way that I'd be able to bring myself to sleep with him. Why hadn't I figured this all out at the coffee shop?

Uh, probably because you were feeling horny as fuck tonight!

Still, this guy wasn't going to do it for me. Maybe I could say that I forgot about an early morning appointment or I could pretend to get an emergency text. Say that my phone was on silent—

But right then, he leaned over.

"You're so beautiful," he said as he grabbed my face with both hands and started kissing me.

What's a girl to do? I kissed him back. Like I said, I was *really* horny that night. And in spite of everything, Ray was a good kisser. So, I tried my best to close my eyes and be in the moment. Just forget about all of those things that had turned me off about him.

He moved on top of me and dry humped me on the couch, occasionally grinding his erection into me.

Okay, okay, I was starting to get into this. This was getting my gears revving.

Ray started sucking my earlobe and that was sort of nice… then he stuck his tongue in—all the way into my ear.

WHAT? Just… *what?*

Ick, ick! Get your tongue out of my ear, get your tongue out of my ear!

Luckily Ray stopped and asked if he could use the restroom.

"Sure," I said, half in relief. "It's right down the hallway. I'll be on the porch smoking a joint if you need anything."

I knew there was no way that I could do anything more with Ray unless I had a little help from Mary Jane.

I went out onto the patio, grabbed the joint a friend had left for me, and lit it up. I took three hits and relaxed into my patio chair. The cool crisp evening air hit me, I could see the seasons changing before my eyes. It felt nice to sit outside. At that moment, I wished I was alone, just smoking weed and relaxing.

Unfortunately, Ray was still in my house and he was ready to go.

I put everything away and went back inside. Ray was on his phone. He had already texted someone three times that night which had irked me. I have so much respect for men (at any age) who can't put their phones down when they spend time with me. When you're with someone, they should be your priority. Ray clearly didn't know what a turn off it was. His texting—at this point in the night, was not getting him anywhere with me.

Ray was attending to his phone when I came in. I turned off all the lights and sat next to him. I already knew I was going to be way more successful with whatever was about to happen, now that I was high and the lights were off.

I sat next to Ray and he was on me immediately, his hands grabbing my breasts and his tongue sticking itself into my mouth. I started kissing him again and tried to forget that I wasn't sexually aroused or attracted to him.

Ray unzipped my sweatshirt and removed my tank top. He played with my breasts for a few minutes and sucked my nipples. He sucked so hard that twice I was startled and let out an 'Ow!' loudly.

Seriously, what was with this guy? Had he never paid attention to what actually turned women on?

Maybe he'd never had to before, aside from his short stature, he did have a firm muscular build.

Still, there had to be some way to salvage this night. I unhooked his belt and undid his pants. Ray got up to remove his clothes. Strange. When he returned, he pushed me onto my back and got on top of me. He was wearing only underwear now. I was still wearing sweats and panties.

He kissed me and grabbed my breasts while grinding his dick between my legs.

Okay, *finally*. I was getting aroused. Being in complete darkness definitely helped with that. I focused on what I was feeling and how he was touching me rather than who I was with. I lied there just feeling him grab my breasts and getting more aroused as he grinded himself between my legs.

I grabbed Ray's dick through his underwear.

Wah, *wah, wah, wah*—as expected, his dick measured up to the size of his hands and feet.

To be honest, he was proportionate to the rest of him, so I wasn't really surprised at all. With that being said, I was still disappointed.

A woman can always hope to be pleasantly surprised. This wasn't one of those times. Because, regardless of what they say, I'd always found that size *does* matter—at least for me it does.

I rubbed his dick through his boxer briefs for a few minutes. Ray was getting very aroused and sat up on his knees to take off my sweats and panties. He dropped them on the floor. He leaned forward, wrapped his arms around my thighs, and laid down on his stomach. He was going to eat me out.

Well damn! Ten points for Ray!

Despite the fact that I give men head almost every time we have sex, often more than once, most men don't perform oral sex back. I'm not sure why. Maybe I need to ask for it more.

It has never been my favorite thing, so I just settle for rarely having it.

I reached my hand down, held back my hair, and spread myself open for him. Immediately after I exposed myself to him, Ray's face was buried between my legs.

Oh! Oh, that felt good. Soooooo damn good.

Everything I thought I knew about Ray flew out the window and before long, he had me begging him to fuck me.

Ray ignored me and continued eating me out while fingering me. He was a little too rough with his finger; I had to ask him to be gentle. If only I had a nickel for every time I had to tell a man to be gentler down there.

I was squirming and repeating, "Oh my God!" over and over again. I didn't want to cum with Ray eating me out, so I was relieved when he finally moved on top of me.

Before he could lie down, I grabbed his underwear and pulled them down. This was the first time that I was able to grab Ray's dick. I confirmed that Ray was a one fister and skinny. Almost a perfect example of a pencil dick, except a pencil had a few inches on Ray.

I worked him up and down, not needing to move my hand all that much or else his dick would fall out of my grip.

Ray moved his body on top of mine. I was still working him off to the side, so it was touching my thigh. Ray started kissing me and grabbing my breasts again. He leaned down and sucked a nipple.

"Ouch. You have to be gentle. You're too rough."

Ray didn't respond, but was considerably gentler the rest of the night.

His hand moved from my breast down to my crotch. He started fingering me once again. I was back to moaning. Oh God, I was *so* turned on. I couldn't believe the complete one-eighty this night had taken.

"I want to go get a condom. I need you to fuck me."

I was back in a flash and resumed my position on the couch.

Ray sat back on his knees. He sheathed himself and started rubbing the head of his dick onto my clit. Ray continued rubbing teasingly before he finally entered me.

I could barely think about anything else at that point. I moved my legs to Ray's shoulders as he began fucking me.

He grabbed my foot and started sucking on my toes and heels. It felt amazing—I screamed out, "Oh my God!"

Ray stopped sucking my feet. As he fucked me, he snuck a finger up my ass. I wasn't quite prepared for this, especially since he didn't use any lubrication. It was one of those *surprise* moments.

I was not a girl who was into that, but in that moment—God, Ray ramming his finger up my ass was actually a turn on. Luckily, he didn't try to move it in and out. He just left it there for a few minutes.

The thought occurred to me, maybe Ray would be a great guy to try anal with. He had a little dick that probably wouldn't feel much different than the finger he had just shoved up there—unannounced. I bet Ray probably got asked to perform anal sex frequently. It's definitely was something I wouldn't want to do with a well-hung man—that's for sure. I wasn't really contemplating asking for anal sex. It was just an observation I made in the moment.

Some doors are exit only and for me, that was one of them.

Surprisingly, Ray felt amazing, largely due to the fact that he performed so much foreplay on me. Ray was definitely a giver; but then again, he had to be. I have been with enough men who were not well-endowed and they all had one thing in common: they learned to compensate for their misgivings in other ways.

Ray was great at compensating with skill—and in the end, he had me absolutely begging to be fucked. Ray also knew not to cave the first time a woman begged for it. He made me wait as he continued to please me until I finally put my foot down.

"Let's go to my bed. I want to lie down and continue this in there."

Ray got off of me. We walked down the hall to my bedroom. He went to the bathroom again. When he came back in, I was lying on the edge of the bed with my legs dangling over it.

Ray stood between my legs. He put his hands around my thighs and pulled me to the end of the bed until my ass was on the very edge. He stepped closer, held my legs up in the air and slid his dick back inside me.

It felt great the way Ray moved me around and took charge. It was interesting how his energy changed while having sex—very take charge and masculine. When we were just chatting, he wasn't like that at all.

I felt on the verge of having an orgasm several times. Ray had me so turned on. I just needed to close my legs and I knew I'd have that orgasm. Before I could ask to close my legs, Ray grabbed me and flipped me over.

"Get on your hands and knees."

I did as he asked. I held onto the headboard as Ray slid himself inside me. He fucked me hard. His dick fell out a few times, but he just put it back in and continued fucking me. I wondered if he realized that having to reinsert his dick on occasion wasn't really normal.

Although, for him it probably was. Hmm.

"Are you close to cumming?"

He was ready to finish and had enough manners to be sure I finished first.

"I have been several times. I need to be on my back with my legs closed."

Ray returned me to a supine position and got back on top. He slid himself into me. As I got more aroused again, I asked him to put his leg over mine. I closed one leg over his. He moved his leg to the outside of mine. He fucked me in this position for a few minutes and seemed to enjoy it.

I say seemed because Ray had not made one peep the entire night. I assumed he was enjoying himself, but I had no idea because he didn't say anything. Nor did he let on that I was turning him on or that I felt good to him.

"Let me close my other leg," I gasped, my orgasm so close now. "Put your other leg over mine."

Ray moved his other leg so that my legs were closed. He was fully straddling me. I was concerned that he wasn't going to be able to fuck me in this position, that he wouldn't be long enough. I was mistaken. Ray fucked me until I was almost ready to cum. He asked again if I was close.

"Yes. You feel fucking great."

Ray started speeding up. Fucking me harder and harder. I was on the verge of blowing. I got so aroused that I finally exploded.

He exploded at exactly the same time. He felt fucking great and he gave me a huge orgasm.

I mean, *huge*.

I was so impressed at Ray's self-control. As soon as I said I was about to cum, he finally let himself go and we were able to cum at exactly the same time.

Simultaneous orgasms were hot and a huge turn on! I think I was able to have an orgasm purely because of how great it felt to cum at the same time as him.

He didn't wait long before grabbing hold of the condom, pulling out, and heading to the bathroom. I lay on the bed ready to pass out.

Ray came out of the bathroom, turned on the lights, and immediately went about putting on his clothes. He had no intention of cuddling or staying any longer. He checked his phone while I lay naked in bed then he gave me some excuse about a birthday party he had to go to.

I really didn't give a shit about what he told me. I had no desire to cuddle him and I was honestly happy he was heading out immediately. I was ready to go to sleep. Once the lights were on, I was reminded that I had almost zero attraction towards Ray.

Not my finest moment.

I walked him to the door. He hugged me. Then I opened the door to let him out.

"Drive safely," I said. "Thanks for coming over."

"Thanks for having me. Goodnight."

"Goodnight."

I closed the door and immediately called Claudia.

"Holy shit, I just had the biggest orgasm from the smallest dick. Go figure!"

Claudia laughed. "Hey—whatever gets you there."

"True enough. I should've asked to try anal. He had a perfect dick for it. Small and thin. It wouldn't have felt any different than the finger he stuck up there."

239

Claudia laughed again. She knew I was joking. "I fucking love you and your stories."

I laughed then cringed. "Yeah I'm a little embarrassed to admit I fucked this guy. I had zero attraction to him. Nothing a little weed couldn't remedy; but fuck, what did I just do?"

"You did nothing different than what drunk people do all the time at bars. They wake up the next morning, see who is in their bed, and say the exact same thing. You just rushed the process—no surprise!"

"Yeah, I guess. It just isn't something that I've really done before. Fucking a guy that I literally had to get high and turn off the lights to fuck." I felt shame creep in. "Then again his foreplay skills were *on point*." I had to give him some credit.

Claudia thought this was hysterical and started laughing again. "Who the fuck cares? You got yours and he got his. You never have to see him again. It's done."

"True. So, what's going on with Mitch?"

"I'm actually going to see him," she said. "He asked me to go down to Arizona for the weekend. His friends are having a big party and he wants me to be his date."

"Really? That sounds promising. Are you excited?"

"Yeah, I am, but… I'm a little worried that I'll be trapped with him all weekend. We've only spent one night together. What if I don't like him as much as I think I do, then I'm stuck with him for the whole weekend?"

"Are you staying at his house?" I asked, going back to my bed and flopping down on it, my phone still in hand.

"No, I was smart enough to get my own hotel room—just in case things got weird or he turns me off somehow."

"Ooh, that was smart. I can't wait to hear how it goes."

"You'll be the first person that I call. I have to get to bed. I'm falling asleep just talking now. Congratulations on your big O. Let's chat tomorrow when I am more awake."

"Ok. Goodnight."

"Goodnight."

I put the phone on my nightstand then went about my nightly routine. When I came back to bed, I was sleepy, but I also couldn't stop thinking about the sex I had earlier. Although I prefer a bigger dick, Ray really did bring it and he knew how to please a woman. He was a smart man for learning how to be a great lover, despite his er— shortcomings.

I knew I'd never see Ray again, because quite frankly I had zero desire to. I was grateful for the experience though. It helped me see that I liked receiving oral sex a lot more than I thought. Especially from a man who knew how to give it— which is rare. Most go at it like they're pounding a hamburger rather than creating a slow and sensuously arousing experience.

Ray reminded me of Darwin's survival of the fittest theory. He learned to adapt and develop the perfect skills that could get the job done.

Ray redefined the stereotype I had about smaller men—in a good way.

Chapter 20: I'm So Excited

I first met Xander on a Tuesday night. He came over on his way home from school. He was a full-time student and worker with an end goal of becoming a police officer.

Xander was really nice to look at with short dark brown hair, a clean-shaven face, and brown eyes. He had a very positive, easygoing personality. He was twenty-five, a little short, and very hard-working, driven, and ambitious. He was also very family oriented.

I checked out his Instagram pictures which were linked to his profile. The majority of his pictures were taken with family, friends, and at events for various police causes. He seemed like a great guy and I was definitely attracted.

We had communicated very little prior to meeting—due to his busy schedule.

Xander's communication style (if you can call it that) was very different from the start. He would send one message each day, either answering or responding to the previous message I'd sent. He didn't put much effort into keeping the conversation going.

I finally got tired of the minimal back and forth so I decided to message him one last time.

Xander wasn't pursuing me and it was obvious.

Me: HEY, YOU SEEM REALLY BUSY. I'M LOOKING FOR SOMEONE TO HANG OUT WITH. IF YOU'RE NOT INTERESTED IT'S FINE. I'LL WISH YOU GOOD LUCK AND UNMATCH.

One of the biggest lessons I've learned through my sexcapades was to notice when a man was pursuing me and when he wasn't. Although at this stage in my life, I had the confidence and determination to pursue men, I had learned than being pursued was also important and I'd begun to enjoy it.

Xander: I'M VERY INTERESTED. I'M JUST VERY BUSY GOING TO SCHOOL DURING THE WEEK AND WORKING FRIDAY AND SATURDAY AT THE HOSPITAL. WHEN ARE YOU FREE?

So, he was trying to put a date on the calendar which showed me he was at least legitimately interested and not just blowing smoke up my ass.

We set a date for next Tuesday.

When Tuesday rolled around, I texted him.

Me: I'M MAKING FOOD IF YOU'RE HUNGRY AND WANT TO EAT. I FELT LIKE FRIED RICE. THE ONLY PROTEIN I HAVE IS SPAM. I'VE NEVER MADE SPAM FRIED RICE AND DON'T KNOW HOW IT'LL TURN OUT. JUST TELLING YOU AHEAD OF TIME.

Xander: SPAM FRIED RICE SOUNDS GREAT! AND YES, I'LL BE HUNGRY.

I waited to start cooking until after Xander arrived so it would be fresh off the stove. He stood in the kitchen watching me cook and chatting with me in the interim.

"How long until you're done with school?"

"In about six months."

"You must be excited."

"I am. I'm ready to be done and start working full-time. I'm ready to make money and get my own place."

"You live with your parents?"

"Yeah. For the most part they give me my space, but it's not ideal when you're twenty-five-years-old."

I laughed because I assumed Xander's comment was referring to bringing women home.

"I can see that. I guess you will just have to stick to older women who have their own place."

At this statement, Xander laughed.

"I think you're right."

Xander brought a six pack of Stella Artois and was enjoying a beer while we chatted.

When dinner was ready, we served ourselves and sat across from each other at the table to eat.

The fried rice turned out great—minus the Spam. I should have gone with ham or pretty much any other protein out there besides Spam. I ended up picking the Spam out, but Xander ate the whole bowl, Spam and all.

"So, you grew up near here?"

"Yeah, I'm just 20 minutes away. We're pretty close. I pass your exit every day on my way home from school."

"That's good to know. I'm glad I'm conveniently located."

We laughed.

Afterwards, we sat on the couch and ate chocolate chip cannoli for dessert.

After eating dessert, I excused myself to use the restroom and brushed my teeth. I returned to the couch and sat so our legs were touching. I could tell Xander was nervous. He seemed to be awkwardly trying to figure out how to situate himself on the couch. That didn't stop him from touching me though. My guess was that he couldn't help himself. It only took a few minutes before his hand was on my thigh. The other was on the couch creeping closer to me.

Xander kissed me after a very short few minutes of continued small talk.

He was a great kisser. Slow, passionate, and tender. We began to make out. I felt myself relax into the couch totally at ease with Xander. Our hands started feeling each other's bodies. My hands went immediately to his arms which were muscular and strong. His face and neck were smooth and freshly shaven. Every part of Xander felt great to the touch.

We enjoyed making out for several minutes. Xander's body was so firm. My hands stayed under his shirt glued to his shoulders, arms, and pecs. Out of character for me—I know.

"You're a great kisser, Xander."

He pulled away and looked intently in my eyes. "Thank you."

Xander immediately went back to kissing me. After a few more minutes, I was ready to get him fully undressed.

"Let's go to my bedroom. I want to take your clothes off."

Xander laughed. I think my forwardness was surprising and humorous to him.

I hopped up off the couch and Xander followed.

Once we got into my bedroom, we stood by the bed making out for what seemed like forever. Xander wasn't very tall so we could kiss easily while standing. It was amazing!

Due to my short stature, I had never really experienced making out while standing up and I really liked it.

Xander began undressing me as we kissed. His hands gave full attention to every body part that was uncovered.

After pulling off my shirt, he kissed and sucked on my breasts and nipples. Xander kissed all the way down my belly as he reached down to pull off my sweats.

Xander liked to take things slow, which is rare—yet a huge turn on. Xander was doing a stellar job of increasing my arousal and desire for him. For the first time in a long time, I felt what it was like for a man to enjoy every inch of my body.

Xander's attentiveness boosted my confidence. He didn't care what size jeans I wore or about any imperfections I thought I might have. His actions showed he thought my body was sexy and desirable. I could tell immediately Xander lived in the moment and enjoyed his time with me. He was like a sponge soaking up every inch of me.

Once I was fully undressed, Xander commented on my unshaven pubic area. He was pleasantly surprised to see hair.

"You don't shave? That's hot. I've never been with a woman who didn't shave."

"Really? That's crazy to me. I don't understand why people shave their pubic hair."

"It gets in the way. It just seems easier to have sex with no hair."

"I guess, but I much prefer my man *au naturel.*"

"Good to know. I'll keep that in mind."

I undressed Xander after our impromptu conversation, paying attention to every newly exposed part of his body like he did with mine. Like most men I'd encountered at his age, he shaved his pubic hair almost down to nothing. I was disappointed at seeing this but not surprised. I refrained from saying anything since I had already expressed my stance.

We moved to the bed and continued caressing each other's bodies until we were both wanting for sex. I gave him a condom and he put it on.

Xander was hard and eager. He slid inside of me as soon as the condom was on. After only a few minutes of thrusting, I could feel his erection was going away.

I frowned. "Did you cum?"

It was either that or he would be the third man to have those kinds of issues. Asking if he came was much safer based on prior experience.

Xander laughed and said, "Yes." I could tell he was embarrassed.

He held the condom as he pulled out and shuffled into the bathroom.

I was just barely getting started and he had already finished. Ugh! By the time he was done cleaning up, I wasn't even in the mood anymore.

Xander joined me in bed and I was relieved I didn't have to ask him to cuddle. He lied down next to me. I turned my body draping my arm and leg over him, then lying my head on his chest.

Although I cuddled up to Xander, his hands weren't touching my body. Cumming quickly might be something he couldn't control but touching me was.

"It isn't every night that you get to lie in bed next to a woman. Your hands should *never* leave a woman's body, especially when lying in bed naked with her."

If there is one great truth I can impart to the men of the world, let it be this! Enjoy every minute with a woman while you're with her. Take advantage and touch her body as much as you can.

Xander immediately started rubbing my body with his hands. He didn't stop the rest of that night.

I loved how Xander listened to what I wanted and immediately responded—thus pleasing me. That was more like it.

"Have you been on any ride-a-longs? If you haven't, I highly recommend it. I have a couple police officers in my family so I've been on a few ride-a-longs. They're fun."

"Yes, I have. You're right; it's exhilarating."

"You have to go at night though. A daytime ride-a-long is boring."

Xander was still rubbing my body while we talked.

After a few minutes, I began rubbing his body as well, moving my hands down to his dick and testicles. Xander was already hard. We were both ready to have sex again. Surely this second time around, he'd be able to last a little longer.

No such luck.

The second time we had sex the same thing happened. We were just getting started and Xander climaxed.

"Holy fuck Xander! Did you cum again?"

I wasn't hiding my exasperation. I was so frustrated that any attempt at sparing his feelings went out the window.

"Yeah. You get me so excited," he said somewhat bashfully.

I felt mildly guilty for displaying my true feelings so candidly. I was just so shocked and disappointed—it was almost impossible to hide.

"Does this happen with other women?" If it did, this guy was fucked.

"Usually only the first time. The second time I typically last a lot longer."

I had the feeling he was probably bullshitting me.

"Well, go clean up. When you can come back, you can take care of me." I was riled up and horny as hell! I was going to make sure I got my happy ending that night, even if I had to give it to myself.

When Xander got back into bed, I was still lying there naked. He laid down next to me. Propping himself up onto his arm, he slid his hand down between my legs and started touching me.

Like almost every man I've ever been with, Xander's hand was too rough.

"Be gentle. Barely a touch. Super soft with straight fingers. Rub back and forth over the clit."

Xander did exactly as he was told. Oh God, *finally*. Yes, right there. He made me cum pretty quickly with his fingers (especially since I just had sex twice with no happy ending).

"That was fucking hot!" he exclaimed. His eyes wide. "I've never done anything like that before."

"Really?" I was very surprised by his revelation. I wondered if all of his sexual encounters consisted of the quick fucks like we had experienced. "Welcome to having sex with a forty-three-year-old woman."

We both laughed.

We cleaned up and cuddled for a few more minutes. Xander wanted to leave by 11 pm because he had school the next day.

At 10:55, I shuffled him off my bed and out the door. I hoped I would hear from Xander again. Our first sexual encounter may not have been the best, but he was a nice guy and good company. And that was something I craved on lonely nights.

I knew only time would tell if I would see him again. Based on past experiences, the odds were not in my favor.

Xander texted me a few days later and wanted to see me the following Tuesday then the Tuesday after. He became my Tuesday guy and I loved it. I looked forward to seeing Xander every week.

This went on for about a month until Xander said he was too busy to commit to every Tuesday night. I hadn't seen him in three weeks and didn't know if I ever would see him again.

So, I broke my own rule and texted him.

Me: I FEEL SAD. I CAN TELL I'M NOT GOING TO SEE YOU AGAIN. I LIKE SPENDING TIME WITH YOU. I DIDN'T WANT OUR FUN TO END.

At this point in my journey, I wasn't afraid of scaring a man off with my bluntness. I knew how the game worked, but I also didn't mind reaching out and being honest. I knew it could go either way and I was finally okay with that. The feeling of desperation I'd felt at the beginning of my sexcapades had dissipated and I was truly okay with not seeing a man again, regardless of how great our night was.

Xander: NOT TRUE AT ALL. I'VE BEEN VERY BUSY AND UNDER A LOT OF STRESS. I ENJOY SPENDING TIME WITH YOU, TOO. I WANT TO SEE YOU AGAIN, IF YOU ARE OK WITH THAT?

I never replied because I really didn't know what to say or believe at that point. I had a hard time believing that a man was simply too busy for sex. I vowed to not reach out again, but failed miserably like the times before. A few days later on a Tuesday, I texted Xander—one last try.

Me: PLEASE COME OVER.

Xander: ALRIGHT. I'LL BE DONE AT THE GYM IN ABOUT 30 MINUTES.

That was the first time I can remember a man agreeing to come over when *I* asked. I learned quickly that men come over when it was most convenient for them. Any time in the past when I reached out to a man (who I had slept with) the answer was always silence or some excuse explaining why they were busy.

Xander was the first man to say yes. It drove me wild with excitement. I was feeling particularly lonely and honestly, I just wanted the company. It wasn't even about the sex for me that night.

He showed up directly from the gym. I opened the door in a tank top and panties. Xander immediately grabbed my waist with both hands and we kissed.

After kissing in the entryway for a few minutes, we walked to my bedroom. It was already late in the evening and I had to work in the morning. Xander sat on the bed and I stood in front of him. We kissed slow and sensually. My hands immediately went under his shirt and up to his pecs and arms

This was one of my favorite things about sleeping with Xander—he enjoyed every moment, which resulted in me slowing down and enjoying it as well. Xander's slow approach lengthened the foreplay and increased my arousal.

He placed his hands on my hips. My top cut off a few inches above my panties allowing my skin to peek through. It drove me wild to feel his hands on my bare skin.

My hands started moving all over his body. I grasped onto his shoulders then ran my hands down his arms and chest. Xander's body was like a sculpture by Michelangelo— absolute perfection.

I started sucking on his ear lobes and kissing his neck. Xander seemed to enjoy this. I heard him moan and his breathing sped up.

Xander let out a loud sigh. He was in heaven. It made me smile. Especially since he usually expressed so little of what he was thinking or feeling verbally. Non-verbal expression can be just as powerful. Xander is the man who taught me this.

His hands moved up my tank top to my breasts. He grabbed both and immediately buried his face in them. He kissed them and started sucking on my nipples gently.

Whatever he did to one breast, he was sure to do the exact same thing to the other.

I had four condoms sitting on the nightstand. I learned to always be prepared with a spare or two. Xander grabbed one and put it on.

I pushed him onto the bed and asked him to lie back on the pillow. I sat between his legs as I gave him head. I was pleasantly surprised to see he had still left his pubic hair untouched. He didn't like having pubic hair, so I wondered why he hadn't shaved.

"Wow, your hair is long."

"You said you preferred men with hair. I haven't touched it since I last saw you."

Huh. So, he was telling the truth. Xander always had the intention of seeing me again. He really *was* too busy to have sex. Go figure.

I felt a ping of guilt for not believing him when he texted me.

Xander loved receiving head. He was more vocal than I had ever heard him before and it fueled me.

"You feel so fucking great."

"Thank you." A compliment from Xander was close to nonexistent. I smiled and savored it.

I didn't want him to cum—we all know that was definitely a concern with him.

I stopped right after I really got him going. I crawled on top of him and straddled him. We kissed some more before he rolled me over onto my back.

"Put another condom on before we have sex." I handed him another latex free condom.

I didn't know it at the time, but using two condoms at once increases the likelihood of them ripping. I thought it was a good solution at the time for his premature ejaculation. To dull some of the sensations and make him last longer. Probably should've Googled it first, rather than risking my own health and safety.

Xander laughed. "That's weird. I've never used two condoms before."

"I've been doing some thinking and I have three different things for you to try. Are you open to trying them so we can have longer sex?"

He seemed apprehensive. "What are they?"

"Number one is to try having sex with two condoms."

"What're numbers two and three?"

"Let me preface this by saying that I have this random pain in my vagina and have lidocaine cream to put on it. It's totally safe for down there. I thought we could put it on your penis to desensitize it—so you can last longer."

"What's number three? I'm *not* putting lidocaine on my dick."

I laughed at how vehemently he made the last statement. The lidocaine cream was clearly a no-go.

"I have Viagra. I thought you could take half and see what happens."

Why the fuck not? *Right?* You'd think the guy would do anything to have more staying power.

"I'm not going home with a fucking boner."

I laughed loudly. "Oooookay…two condoms it is."

Xander was agreeable to testing out my theory and put both condoms on.

I'm happy to divulge it worked like a champ. I was quite surprised by how long he lasted. I was super happy. Not only because it worked, but also because Xander and I were going to have much better sex from now on.

Again, please do not try this at home as two condoms create friction which increases the chance of the condom breaking. If you're like me, your hands are full enough with the kids you already have. I've since learned they make specific condoms for lasting longer, so don't risk yourself doing what I did and buy those instead.

Back to Xander.

I liked spending time with him, but the sex wasn't as good as it could be and I knew it.

After we cleaned up, we cuddled in bed.

"Fist bump for the two condoms working?" I grinned holding up a fist.

He laughed and gave me a fist bump.

"So how is the writing going?" he asked.

Xander was one of the few people I told about my dabbling into writing. Well, it was more than dabbling. I wanted to write a book. I *was* writing a book. You're reading it right now.

Writing was something I'd loved ever since elementary school. I'd write in my diary every night to process my thoughts and feelings. Oddly enough, I'd never taken a formal class, nor did I have the desire to. It was just something I found therapeutic.

It had never seemed like the right time before to attempt writing a book. I was either too busy or I didn't have good enough ideas. There were always a million excuses not to do it.

I now had some entertaining stories to share and had the desire to do just that. My friends ate them up and they unanimously agreed that I had to write a book—they literally pressured me until I finally set the gears into motion.

I told Xander I had started my book and he was very positive about it and thought it was really cool.

"I tell my daughter all the time that we can truly have anything in this life as long as we work hard for it. Yet, it feels surreal for me to finally be writing a book. For as long as I can remember, I've always thought the greatest career would be that of an author."

Xander was a great listener, but not one to offer up much about himself. I was surprised when he opened up to me about his past.

"I used to go out all the time partying and drinking with my friends. I wasn't serious about school and didn't know what I wanted to do with my future." He looked at me. "Not many people know this, but I failed out of the police academy the first time I enrolled. It was a horrible time in my life. After failing, I knew I wanted nothing more than to be a police officer. I had to get serious about it."

"You should be proud of yourself." I squeezed his arm. "You are very hard-working and committed to both your school and work. You are a great man, Xander."

Everything about our interaction was positive. This was what I had been looking for, what all of this was all about. Genuine human connection. Mutual enjoyment. Companionship—even if it wasn't that long-lasting. Both of us were feeling better since we had met.

We cuddled and chatted a little bit more. His hands started wandering around my body and we started kissing again. I could tell we were both in the mood for round two.

Chapter 21: Despacito

After months of Bumbling, I'd finally found a somewhat steady lover. Even though Xander wasn't coming over every Tuesday anymore, I could still count on him here and there to meet my needs. Unfortunately for me, my hormones were raging. I really needed to have sex more than every once in a while. I was still searching for someone to spend time with—shall we say a little more frequently.

Urban Dictionary defines Latin Lovers as 'The best men out there. They're not only very sensual and manly, but they're gorgeous with warm golden skin, dark bedroom eyes, and full sensual lips.'

After sleeping with Antonio, I couldn't agree more. In hindsight, I should not have stereotyped Antonio as the Latin Lover. I was so taken aback by his bedroom skills that I grasped for a label.

"Oh my God," I screamed. "Thank you! I needed that soooo badly!" I let out after having sex with Antonio for the first time.

Antonio had been trying to pin me down since last week. Honestly, I had been too busy for men lately. I knew from Xander that when some men say they're too busy for sex, they may actually mean it—this went for me as well. I had been busy all weekend long. I even had to cancel my encounter with Antonio which I never do.

Monday evening started with me sitting at my kitchen table writing this very book. I was engulfed to the point that I didn't want to hang out with anyone. My priorities were shifting and it felt good to be moving on to the next phase of life—whatever that may look like.

Antonio's name popped up on my phone and it took me a minute to remember who he was. We hadn't communicated since I had to tell him that I was busy last Saturday.

Antonio: HAPPY MONDAY! WHAT'S YOUR SCHEDULE LOOKING LIKE THIS WEEK? WHEN WOULD YOU BE DOWN TO CHILL?

I wanted to write some more. Still, you know what they say—all work and no play...

Me: TONIGHT OR TOMORROW NIGHT GOOD FOR YOU?

Antonio: OH, OK. I'M ACTUALLY ABOUT TO JUMP IN THE SHOWER. IS IT OK IF I COME BY AROUND 6:30-7 TONIGHT?

Me: SURE.

Antonio texted me when he parked. I walked out to greet him. Immediately I noticed he was dressed like he lived in another state. Antonio was wearing pants and a long-sleeved sweater. I was wearing a skirt, tank top, and flip-flops— normal attire for warm weather.

Immediately after waving hello I exclaimed, "Holy shit, you must be sweating!"

He laughed then said, "I'm fine."

We walked back to my condo and I introduced him to Chewie

Antonio brought some sort of alcohol to mix with coke. He was very nervous. His hands were shaking a little. He needed some liquid courage for sure. I offered him a hit of weed, but he declined.

I liked that Antonio knew what he needed to relax himself and open up. Also that he had made sure to bring it with him. We stood in the kitchen as he sipped on his drink and I smoked weed.

Somehow, we got on the topic of discussing our current situation—online dating that is.

"I can't stand how women never reply to my messages. I think there are too many men on Bumble and women just have too many to choose from."

"I'll bet you're right. I have a ton of matches," I said. "I'm not going to lie, but I am only actively talking with two of those matches. I realized that all the men I was spending time with recently had similar attributes. They all pursued me, took the lead on making conversation, and gave me a reason to make them a high priority. Those are the men I make time for."

Antonio nodded. "In sales it's called consistent and persistent. So, what you're saying is that online dating is kind of like sales."

I laughed. "Yes, that is *exactly* what I'm saying. So, you've had women who aren't responding to you?"

"Yes."

"Tell me what you've said to them. I'll let you know what I think." I looked at his expression and saw the hesitation so I decided to ask, "Only if you want my advice?"

"Yes," he paused, "but you're going to laugh at me. I probably said something like: *Hey, what's up?*"

I broke into immediate laughter. Antonio started laughing too. He looked a little embarrassed but was being a good sport.

"I'm sorry, I'm not meaning to embarrass you. What's up is something you would say to a guy. That's not how you talk to a woman."

I tilted my head to the side thinking of how to best phrase what I wanted to say next. "If you want to pique a woman's interest, give her a genuine compliment. For example, tell her you were happy when you matched with her and that you really want to get to know her. Tell her she looks interesting or fun, maybe notice something special about her profile or photo. Say something to turn her head. Don't make a general comment that you could just as easily copy and paste into a message with another woman."

Antonio looked skeptical. He kind of laughed nervously in response to my advice.

"Please don't be upset at me for saying so, but all that sounds a bit cheesy."

"Well, it would work on me." I shrugged unbothered by his words. "I can't tell you how many men start their messages with something like 'hey beautiful' or 'hi sexy', something along those lines." I rolled my eyes. "They say that to every woman they message, it means nothing to me. When a man genuinely compliments me—notices something about me—it actually makes me smile and take notice. Needy, insecure women, who lack confidence take the 'hey beautiful' bait—not women like me. Although, with that being said, I all too recently *was* that woman, so I'm speaking from my own experience."

"Well, I guess I'll try it."

We moved to the couch and continued talking. Antonio immediately put his hand on my thigh. I was pleasantly surprised as he was so nervous in the kitchen. I guess the alcohol was starting to kick in.

Antonio put his arm around me and pulled me closer.

We moved on to talking about compliments. "I'd rather get a compliment on a character trait than my physical appearance any day of the week."

He looked skeptical.

Oh my God, did most men think this way? Or maybe it was just younger men?

"I can tell you disagree with me. I'm going to ask my friends and family on Facebook."

I grabbed my phone, opened Facebook, and typed out: *Would you prefer to be given a compliment on a character trait or on your physical appearance?*

What percentage of people do you think voted for which?

One hundred percent of my friends and family chose character trait. One man even replied that a compliment to your character carries so much more weight than a compliment on your physical appearance. Antonio and I both agreed with the results of my Facebook survey, there's so much more depth to the compliment.

Antonio's hand was still on my thigh. He was rubbing up and down my leg. When Antonio was finally ready to kiss me, he pulled me as close as I could get—our chests touching.

I wasn't sure about how the night would turn out. I was pleasantly surprised when he initiated our first kiss. The problem was our kissing styles weren't very compatible.

I tend to kiss passionately, tenderly, slowly—enjoying every moment. Antonio kissed harder and faster—also wetter than I would have liked. Here we go again. It was slightly turning me off.

I tried to put it out of my mind and focus on his body. I placed my hand under his shirt and started rubbing his waist. I ran my hand up his belly and over each peck, gently pinching his nipples.

He let out a moan. Ooh, Antonio was expressive. One of my top turn-ons.

As our foreplay progressed, I quickly learned Antonio was very skilled. He felt my breasts through my shirt, rubbing and squeezing both. I felt his arousal increase from the excitement and anticipation. He ran his hand over my clothes feeling every part of my body. There was something titillating about the barrier of clothes that separated our flesh. He started rubbing between my thighs—under my skirt. He moved his fingers over my panties and started rubbing my clit. Not surprising, Antonio was too rough and needed a little direction.

"Barely touch it," I whispered. "It's sensitive."

Antonio did exactly as I asked which increased *my* arousal tenfold.

"Do you want to move to the bedroom?"

"Yes."

I grabbed his hand and walked him down the hall into my room. I gently pushed him into a sitting position on the edge of the bed. Standing in front of him as he sat on the bed was one of the most comfortable ways for me to kiss him or really any man as it brings them down to my level.

Antonio and I started kissing again. We were still fully clothed and I was ready to do something about that. I lifted his shirt over his head and dropped it onto the floor. He grinned at me.

"A shirt for a shirt?"

I laughed. "Of course."

Antonio took off my tank top. He didn't immediately go for my bra like other men. He kissed my neck then continued kissing along my bra strap down to my breast. He played with my breasts, kissing the flesh that was bulging out of my bra.

Antonio moved his hands under my skirt and firmly grabbed my thighs.

His foreplay game was driving me through the roof. Antonio was going to be a great fucking lover! I already knew and I was insanely turned on.

Finally, he decided it was time for my bra to come off. The greatest compliment of the night was when he removed it and said, "Oh my God. Your tits are amazing."

I smiled. "Thank you."

Antonio had a love affair with my breasts that night. I honestly don't think they ever left his hands until morning.

After running his hands down my body as far as he could reach, he'd slide them up my side, to my arms, over my shoulders, then back down to my breasts. It was incredibly sensual and stimulating to feel Antonio's hands on me.

His hands never stopped moving. Antonio made me feel like he was in love with my body. It felt amazing!

After letting Antonio explore my body, I decided to undress him from the waist down. I had to crouch down to pull off his pants and socks while he put on a condom. As I stood back up, I licked his dick from bottom to top and started giving him head.

Antonio was *very* expressive. He moaned and said, "Oh my God—Oh my God. Lacie—fuck!"

I loved it. The sound charged me up and made me want to give him even more.

Antonio grabbed me. "I want to fuck you, Lacie. Right now."

I laughed a little at how abrupt and forward he was. But he'd gotten me more than ready. I was right there with him.

Antonio's dick was a little different than others. He fluctuated from hard to soft. Most young men get an erection and it stays that way until they cum. (Thank you, God!)

He initially put on the latex free condom I purchased. He complained of it being too tight. I kind of thought it was weird because his dick didn't seem that big when I was handling or sucking it.

I found a Trojan Magnum in my nightstand and he put that on instead.

Antonio slid his dick into me very slowly.

I thought his caution was weird at first, but quickly realized his dick kept going and going.

Antonio was hung. It was hard to tell because he was never one hundred percent hard during foreplay. Antonio was definitely more of a grower than a show-er!

Now that I could feel the size of his fully hard dick, I could tell by the way Antonio was holding back that he was probably accustomed to women asking him to be gentler.

Antonio was an amazing lover. He fucked me in missionary with his arm under my back, holding me close. He liked being face to face. He kissed me, moving his lips to my ears then neck. Any and all problems with kissing had worked themselves out as he'd finally relaxed and aligned with my kissing style.

The way Antonio adapted his kissing was beyond impressive.

Antonio was an intensely passionate lover and it was just the kind of sex I needed.

Oh God, *yes,* how I'd needed this. Finally, a lover who knew what he was doing and could satisfy me completely.

Afterwards, we cuddled and got to talking again.

"So, tell me your go-to line for picking up women at bars or while you're out with friends."

"I don't."

"You don't what? Hit on women?"

"Yeah, I don't go out to bars often and I don't really hit on women."

"Are you kidding me?" I looked up at him "It's because you're nervous huh?"

Antonio smiled bashfully and said, "A little."

"Antonio, you have everything to be confident about. Not only are you hot, you're fucking amazing in bed. You should hit on women right and left because you can bring it."

Antonio laughed.

"Is this the kind of thing you talk about with other men?"

"Well, kind of. I like talking about deeper things. And, I like talking about sex. We're both here to fuck, why not talk about sex."

"Give me an example of what you talk to other men about."

"Well, often times we talk about their lives. Their hopes and dreams. The goals they have for their futures."

"Do you ever talk about your fantasies?"

"Sometimes."

Antonio couldn't keep his hands off my body. We were soon fooling around again. I gave him head, this time he was completely hard and I could finally experience all of him.

"Holy shit, you can suck a dick!"

I giggled a little at his outburst.

When my mouth started to tire, Antonio pulled his condom off and I used my hand to finish him off. Antonio sprayed cum all over himself and me. We laughed at his explosive orgasm then cleaned up.

We cuddled more afterwards. Soon, I'd need to set a time limit for him to leave since we were both getting very relaxed. I'd learned after Jeremy ghosted me that I wasn't too keen on men spending the night. I tried to avoid making the same mistakes. Sleepovers, in general, were a big no-no for me.

Antonio and I got to talking about our fantasies again, so I got distracted and forgot to mention that I wanted him to leave soon.

"What are your top three fantasies?" I asked.

"Really the only fantasy I have is to sleep with an older woman."

"Yeah but you've already done that so what's a *current* fantasy you have?"

"Yeah, but I *just* did that."

"What do you mean?"

"*You* were my fantasy."

"Are you kidding me? Why didn't you tell me? I would've kicked it up a notch."

"You're able to kick it up a notch?" His eyebrows rose with the question.

I laughed and said, "Yes! So, tell me, what do you think of older women now that you've finally slept with one?"

Antonio shouted out, "I fucking love older women! Lacie, you've made me love older women."

My smile couldn't get any bigger. I was giddy with excitement. "Are you fucking kidding me? Thank you for telling me. That's awesome. It makes me sooo happy."

I hugged him. I was this man's first MILF and honestly it felt good to have made a lasting impression.

"So, now that you've fulfilled your MILF fantasy, you've got to have a new fantasy. What would it be?"

"Hmmm, I guess to make a video with a woman. I've never done that."

"I've never done it either. Sounds sexy."

Antonio and I laid in bed together for a bit longer before I told him he had to leave in five minutes.

Antonio was a little surprised when five minutes later I declared, "Time's up. You gotta go. I have to get some sleep."

"Wow, you weren't kidding about the five minutes!"

I laughed. "No. I wasn't."

Antonio wasn't going to be sent home and continued to cuddle me. I didn't bring up the time limit again. I could tell *he* wanted to decide when he left. I was fine with letting him make that decision—within reason. He left about thirty minutes later. No kiss. No hug.

I guess the alcohol had run its course.

"Thank you, I had a great time."

"Me too. Goodnight."

"Goodnight."

Antonio texted me when he got home which was extremely rare for the men I'd spent time with. His text brought a smile to my face.

Antonio: HAD A GOOD TIME TONIGHT. YOU'RE FUNNY. THANKS FOR HAVING ME OVER.

Me: I HAD A GREAT TIME AND APPRECIATE YOUR TEXT! GET TO BED SO YOU DON'T BLAME ME TOMORROW WHEN YOU'RE TIRED!

Antonio: HAVE A GOOD NIGHT.

Me: YOU TOO!

Antonio would be back. I was certain.

***

Sure enough, Antonio returned exactly one week later.

Antonio: HI HONEY.

266

Me: HI. HOW ARE YOU DOING?

Antonio: GREAT. HAVEN'T SEEN YOU IN A WHILE AND I WANTED TO SAY HI.

Me: SUPER SWEET AND THOUGHTFUL OF YOU.

That was Monday night.

On Friday night Antonio texted again. I was home alone writing.

Antonio: WHEN DO YOU WANT ME TO POUND THAT KITTY OF YOURS?

I literally laughed out loud when I read the text. Antonio. Sweet shy Antonio who had to spend an hour drinking before laying a finger on me. He was now asking about pounding my kitty?

Despite thinking his text was hilarious and out of character, I went with it.

Me: RIGHT NOW, BABY. TAKING MY PANTIES OFF AS I TEXT.

I had a knack for being able to get men riled up. I knew those words would put a visual in his mind and would drive him wild.

Antonio: TONIGHT?

Me: YES, PLEASE.

Antonio: REALLY?

Me: ABSOLUTELY. TELL ME WHAT YOU WANT ME WEARING.

Antonio: ARE YOU AVAILABLE AROUND 9?

Me: ANYTIME.

Antonio: OK. 9ISH.

Antonio: AND WEAR SOMETHING SEXY. SURPRISE ME.

Me: I'M GOING TO GIVE YOU THE BEST HEAD OF YOUR LIFE AND THEN I'M GOING TO SHOW YOU THE MILF I SHOULD'VE SHOWN YOU LAST TIME.

Antonio: OMG. YES. I'M READY FOR A SEXY DIRTY MILF.

After a few minutes of silence, our conversation seemed to have ended. I walked into my closet and grabbed my bin of lingerie. I hadn't worn a single item from this bucket in six years. Everything in it was purchased and worn for 24. I didn't even know if any of it would fit.

I pulled out the piece I was thinking of wearing. A sheer black baby doll negligee. The bust area was gathered and it had frills sticking out of the top. It had half-cup coverage, which meant the girls would be on full display. Only the nipples and lower half of my boobs would be covered. I found the matching thong. I hoped they'd fit after six years.

They did! I pulled out my black leather heels and was ready to knock Antonio's socks off.

The thought occurred to me, this was the very first time I was owning up to the fact that I'm a MILF. I've known for a while how highly attracted to younger men I was, but tonight was the first night I was really embracing it.

I was going to give Antonio the night of his life.

How did I get here? From not kissing on first dates to feeling like a sex goddess—abounding with confidence!

The transformation was amazing, I was overcome with gratitude for my journey and the experiences I'd had along the way.

I thought back to the last time I was with Antonio. He declared I made him love older women. He couldn't stop thinking about me. It felt great to be able to have that kind of impression on a man.

I couldn't stop smiling. I loved my life—the fact that I had made the conscious decision to actually live it and learn from my experiences! How many people could genuinely say that?

Antonio: I'LL BE THERE AT ABOUT 9:30.

Me: OK. PLEASE TEXT WHEN YOU'RE ON YOUR WAY SO I CAN GET READY.

At 9:15 pm, Antonio texted to say he was on his way. I hopped off the couch and went to my room to get ready. I slipped the thong on and it fit like a glove. I felt confident and sexy. I put on my black heels and walked into my closet to look in the mirror.

Holy shit! I looked sexy as fuck!

Standing there at the mirror, I was looking at a woman in her mid-forties. Curly hair falling over my shoulders. Like many women, I spent the majority of my life ping-ponging back and forth between loving myself and pointing out every single flaw. A mirror is not very forgiving when you have extra weight, thighs that touch in the middle, and a very visible C-section scar.

On this night, I didn't see any of those things. I looked in the mirror and saw what Antonio would see—a sexy as fuck MILF in high heels and lingerie.

I have yet to meet a man who didn't find my body sexy; because of that, *I* was finally able to see my naked body as sexy and desirable, too. The most important thing I've learned is that confidence is the single most attractive quality a woman can possess. Let me repeat that… *confidence is the single most attractive quality a woman can possess*. Period.

I looked one last time in the mirror. The lingerie was flattering on me, covering the tops of my thighs (one area I'm not particularly proud of) and showing off my breasts. My hair was already in an organically messy ponytail after a long day. Some deodorant, perfume, mouthwash, and blush followed suit—I was ready to rock and roll.

Antonio: I JUST PARKED. ARE YOU READY?

Me: YES. I'M AT THE DOOR WAITING FOR YOU.

I unlocked the screen and cracked the front door open about six inches. I hid behind the back of the door so as not to be seen by my neighbors.

A few minutes later, Antonio opened the screen door and stepped inside.

He immediately looked me up and down not attempting to hide the emphasis of his mannerisms. "Holy shit. You are sexy as fuck."

I smiled coyly. "Thanks."

Antonio leaned down to give me a kiss. I responded in a way that said, *I want more than just a peck hello.*

He continued kissing me gently giving me a little tongue. His hand grabbed the outside of my thigh and moved up under the negligee to my ass. He rubbed my ass for a minute while we continued to kiss in my entryway.

We finally stopped and moved to the kitchen. I got him a glass for his alcohol then grabbed my pipe and lighter.

I was anticipating smoking by myself while Antonio drank.

"Hey, can I have a hit? I've never smoked weed before and I'd like to try it."

"Really? Of course you can. You will be hanging out a while, right? I want to be sure you're sober before you leave."

"Yes, I'm going to hang out a while."

I took a hit and gave Antonio his first shotgun. He wasn't prepared to inhale the smoke I was exhaling; but he caught on right away and took the hit. Then it was back to the kissing. *God* could Antonio kiss once he lost those nerves of his.

He leaned over to kiss me slowly and gently. It was hot and made me want more. I wanted to rip his clothes off. My hands started rubbing his chest and belly. I moved them down under his shirt and back up to his pecs, pinching his nipples once my fingers found them. Antonio moaned with pleasure. I grabbed the bottom of his shirt with both hands.

I was ready to undress him right there in the kitchen.

"Already?" He sounded surprised.

"Fuck yeah. We don't have to have sex, but I want your shirt off. I want to touch your body."

Antonio laughed. "Ok."

I pulled his shirt off and set it on the kitchen counter. We continued kissing while my hands started rubbing his chest.

Antonio wasn't ripped or muscular like most of the men I spent my time with. I would say his body best resembled a dad bod. He felt amazing and I was wildly attracted to him nonetheless.

After a few minutes of kissing and rubbing Antonio's body, I squatted down in front of him. I reached for his belt buckle and unbuckled it.

"Already?" he asked again, sounding out of breath. "You want to do all of this already?"

"Fuck yeah. It's Friday night. You've got to be packing more than one in the chamber. Let's have some fun. I'm ready."

"What if I'm not packing more than one in the chamber though?"

I just smiled. "Trust me, a little recovery time and you'll be just fine."

The thought never occurred to me that Antonio might not be able to have sex consecutively, since I was used to it being the norm with other men.

"Where's your restroom?"

"Down the hall to the right."

While Antonio was taking care of business, I adjusted the lighting so that only the dim light above the kitchen table was on.

I walked over and sat on the edge of the table. Then I slid my hand down my panties and started playing with myself. I knew it would be a huge turn on when Antonio came out and saw me.

I wanted to be ready to go and wet by the time he came back. I knew I could get myself there.

Antonio came out of the bathroom and walked down the hallway. As soon as he saw me on the table, he shook his head and said, "Oh my God. You are sexy as fuck sitting there playing with yourself. Fuck!"

I smiled, bit my bottom lip, and continued rubbing.

Antonio walked right up to the kitchen table and stood between my legs. I continued touching myself. He stood so his erection was right against the hand that was in my panties. I pulled my hand out and grabbed his dick then started stroking it. Antonio's breathing was so heavy, I knew he was off-the-charts with arousal.

He kissed me then took my head and gently pushed it down to his nipples. (Antonio loved his nipples played with more than any other man I'd been with. He constantly encouraged me to suck, bite, and play with them. I made a mental note to give them a lot of attention throughout the night.) I gently sucked his nipple then bit down and pulled on it firmly.

Antonio exhaled loudly. The change in his breathing only encouraged me to give him more of what he wanted. I moved to his other nipple and repeated the same thing.

"Do you want me to go get a condom or do you want to stay here and fool around for a bit, then go to the bedroom?"

"Let's just fool around here for a little bit then go to your bedroom and fuck there."

We continued our foreplay on the kitchen table. I started playing with his dick while he grabbed my breasts and buried his face into them.

"God, I fucking love your tits. They're amazing."

"Thanks."

As things heated up, we couldn't wait any longer.

I broke first. "Let's go to the bedroom, please," I moaned. "I want you to fuck me."

"Ok."

I hopped off the table, grabbed my phone and started playing mellow classic rock music while I walked to the bedroom. I closed the door, turned my closet light on, and cracked the door for perfect mood lighting. I grabbed condoms out of my nightstand and set them within reach. Antonio was lying naked on the bed.

"I have this feeling you would be great at giving a massage. Just a hunch." He did always have his hands on me. "Do you want me to get out the massage oil? You can touch me everywhere."

"Sure."

I got the massage oil out from my nightstand and set it on top of it. I crawled onto the bed, rolled a condom onto his erection and started giving Antonio head again. I was taking his dick as far down my throat as I was able to. He put his hand on top of my head moving me up and down.

Antonio started moaning and shouting, "Oh my God!" I sucked him enough to get him very aroused then grabbed the massage oil and handed it to him.

I took off my lingerie and panties, dropped them onto the floor and lay face down on the bed.

"Do I put the oil in my hands or on your back? I've never done this before."

Wow, another first for Antonio.

I laughed and said, "Whatever you're comfortable with."

He straddled my ass. I heard the click of the bottle opening then he squeezed some into his hand. Antonio rubbed the oil onto his palms and started massaging my back with both hands.

It felt great. His hands were strong and warm as they moved slowly over my back, shoulders, and arms. Antonio sat in that same position as he massaged my upper back and shoulders. Next, he moved down and straddled my legs while continuing to massage me.

In this new position, my ass was exposed. He squeezed more massage oil into his hands and started rubbing my ass.

Antonio ran his hands all the way up my back to my neck, on the way back down, he slid his hands between my ass cheeks then up and down between my legs—where I was dripping wet.

I moaned every time his fingers brushed over my ass and between my legs. I was dying for him to finger me. After waiting in anticipation, I finally begged him flat out.

"Please finger me."

Antonio moved his hands up my back again. On the way back down, he slipped both hands between my ass cheeks, down to my wetness, and slid a finger deep inside me.

"Oh my God. Fuck that feels good."

Antonio kept doing this for a few minutes. Massaging me and fingering me, taking the time to rub my clit with his oiled fingers. It was all so damn erotic. I finally turned over and begged, "Please fuck me!"

I grabbed his dick and started stroking. He placed his hands on my inner thighs and spread my legs open.

Then he slid himself deep into me.

God, there is nothing like the first few moments when a man puts his dick into you. Especially since I was begging for it. Antonio felt great and his dick was so hard.

He kneeled between my legs and fucked me. I was spread wide open to him. I pulled him on top of me as he continued pounding. We had amazing chemistry and Antonio knew instinctively to grab my breasts. He knew all the right places to touch without having to be told and that, in itself, was a major turn on.

"Go get your phone," I said. Tonight, was all about making his fantasies come true. Because the truth was, being somebody's fantasy was a fantasy of mine, I just hadn't even realized it.

Antonio clearly didn't understand why I was asking. He exhaled loudly and said, "It's all the way out in the living room."

"Well, you said you had a fantasy of making a video with me. Let's do it." I was so fucking turned on. I wanted to take this as far as it could go. Make this a night Antonio would never *ever* forget.

Antonio abruptly pulled himself out of me, hopped off the bed, and hurried to the living room for his phone. He came back, kneeled in the same position he was in previously, and turned it on. A bright flash lit up. He flipped me onto my hands and knees. I stayed on all fours because I knew it would make for a better angle.

"If you get anything other than my ass and your dick in this video, I will make you delete it. Understand?" Fulfilling a fantasy was one thing. Ending up with my face on *PornHub* was another. I wasn't an idiot.

"Yes. Don't worry—I won't. It'll be a close up only."

"Ok. And, we're watching it together after so I can be sure there's nothing in it that shows who I am."

"Ok."

Antonio pointed his phone towards my ass. I could feel him start to put his dick into me. He started fucking me and it felt amazing. A well-hung man feels absolutely mind blowing, regardless of his ability to perform in any other area. Antonio was definitely well-hung and I was in heaven.

He continued fucking me and filming his dick as it moved in and out of me. I had a feeling the video was going to be sexy as hell. Antonio started rubbing my asshole and spanking me periodically.

God, why was that so hot?

"You feel fucking amazing. I want you to cum in me. I want to feel you cumming. Your dick pulsing inside of me." The dirty talk was just spilling out of me. It all just felt...

So. Damn. Good.

"Fuck yeah. You want me to cum in you?"

"Yes. Please cum in me."

As Antonio continued fucking me, I could feel that he was harder than ever. I knew he was close to cumming, I continued to talk dirty to help push him over the edge.

"I want you to fuck me on the kitchen table next and film your dick moving in and out while my legs are spread wide open. Will you?"

"Fuck yeah. You're going to make me cum baby."

"Cum for me. Please, cum for me."

Antonio came right then. He continued filming as his pace slowed. His dick slid in and out of me slowly. He basked in the glory of his orgasm. He left himself inside me while he kneeled there for a minute. He turned the phone off and said, "That—was fucking amazing!"

"Yes, it was." It *so* was.

He got up and went to the bathroom to take the condom off. After we lay in silence. I think we were both exhausted and trying to cool ourselves down a bit.

Antonio broke the silence. "What did you think about our sex?"

I threw the question right back at him. I was just as curious about his reply. "What did *I* think about our sex? It was fucking amazing. What did *you* think about it?"

"Fucking incredible."

"I'd imagine you don't have sex like that with every woman."

Just to clarify, I wasn't saying this out of cockiness. I had been with enough younger men by now that I knew sex with a woman in her forties was drastically different than sex with a woman in her twenties. Being that I was Antonio's first older woman, I knew it was likely that he hadn't experienced the caliber of sex we were having.

"Definitely not."

"I'm cooled down now. Let's watch the video."

I rolled over and laid on his chest. He lifted up his phone so we could both see the screen. Antonio pressed play and I immediately saw my ass and his dick moving in and out of me. I wasn't quite sure what to expect; but I have to say, the video was fucking hot.

I thought I'd be embarrassed or turned off, but it was the complete opposite. Antonio did a great job filming. The video was super clear and well-lit. It was a perfect close up of just my ass and his dick. It turned me on.

"Holy shit," I said. "It's so fucking hot!"

Antonio smiled. I could tell he was very happy with it by the grin on his face.

"Are you going to watch that at home while you masturbate?"

I'm a naturally curious person and the questions I asked were things I was legitimately wanting to know.

"Fuck yeah!" he said.

"That's so hot." I could only shake my head, not sure which was sexier. Watching the video or thinking about Antonio watching the video.

We finished the video and fell asleep. Around 3:45 am, I woke up slightly startled to find Antonio asleep in bed next to me.

I placed my hand on his arm and gently shook him.

"Antonio. You have to wake up and go home. We fell asleep."

Antonio was groggy, but I knew he was sober. It had been hours since he smoked and drank. He sleepily got up and dressed then left quickly.

My body was fatigued. I knew Antonio, the Latin Lover, was one of the best lovers I have ever been with. I hoped we'd have another fun night with each other. I was already fantasizing about what we'd do next.

After Antonio left, I crawled back into bed and tried to get back to sleep. The only problem was that my bed didn't have the same warmth as when Antonio was lying in it.

Going to bed alone after that night felt lonely and cold. I was longing for a night when a man stayed in my bed. Not a booty call—but Mr. Right.

After tossing and turning for close to an hour, I decided to text Claudia. She was the only person I knew who would be up at this ungodly hour. Plus, I was dying to hear about her trip to Arizona and how things went with Mitch. She had been MIA since she left to visit him. I was chomping at the bit to talk to her. Especially now that she was home.

Me: ARE YOU UP?

Claudia: YES.

I stopped texting and called her.

"Good morning. How was Arizona? How was Mitch the second time around?"

"Honestly, it was a great time. He's definitely a man to just have fun with—but I'm open to hanging out with him again—maybe the next time he's in my area. We have fun together, not to mention our off the charts sex."

"That's great! I know you're probably disappointed that he doesn't have that potential to be something more, but I'm glad you're getting back out there and opening yourself up to men. Admittedly, I'm really glad you're finally having sex again."

"Yeah, he said he'll let me know when he's here in Colorado again. I'm not holding my breath though."

"Great attitude."

Claudia redirected the conversation towards me.

"So, how was your weekend?"

"It couldn't be better. Antonio came over last night and I can tell he's going to keep coming back. I finally found a man that I know I can text when I'm wanting company. He will definitely try and make it happen.

"Also, last night was a first for me. We made a video. Only my ass was showing so nobody would know it's me. Do you think I'm crazy? It was hot in the moment, but I feel a little regretful now."

"NO! Not at all. I don't know a single friend who hasn't made a video with her husband or boyfriend. So, you go girl. You made sure you weren't identifiable and had fun. And, how perfect, you have two men to sleep with now—are you gonna get off Bumble."

"Oh, trust me, I've already done that. I just don't feel as happy and excited as I thought I would be about it. Sure, I can't wait to see Xander and Antonio again. I have a great time with them. It's just that they leave and I'm in the same position again. I'm ready for a man who never wants to leave."

"I'm so sorry. I feel your pain really—I get it. When you're done with twenty-five-year-olds, the man who is meant to stay will come. Trust that."

"I do. I'm just surprised I finally got what I wanted and I don't feel any more satisfied or fulfilled than I did when this all started. If anything, I feel just as empty—just with a side of the occasional fun."

"Sounds to me like you're finally ready to move on."

"I think you may be right."

I hung up with Claudia and lay in bed thinking about her words. I knew she was right. I was ready to move on.

After nearly a year, I finally found what I thought I was searching for. Don't get me wrong, I wasn't ultimately searching for a booty call when I began this journey. While my hormones were raging and Mr. Right was nowhere in sight—I felt it was the perfect solution to online date and at the minimum get my needs met. In the end, I was in the same spot I was a year before: lonely, empty, and wanting more.

Albeit, I was definitely more confident, knowledgeable— and ahem, shall I say skilled?

Chapter 22: Confident

After a year of sexcapades and sexual exploration, I had the sense that I finally acquired what I set out to get—a couple men I could reach out to when I needed some physical connection.

When I first lowered my age range on Bumble, my intention was for sexual gratification; however, I was not at all looking to have a variety of sexual partners. I truly would've been happy if that first man—the young single dad, would've just kept coming back to meet my needs. Alas, that's not how thing were meant to go, so I was forced to adapt.

I continued hanging out with Xander and Antonio for many months to come. I'd only see them about once or twice a month if I was able to carve out the alone time.

My internal sex drive which had been voracious at the start of all this had dissipated to almost nothing. It was like an internal switch went off inside me. My body no longer needed sex as if it was the air that was keeping me alive. I was completely done having casual sex and the thought of sleeping with random men returned to being a turn off.

I was finally ready for something real. Although I had learned so much from my experiences, casual sex really wasn't meeting my emotional needs.

What I wanted now was a strong, confident, intelligent, and responsible man who wanted to commit to Aubrey and me for a lifetime. It had been nine years since my divorce, I could finally say I was ready for Mr. Right.

I'd learned enough about men, myself, and dating, I was one hundred percent confident that I would not make mistakes by dating the wrong men again. I wholeheartedly believed this. For the first time in my life, I trusted myself when it came to dating men. I knew I finally had the tools to make the right choices and to see the red flags.

I thought back to how therapeutic and eye-opening the past year had been. I learned countless life lessons and was better in bed than I had ever been before.

I thought about the woman that I was at the beginning of it all. Insecure, needy, clueless. Did I already say clueless? I knew very little about men and dating, but I'm proud to say that's no longer the case.

Antonio reminded me of how visual men are. Dressing up for a man can really kick the sex up a few notches and will turn on any man—guaranteed. Whether it's a Snow-White costume or sexy lingerie, men love something out of the ordinary. Something that allows them to fantasize and get off in a different more exciting way.

I also learned how much men crave intellectual stimulation. Although men in their twenties are primarily driven by their sexual desires, most of the men I hung out with spent more time talking with me than having sex with me.

Twenty-something-year-old men might not have all the worldly knowledge of a forty-something-year-old, but they sure are intelligent and have a lot on their minds. They're just looking for someone to share it with.

I also noticed how nearly every man I encountered wanted to please me. They were eager to know what I needed, liked, and wanted sexually just so they could give it to me. If there was one piece of advice I could give to women, it would be:

Don't be afraid to tell a man what you want. They prefer straightforward communication and are not looking to guess what turns you on. Take the guessing out of it and just tell them.

My experience with Ray taught me that size really doesn't matter and a man who is passionate and motivated will get the job done by any means possible. Sure, there isn't a woman I know who doesn't prefer the feel of a big dick, but as long as the ending is happy—then it's a win.

My sexual experiences also taught me the importance of foreplay. Maybe it's because I'm older—I'm not sure—but I was keenly aware during this past year that if I didn't get decent foreplay before the sex, it was not as satisfying. Period.

If there's one piece of advice I could give men it would be this: have a woman begging for your dick before you actually give it to her. Great foreplay and slower drawn out sex will guarantee better sex for both partners. That's not to say that changing things up isn't hot, because it most definitely is. I just learned for me, slower is sexier, more arousing, and hands down more fulfilling.

One of my greatest revelations was that lots of men LOVE a curvy woman's body. It's insane to me how many women strive for a perfect body, when a perfect body isn't what most men are looking for. When a man sees a naked woman in front of him, he doesn't see the stretch marks, extra pounds, or scars. Most men see a sexy naked woman with a beautiful body.

The men that I spent time with helped me fall in love with my body. Helped me realize I was sexy all along and I just didn't realize it.

I am most grateful for this personal revelation, because it's what helped me not care what other people think of me—I choose to live my life instead.

The final and most important lesson I learned is that casual intimacy can also be very damaging. I know there are many people (namely men of any adult age) who will disagree with me; but after my experiences, I am one hundred percent convinced.

What I saw in the men I spent time with was one strategy after another to stay detached from their partner. The behaviors they had developed may never go away and that's a very scary thought.

It is a proven fact that oxytocin is released during sex and plays a role in bonding people who are intimate. It's called the *Love Drug* for crying out loud!

People who choose to have casual sex are fighting the powerful bonding effects of oxytocin. It's a constant battle to not get attached—which is partly why, aside from the whole seed sowing thing, men go from one woman to the next even when the sex was great. If they stay too long, they *will* get attached. It's a vicious cycle I fear many can't escape, thus stifling many people's abilities to make real, meaningful, and intimate connections.

So, when all is said and done, I found a couple of hot motivated men I could call if I wanted company. But by and large, I have much bigger goals. I don't want to just have a good time for a night. I'm not opposed to it, but I've begun to realize that this journey has always been about something far bigger than I ever expected.

I thought I was looking to just ease boredom, have a good time, or hell—to just deal with the constant horniness! But somewhere along the way, I've rediscovered myself and learned to love everything that makes me who I am.

However, I am left with some final questions to answer. What do I *really* want this next phase of my life to look like? What are my dreams and how the hell do I make them come true?

I've always wanted to be a writer. So why can't I be one? What's stopping me?

Nothing.

This past year has proved to me that I can do the impossible. I can put myself out there. I can learn new things and demand respect when it isn't given. And, I can now drop a man like a hot potato if he makes the poor choice to not treat me right. I can meet people where they're at and take them as they come.

It amazes me how far I have come.

I have life in abundance—joy and happiness.

And there was only one person who could make it happen—*me*. Taking control of the reins of my life was the best thing I could do along with a whole heap of grace from God.

I was in a great place by the end of 2018—the best place I could ever remember being in emotionally, spiritually, and mentally. I hadn't had a thought about 24 in a *very* long time. Honestly, I couldn't remember the last time I thought of him. For me it was a sign of being healed. Finally.

Of course, just at this time of true contentment in my life, I heard from him again. I was surprised to see I had received an email from him one night.

Lacie,

I want to thank you for everything you have done for me. I have been in recovery and am sober, despite some bumps along the way. I was angry with you at first for talking to my family, but now I see that you saved my life. I thank you from the bottom of my heart for putting up with my selfishness and for having the courage to talk to my family. Because of you, I am alive today. I wish nothing but the best for you and Aubrey. Thank you for everything you have been in my life.

Thank you for saving my life,
24

Wow. I was genuinely floored. I never expected to hear from 24 again. I thought he hated me and would never be able to see past his anger.

I was wrong.

I felt a wave of relief. My body literally felt lighter. It was as if someone physically removed a weight from my shoulders. I was overwhelmed with happiness. He was sober and healthy. I hoped and prayed he was happy with his new substance-free life. I wiped tears from my eyes and sent a reply.

24,

Thank you so much for your email. It is one that I never expected to receive and it came as a pleasant surprise. I am so glad to hear you are sober and healthy. Thank you for your forgiveness. It is a weight lifted off my shoulders. I hope you know that everything I have ever done including talking to your family came from a place of love.

Take care and best of luck to you in your life,
Lacie

I never felt such a genuine sense of closure with anyone else in my life as I sent that email. I was happy and in a great place. I hoped 24 was as well. I truly wanted him to live the best life possible. Now that he was sober, I was hopeful he could do it.

Although I would not suggest sleeping with strangers to anyone. It was risky, dangerous, and emotionally unhealthy, I am grateful for every experience I've had as it shaped me into who I am today.

I'm grateful for the men I met, the connections I made, and the countless life lessons I learned during that time in my life. They are all so priceless.

I became a woman who says *yes* to living life, says *yes* to taking chances, *says yes* to trying new things. There isn't a thing I would change about the life I have lived nor the life I'm currently living.

Life is short and I've made the choice to live mine to its fullest.

That night, I went to bed and prayed for the first time in a very long time:

Dear God,

Thank you for the closure I have received from 24. Thank you for helping him on his path to sobriety and for using me to help him. I'm ready for something real in my life. I'm grateful for all of the positive and negative experiences you have sent my way. I am grateful for everything you have done in my life and I'm proud of the woman you've helped me become. I'm ready for my man. I've been patient. Please don't make me wait any longer.

I know that not all prayers are answered, but I felt deep down a change was brewing in my life. I knew with certainty that Mr. Right was just around the corner.

Want More?

If you enjoyed reading *Lacie's Lessons In Dating: Confidence is Alluring* and would like to continue following Lacie's journey, please look for book 2...
Lacie's Lessons in Dating: Self-Trust is Key...coming in the fall of 2021

To stay connected and receive email updates about future publications and a sneak peak of *Self-Trust is Key*, visit:
Laciemaegabor.com

Acknowledgements

In acknowledging my friends and family, I'd like to express who they are to me and what they do to support and inspire me every day.

To Aubrey: I admire your intelligence, strength, warm nature, problem-solving abilities, thoughtfulness, open-mindedness, artistic talent, confidence, and fortitude. You are quite simply amazing. I couldn't love you a drop more! Follow your strengths, interests, and passions—you too, will live a happy and blessed life. Thank you for believing in me. I persevered during the toughest of times because of you. Since the moment I knew that I was pregnant, you've been my Northern Star. Keep shining bright love bug!

To My Parents: Thank you for your support and non-judgmental acceptance of this book. I am proud of the woman that you helped me become and will forever be grateful that you were chosen to be my parents. Thank you from the bottom of my heart for every single thing you've done to help me to get to this point in my life! I love you!

To Chloe: You are an amazing woman! This book would never have happened if it weren't for your unwavering support. You believed in me when I wasn't sure I could make it happen. You reassured me that WE would make it happen and guess what... WE did! I admire your ability to juggle everything in your life and still have time to help me publish this book. You are beautiful, strong, hard-working, and the most supportive friend I could ever ask for. I am beyond blessed that we crossed paths and that an everlasting friendship blossomed because of it. Thank you for always being there for me.

To Claudia: You are the woman every woman wants to be. Self-assured, determined, resilient, hard-working, and drop-dead gorgeous. You have been one of my closest friends—for what seems like forever. I will be here for you until the end of time, my friend. I look forward to many more memorable moments.

To Alex: You are beautiful inside and out! Thank you for your encouragement, support, and unconditional love. I am grateful for our friendship. Aubrey and I are blessed to have you and your family in our lives.

To Ingrid, Sarah, and Maria: Our girl's weekends are everything to me! I love spending time with you ladies at any cheap place we can find. Fuck the no smoking sign! We're smoking a joint on the patio! Room 69 forever ladies!

Sam: I will be forever grateful God brought you into my life. You amaze everyone with your ability to turn your hardships into opportunities with which you can provide help to others. Stay the course. God will help you understand the reason for your suffering one day.

My Cousin: Misfortune brought us closer together. For that we are blessed. Your work ethic is inspiring and you are a mother that I emulate. Loving, kick-back, involved, supportive, and caring are all qualities that I see in you which I hope to always have prominent in myself. Thank you for your unwavering love and support!

Shelley and Eddie: Thank you for welcoming me with open arms. I appreciate your friendship and advice.

My Editor: Your attention to detail and patience is greatly valued. Thank you for educating me! Your help with my book is a blessing.

Lyz Kelley: I'm beyond grateful for your advice. Your willingness to help others is a gift. Thank you, thank you, thank you!

My Dear Readers: Thank *you* to every single person who read this book and didn't judge me. Thank you to every single person who can say:

I've been there before, I know your heartache, your loneliness, and your pain. At some time or another—your pain was my pain.

I understand you and I'm here for you.

To those of you who can say these things, I say thank you. Thank you for seeing me as a whole person, flaws and all. May God bless you!

Last but certainly not least, I want to give thanks to God. My path may not have been righteous or godly; but in the end, I have acquired emotional healthiness, empowerment, self-love, and discovered that only *I* have the power to make myself truly happy.

"The one who gets wisdom loves life; the one who cherishes understanding will soon prosper."

Proverbs 19:8

About the Author

Lacie Mae Gabor lives happily in an undisclosed location in the United States of America. She is a hard-working, adventurous single mom who is trying to live her best life possible. You can find out everything you need to know about her by reading this book and subsequent publications. This is Lacie's first book, but she plans to publish two additional books, one about her life leading up to her sexcapades and one about her life after.

Looking for more information about Lacie and her books? **Visit:**

LacieMaeGabor.com

@LMGaborAuthor on Instagram

http://facebook.com/LMGaborAuthor on Facebook